£ 40

MELANIE KLEIN

Volume I
First Discoveries
and First System
1919–1932

MELANIE KLEIN

Volume I

First Discoveries and First System 1919–1932

Jean-Michel Petot

Translated from the French by
Christine Trollope

International Universities Press, Inc.
Madison   Connecticut

This book is a translation of *Mélanie Klein: premières découvertes et premier système 1919–1932*, by Jean-Michel Petot, published by Dunod, Paris, 1979.

Library of Congress Cataloging in Publication Data.

Petot, Jean-Michel.
    [Mélanie Klein—premières découvertes et premier système, 1919–1932. English]
    Melanie Klein—first discoveries and first system, 1919–1932 / Jean-Michel Petot; translated from the French by Christine Trollope.
      p. cm.
    Translation of: Mélanie Klein—premières découvertes et premier système, 1919–1932.
"Volume I."
    Includes bibliographical references.
    Includes index.
    ISBN 0-8236-3328-4
    1. Child analysis. 2. Klein, Melanie. I. Title.
    [DNLM: 1. Klein, Melanie. 2. Psychoanalysis—in infancy & childhood. WS 350.5 P492n]
RJ504.2.P4713 1990
618.92'8917—dc20
DNLM/DLC   90-4781
for Library of Congress   CIP

Manufactured in the United States of America

CONTENTS

Foreword

Although today the true value of Melanie Klein's work is increasingly recognized, not until now has she been the subject of a comprehensive study. The present work traces the formation of her ideas in a threefold movement: the building of concepts in accordance with the needs of her theories; the incorporation of facts gathered in clinical work; and constant reference from one to the other.

Since the article devoted to her by J.-B. Pontalis (1954) almost twenty-five years ago, which lays greater stress on the problems her thought addressed than on the form in which it was expressed, a few works have appeared, but most of these simply restate Melanie Klein's ideas or are content to criticize them. Such work admittedly has its uses; though Freud took the trouble to introduce psychoanalysis and keep it in the public eye by means of publications and lectures (Freud, 1916–1917, 1933), Melanie Klein troubled only once in her lifetime to assemble her ideas in systematic form. This was in 1932; after that she never thought of revising her work in accordance with her more recent discoveries. As a result, *The Psycho-Analysis of Children* presents difficulties for the reader who is not entirely familiar with her later ideas. Should he consider such and such a passage, describing the earliest forms of defense of the ego, or such and such a disquisition on the second anal stage, as a theory still valid, or as a long-abandoned hypothesis? That is why a clear, concise explanation of Melanie Klein's later theories is invaluable. This task is not that of the work in hand, especially as there exists an admirable *Introduction to the Work of Melanie Klein* written by one of her closest disciples, Hanna Segal (1964).

It is in its process of formation that the present work will try to understand Melanie Klein's thought. It seems therefore legitimate to assume that the truth of what she said and wrote in her lifetime is to be found in the final stage of that formation. From this point of view an historical or even epistemological study could contribute to the understanding of her work by showing how, and in what order, the main ideas appeared. We should then have to go through the successive stages of what might be called her doctrine, indicating as we go what is merely an approximation of an idea that will appear fully only later, what is a stable and definitive acquisition, and what is held or simply considered only to be given up in short order. Such a work would also be very useful, and has been largely carried out by Willy Baranger (1971). But since the renewal of Freudian studies through the work of Ernest Jones, Alexander Grinstein, and, in France, J. Laplanche and J.-B. Pontalis (and, following them, Didier Anzieu), we know how knowledge of the origins, even the initial glimmerings, of an idea, can shed light on the structure of the theory to which, at a certain moment, it gives birth. We have learned that to take seriously the most apparently obsolescent notions of the creator of psychoanalysis, to look for the meaning of his most aberrant meanderings—phylogenetic traces, the primitive horde, the death instinct—does not always lead us away from living theory and clinical experience; on the contrary, it often takes us back to them. Notions of heredity become but a way of stressing the typical nature of these fantastic structures which appear to be largely independent of individual or even cultural contingencies, as if human nature were written into biological programs, while the death urge serves to give an adequate account of such phenomena as negative therapeutic reactions. That is why, upon embarking on a study of how Melanie Klein developed the ideas on which her therapy rested, care must be taken not to be selective regarding the ill-defined hypotheses, uncontrolled beliefs, and ideas in prospect that we find in her early writings. Here everything will be accepted as equally necessary. The inner links and coherence of this material will be explored so as to bring out, at every stage in its scientific evolution, the unity of Melanie Klein's clinical project, the coherence of her theoretical methods, and the suitability for their purpose of the therapeutic tools she in time perfected.

What was Melanie Klein's starting point? What did she especially endeavor to do and say? How did her successive discoveries transform her initial beliefs, her deep-rooted attitudes, and even her project itself? What were the indispensable functions temporarily fulfilled by those of her theses she did not finally retain? And what, if they exist, are the constants of her clinical, theoretical, and technical approach? These are the questions that must be asked, even if we cannot hope to answer them all.

Sigmund Freud, a neurologist of repute, discovered psychoanalysis by analyzing his own dreams. He created a situation in which the patient speaks, without seeing him, to a therapist, relatively silent, as motionless as himself. This device was intended to relieve suffering clearly characterized as sexual and theoretically rooted in his discovery of the oedipus complex. It took Freud a long time to admit that unsatisfied sexual urges are not all to be explained by the social repression of sexuality. Melanie Klein, housewife and mother with no university training, having given up, on leaving her teens, her intellectual and medical aspirations, came to psychoanalysis during the First World War, first undergoing analysis and then undertaking to apply the doctrines of psychoanalysis to the education of her children, most particularly her youngest son. For her it was a question not of treatment but of prevention. The pain from which she wanted to save her son was not sexual but intellectual, not imminent but simply potential. She sought above all to protect him in advance from all danger of intellectual inhibition, giving him the kind of education which, following the psychoanalytic ideas of the period, she believed would ensure the full use of his intellectual faculties, in the context of a normality which to her was the untrammeled combination of all his talents and aptitudes.

With this in mind she sought to liberate the child as much as possible, and above all to free him from the repression of sexual curiosity, considered to be the source of all denials of intelligence. She spent herself, without counting the cost, in order to fight anxiety, the outward sign of repression, and to facilitate all the expressions, direct or indirect, of the child's spontaneity. It was from this point of view, initially more prophylactic and educational than psychoanalytic, that play became the center of her interest. But Melanie Klein soon lost her educational illusions. Passing from her son to other children, from Hungary to Germany, from the encouragement of the ebullient Ferenczi to the supervision of the cautious Abraham, she fixed the boundaries of her knowledge and abilities, constructed her first theories, and became more confident in her use of her originality in interpretation.

Thus, having taken the measure of the resistance of inhibiting and repressive forces, and having also observed the modes of development of sublimations, she was able to build, around 1923, her first theoretical system, of which it may be said that on certain points it went beyond the Freudian ideas of the period, especially with regard to anxiety; here she kept, however, the essential, durable element, the bond between anxiety and repression. In Chapter 2 of this work it is established that it was this system of 1923 which made possible the discovery of the play technique and, more indirectly, that of the archaic stages of the oedipus complex and the superego. In order to mark its strength, coherence, and utter originality, as well as its perfect suitability for the clinical problem it was intended to solve, it is designated here the "proto-Kleinian system."

The fact that Melanie Klein played spontaneously with her son and with her other child patients before making this a studied technique is explained by the nature of her objective and the circumstances of her approach; in any case, there was nothing extraordinary about it, and we shall see that around 1920 she was not the only one to consider it. But where she differed from many others was that she was capable of theorizing about what happened between herself and the child, thanks to the early concepts she had forged to that end; whether they were true or false matters less than their fruitfulness. Thanks to the status such ideas gave her, play could be considered not only as an instrument for easier communication, not only as material to be interpreted—we shall see that in 1920 two important psychoanalysts each held one of these two partial truths—but as both at once, and thus as the equivalent of the verbal associations produced by the adult in analysis.

Once in possession of the play technique, Melanie Klein could make, in a few months, the three great discoveries on which Kleinian psychoanalysis was always to rest, and which many people have more or less surreptitiously accepted: the normal and regular existence of an "early" oedipus complex at the end of the first year of life; the existence of an archaic form of the superego at this same period; and the possibility and daily reality of transference in the analysis of very young children (see Bolland and Sandler, 1965). Once these essential facts are grasped, the universe of the archaic unconscious can be explored. What Melanie Klein first found there was the nucleus of the psychotic part of the personality, the incoherent world of the phantasms of oral, anal, and urethral sadism, and the incessant struggle of the ego to escape from the assaults of sadism and anxiety by bringing into play such defense mechanisms as splitting and, most especially, reparation. The first coherent geography of these unknown continents was *The Psycho-Analysis of Children*, published in 1932.

It is this first part of Melanie Klein's career, perhaps the most fascinating part, even if it is not the one which has most enriched psychoanalysis, which is examined in this volume. Chapter 1, after briefly relating what is known of Melanie Klein's life before she became a psychoanalyst, is aimed at reconstituting, as accurately as possible, the story of her first attempts at psychoanalytic education, whereby the vocation of the future creator of the play technique began to take shape. The object of the second chapter is to show explicitly the elements and forms of the first Kleinian system, which remained largely implicit in her earliest writings, or was stated only in concrete descriptions, in terms which laid no claim to general application. Special emphasis will be placed on the fact that before being finally and completely abandoned, this system, by virtue of its most intrinsic aspects, made possible the very discoveries that occasioned its supersession. The remainder of the work deals with the concrete history of this progress: the discovery, through the psychoanalysis of little Rita, of the archaic form of the oedipus complex; the perfecting of the play technique, to be finally adopted some months later; and her difficulty in specifying the exact form of the archaic phase of the male oedipus complex—a difficulty exactly symmetrical to Freud's in conceiving the female oedipus complex without passing through the archetype of male development. It will be shown how this abundance of fact and ideas was arranged in a coherent and even systematic form in the work of 1932, marking the end of the evolution this work endeavors to analyze.

1

The Origins and Emergence of Melanie Klein's Psychoanalytic Vocation

CHILDHOOD AND YOUTH

Melanie Reizes was born in Vienna on March 30, 1882. The family was Jewish, the father a doctor, but the Reizes family does not appear to have moved in the same circles as the Freud family. In any case Melanie Reizes, who became Melanie Klein, knew nothing about psychoanalysis until, shortly before the First World War, she happened to read one of Freud's books. Melanie was the youngest of four children. We know practically nothing about her eldest sister; we know more about her brother Emmanuel, born in 1877, and her sister Sidonie, born in 1878. Her father, who was over fifty when she was born, was of an orthodox Jewish family, and he had devoted his earlier years to religious studies with the intention of becoming a rabbi. At the age of thirty-seven he broke with his origins and began medical studies, probably under difficult conditions. Such a past must have won him the admiration of his youngest daughter for his independent spirit and scientific attitude (Bion, Rosenfeld, and Segal, 1961).

Dr. Reizes practiced in the Austrian capital. We know from Freud's correspondence with his fiancée that it was difficult for

1

a doctor without prestigious university qualifications, especially a Jewish one, to build up a practice in that city. In all likelihood, Melanie Reizes's father was not very successful. In any case, his wife had to open a shop to supplement the family income. This fact reveals some financial embarrassment, as it was contrary to the customs of the period for a doctor's wife to work. It shows also the energy and independence of spirit of a woman who could set aside deep-rooted prejudices to help her husband and ensure a good education for her children.

During her early years little Melanie was deeply attached to her mother and, in tragic circumstances, to her sister Sidonie, who became seriously ill in 1886, when she was eight and Melanie four. As she had to stay in bed, she undertook to teach her younger sister. In her fifth year, then, Melanie learned reading, writing, and the rudiments of arithmetic for love of her sister, with whom she had an intense emotional relationship which left its permanent mark. Sidonie died in 1887. This was the first of the sorrows which haunted the life of Melanie Klein.

A few years later she had a similar relationship with her brother Emmanuel. When she planned to enter the Gymnasium (the Middle European equivalent to secondary school), he helped and encouraged her. Thanks to lessons from her brother, who proved an excellent tutor, she passed the entrance examination of a reputable school, the only one which prepared girls for entering university. As an adolescent she shared the literary and artistic tastes of her brother, who seems to have been a brilliantly gifted young man, both pianist and writer. In the intellectual circle of her brother's friends, she developed her interests and curiosity, and was stimulated by Emmanuel's openly admiring confidence in her burgeoning gifts. But again an intense emotional relationship was broken by death. Emmanuel had suffered from heart trouble since his childhood, and his sister knew, as he did himself, that he was doomed to die very young. He died in 1902, at the age of twenty-five.

At this date Melanie Reizes had already been engaged to Arthur Klein for almost three years. Instead of going to medical school as she had planned, she attended courses in art and history at the University of Vienna. She married in 1903 and went with her husband, a chemical engineer, to various parts of Central Europe, where his work took him. Over the years she had three children: Melitta, born in 1904, Hans, born in 1907, and Erich, born in 1914. We know that the Klein family settled in Budapest a few years before the First World War and remained there until the revolution of Béla Kun. It was at Budapest that she began to read the works of Freud.

1. The Meeting with Psychoanalysis

We know that Melanie Klein was psychoanalyzed by Sandor Ferenczi during the First World War. The "biographical landmarks" accompanying the French edition of *Contributions to Psycho-Analysis* (Klein, 1948, 1968) give us the following information: "1916. In Budapest. After reading Freud's works and undergoing a personal analysis with Ferenczi, she began her career as a child psycho-analyst in a Budapest polyclinic under the direction of her former analyst" (p. 19). In fact, this could not have happened. Freud and Ferenczi had indeed hoped to found a polyclinic and a psychoanalytic institute in Budapest, thanks to a substantial gift from one of Freud's disciples, Anton von Freund, a rich Budapest brewer, who was to become a member of the famous secret committee set up, after Jung's defection and at the instigation of Ernest Jones, to defend psychoanalysis and its founder, and to administer the movement. Budapest would thus have become the main center of psychoanalysis. But these plans were made only in 1918, during the exciting weeks of the Congress of Budapest, when the new science seemed close to enjoying the support of the authorities because of its contributions to the treatment of shell shock cases (Jones, 1955, pp. 222–223). On August 27, 1918, a month before the congress, Freud wrote to Karl Abraham, who did not know Anton von Freund: "I think Sachs has already told you something about Dr. von Freund, whom I am here describing. . . . It is to be expected that Budapest will now become the head-quarters of our movement" (Freud and Abraham, 1907–1926, p. 278). In fact the donation of one million crowns which von Freund had led them to expect was reduced to a smaller sum owing to the illness and death of the donor, and

its real value fell very low because of the collapse of the mon-
etary system of the empires of Central Europe after their defeat.
Thus Budapest did not become the center of the psychoanalytic
movement, and the plans for founding a polyclinic came to
nothing. In fact we know now that Melanie Klein never practiced psychoanalysis in Budapest. We shall return later to the
question of the nature of her psychoanalytic activities in Hungary.

The fact of her analysis with Ferenczi, by contrast, is well
established. What we cannot be certain about is when the treatment took place. We can very definitely exclude certain periods.
It is not impossible that Melanie Klein consulted Ferenczi,
Freud's principal Hungarian disciple, who already enjoyed a
flattering reputation in his native land, in the months following
the onset of the war. But the treatment could not have begun
then: around October 20, 1914, Ferenczi joined the army as a
doctor, with the rank of major, and was attached to a regiment
of Hussars. He was posted with his unit to Papa, a town almost
a hundred miles distant by rail, and had to leave his patients
(Jones, 1955, p. 195). He remained there until January or February 1916, when he was appointed medical superintendent of
a military neurological clinic. It is not impossible that this man,
overflowing with energy, returned then to taking patients in
analysis. We know that Karl Abraham, who was responsible for
an army psychiatric center in Allenstein, near Koenigsberg, had
taken a few patients for treatment in that region (Freud and
Abraham, 1907–1926, pp. 277–280). It is possible, then, that
Melanie Klein's analysis took place at that time. According to
this hypothesis it would have been either interrupted or terminated in the middle of February 1917. At this date Ferenczi
fell ill with pulmonary tuberculosis. He suffered also from ex-
opathalmic goiter, and had to spend three months in a sana-
torium on the Semmering, a high-altitude resort about forty
miles south of Vienna. He returned to Budapest at the end of
May, after long interviews with Freud during which they discussed Lamarck's views on evolution; this was the starting point
for Freud's *Beyond the Pleasure Principle* (1920) and Ferenczi's
Thalassa (1924). From then on, Ferenczi lived in Budapest. He
arranged Freud's summer holidays in the Tatras in 1917 and

set up the psychoanalytic congress which took place in Budapest on September 28 and 29, 1918. Melanie Klein's analysis may, then, have been started or resumed in May 1917.

We do not know what this treatment was. Sandor Ferenczi was working out during the war years the principles of his "active technique," which consisted of injunctions and prohibitions addressed to the patient. We may suppose, without any great risk of being mistaken, that this direct, enthusiastic man, who never did things by halves, applied his technique to all his patients, and that Melanie Klein was treated in this way. This technique was intended to speed up the blank periods in analysis. In the first phase, the analyst called on the patient to put into effect his previously repressed sexual tendencies. In the second phase, these satisfactions were forbidden, and analyzed by relating them to infantile emotions and experiences. Ferenczi had been approved by Freud, who, however, did not formulate the abstinence rule explicitly until 1918, at the Budapest Congress (Freud, 1919). In addition, Ferenczi (1919b, p. 37) was very circumspect in his technical writings about the indications for his method. At any rate Melanie Klein was impressed by her analyst's brilliant personality. In the preface to the first edition of *The Psycho-Analysis of Children*, she wrote,

> Ferenczi was the first to make me acquainted with psycho-analysis. He also made me understand its real essence and meaning. His strong and direct feeling for the unconscious and for symbolism, and the remarkable *rapport* he had with the minds of children, have had a lasting influence on my understanding of the psychology of the small child. He also drew my attention to my capacity for child analysis, in which he took a great personal interest, and encouraged me to devote myself to this field of psycho-analytic therapy, then still very little explored. He furthermore did all he could to help me along this path and gave me much support in my first efforts. It is to him that I owe the foundations from which my work as an analyst developed. [Klein, 1932, pp. x–xi]

We know from Willi Hoffer (1961) that Melanie Klein attended the psychoanalytic congress in Budapest in September 1918. But so did quite a number of other people: the congress was not restricted to psychoanalysts, and the lectures took place in the great hall of the Hungarian Academy of Science. There she saw Freud for the first time. He read—contrary to his custom of speaking without notes—the article "Lines of Advance in Psycho-Analytic Therapy" (Freud, 1919). Melanie Klein was certainly enraptured, for this congress was exceptional, not only by the quality of the papers read, but above all by its atmosphere. Psychoanalysis was apparently on the point of being recognized by the authorities, its members were officially received by the municipality of Budapest, and a petition was circulating among the students of the university asking for a chair of psychoanalysis to be created for Ferenczi. Anton von Freund's gift raised great hopes. All this was to evaporate hardly two months later, following the collapse of the Central Powers.

When, the following year, Melanie Klein read her first paper to the Hungarian Psycho-Analytical Society, she aroused much interest and was praised by both Ferenczi and von Freund, whose pertinent questions aided her in bringing certain of her ideas to maturity. Ferenczi then introduced her, at the International Congress of Psycho-Analysis at The Hague in September 1920, to Karl Abraham, who invited her to Berlin. But it seems to be established that Ferenczi did not guide her in her studies; in particular, he did not supervise her first psychoanalytic work. His help was confined to encouragement and the lending of books (Hoffer, 1961, pp. 1–3). She was elected a member of the Hungarian society on July 13, 1919, immediately after reading her first paper. She had not yet begun to practice psychoanalysis, at least not in the sense in which we understand it today.

In fact she had left Budapest in March 1919 because of the political situation. The defeat of the Central European powers had brought about the fall of the Austro-Hungarian Empire on October 31, 1918. The Hungarian Republic had been proclaimed on November 16th, and a temporary president, Mihàly Kàrolyi, had been appointed. The defeat and the Allied occupation led to economic difficulties and to political disturbances when it came out that the conquerors intended to deprive Hungary of two-thirds of her former territory. This was the setting for the revolution of Béla Kun and the Communist

Party, which set up the Hungarian Soviet Republic. Kun's revolution set up, for four months, a regime which was very favorable to psychoanalysis: a chair of psychoanalysis was created for Ferenczi, and Géza Róheim was appointed to a chair of applied psychoanalysis. All the same, Melanie Klein, with her husband and children, probably urged by the former, left for Ruzomberok, a small Slovakian town where her husband apparently had family ties.[1] From there she returned to Budapest in July to attend the session of the Psycho-Analytical Society at which she read her paper. She was to remain at Ruzomberok for about a year.

Her first paper, to appear later as part of "The Development of a Child" (Klein, 1921),[2] was based not on data collected in the course of a classic psychoanalysis, but on the observation of a child's development during the period in which his mother was giving him explanations to satisfy his sexual curiosity, which he had expressed in numerous questions. This child was no other than Erich, Melanie Klein's second son, then aged five. The child's sexual education began in March 1919, immediately after the Klein family's arrival in Ruzomberok, and continued after the reading of the paper. It then became true psychoanalytic therapy of the child by his mother, first at Ruzomberok and then in Berlin. This psychotherapy lasted until 1922. Melanie Klein, describing Erich's therapy—and giving him the pseudonym of Fritz—stated specifically on several occasions that she had analyzed no other children when she arrived in Berlin: "My first patient was a five-year-old boy. I referred to him under the name 'Fritz' in my earliest published papers. . . . Between 1920 and 1923 I gained further experience with other child cases . . ." (Klein, 1955, pp. 122–124). Between 1920 and 1923, she was already in Berlin, where she began the analysis of other children besides her son.

We have scarcely any documents relating to the end of

---

[1] Hoffer (1961) gives her address in 1919 as "Fr. Melanie Klein, %Director Julius Klein, Ruzomberok, Czechoslovakia."

[2] The text read in 1919, announced in 1920 in the *International Journal of Psycho-Analysis (1:370)* as "July 13th. Mrs. M. Klein: Remarks on the Intellectual Development of a Child," corresponds to pp. 1–25 of the 1921 paper.

1919 and the beginning of 1920. From September 8 to 10, 1920, she attended the psychoanalytic congress at The Hague, the first to take place in Freud's absence, and also the first after the war to unite Central European psychoanalysts with those of the Anglophone world. During the congress Ferenczi introduced Melanie Klein to Karl Abraham, head of the Berlin society. She impressed Abraham, a prudent and thoughtful man but rather given to immediate enthusiasms, sufficiently for him to suggest to her during the congress that she might settle in Berlin and practice child psychoanalysis. She accepted the invitation and prepared to go to Berlin. At the congress she also had the opportunity to hear and approach Hermine von Hug-Hellmuth, then considered the chief specialist in child analysis. Their contact was very cold: reserve on the part of the older woman, faced with this enthusiastic novice without a university background, and disappointment on the part of Melanie Klein, who soon realized that her older colleague had little to teach her. The two coexisted in the Berlin society without collaborating.

At the beginning of December 1920, Melanie Klein was in Budapest. She attended a scientific session of the Psycho-Analytical Society on December 5 and, according to the *International Journal of Psycho-Analysis* (1:370), read a paper titled Contribution to Analysis in Early Childhood. Toward the end of the year her first published article appeared in the *Internationale Zeitschrift für Psychoanalyse* under the title "Der Familienroman in Statu Nascendi" (Klein, 1920); it reported a a separate episode in the analysis of Erich and not the material presented in the paper read in July 1919 and published in *Imago* in 1921. On December 14, having left Budapest, she wrote Ferenczi asking him to send her a book. She spent the Christmas holidays in Ruzomberok and then left for Germany. Her children went with her, but not her husband, who had found a situation in Sweden and gone to live there. This separation was to be a final one; they were divorced soon afterward.

2. The Years in Berlin

Melanie Klein arrived in Berlin in January 1921. She continued Erich's "psychoanalysis" and received valuable advice from Abraham (Klein, 1955, p. 122). As early as February 3, a session of the Psycho-Analytical Society was devoted to her account of the second part of Erich's psychoanalytic education, and the following week's session was entirely devoted to the discussion of this paper. On May 5 she gave a lecture on disturbance of orientation in children. This lecture remained unpublished, but its content was used in "Early Analysis" (Klein, 1923).

In 1922 her name appeared on the list of associate members of the Berlin society, and she began work at the polyclinic. She continued Erich's psychotherapy, and read a large number of papers, generally short and dealing with clinical points, at the scientific session of the society: "An Anecdote Taken from the Life of Walter Scott" on January 24; " 'Sunday Neurosis' in a Child" on February 24, a report on a case seen in the polyclinic which confirmed Ferenczi's views on Sunday neuroses (Ferenczi, 1919a); "Some Observations on Latent Anxiety" on March 21, a text surely identical with the paper entitled "Infant Anxiety and Its Importance for the Development of the Personality (the bibliography of the *Essays*, compiled by Lola Brook, Melanie Klein's secretary and intimate friend for the last fifteen years of her life, indicates that it existed and was used in "Early Analysis"; "Some Observations on a School Exercise" on April 11; and "Compulsive Dissimulation and Mythomania" on May 2. In late September the International Congress of Psycho-Analysis was held in Berlin; Freud was there and read an unpublished text, "Some Observations on the Unconscious." This was to be his last congress. The scientific level on this occasion was particularly high, and some of the papers very evocative: Abraham read his work on melancholy (1924b, pp. 422–433), Ferenczi presented and summarized *Thalassa (1923)*, and Géza Róheim read "After the Death of the Primal Father" (1923). Melanie Klein had the immense pleasure of reading, in Freud's presence, a paper titled "The Development and Inhibition of Aptitudes in Children," which later formed the core of "Early Analysis."

During 1923 Melanie Klein continued to read scientific papers to the Berlin Psycho-Analytical Society: "Remarks on the Analysis of a Child" on February 13; "How Children Play at Doctors" on April 10; and a short clinical paper on May 8. On February 20 she was elected a titular member of the society. But her essential contribution certainly did not lie in these papers on points of detail. In the course of this year she entered upon another exceptional psychoanalytic experiment (the first being the analysis of her son) and invented the play technique, which became the foundation of all her subsequent discoveries. Karl Abraham told Freud, who did not react, on October 7, 1923: "In the last few months Mrs. Klein has successfully conducted the psycho-analysis of a three-year-old" (Freud and Abraham, 1907–1926). It was in fact the summer of 1923 that Melanie Klein had analyzed little Rita, whose age was two years and three months at the beginning of the treatment, which had lasted three or four months. The analysis took place in the child's home; she played spontaneously with her toys, and Melanie Klein analyzed her play, as she had done with Erich. The play technique was thus in a way imposed by the children themselves. It was only during a second period in the course of this same year that Melanie Klein, learning from the beginning of Rita's analysis, decided to analyze the children in her own house, in order to avoid the interference of the family in the treatment, and had the idea of providing them with toys, thus transforming a spontaneous phenomenon into a studied technique. Rita's analysis confirmed the data collected during Erich's and also provided proof of the existence and severity of an inner compulsion to self-criticism at a very early age, the importance of anal and urethral sadistic fantasies, the first glimpses of the anxiety situation typical of girls. This analysis marks the true beginning of Kleinian psychoanalysis as we know it. The year 1923 was also that of the completion and publication of two extensive articles (Klein, 1923a, 1923b) based on the material collected during the experiment with Erich and the first analyses carried out in in 1921 and 1922. We shall see later (in Chapter 2) that these texts contain a very original conception of the relationships of repression, inhibition, and sublimation—a conception which Melanie Klein was later to modify, but which provided the theoretical basis of the play technique. But the results of the latter caused her to abandon the idea. The year 1923, then, was a decisive turning point.

We know little of Melanie Klein's private life during this period. Although no connection can be established between the two facts, she divorced her husband shortly after 1921 and entered upon an analysis with Karl Abraham at the beginning of 1924. On April 22 and 23, 1924, she took part in the Salzburg International Congress, the second to be held in that city. Freud, worn down by illness, was not there. During the congress Abraham was elected president of the International Psycho-Analytical Association. Melanie Klein read a paper entitled "On the Technique of Infant Analysis." This paper, never published, was the first version of the famous article of 1926, "The Psychological Principles of Early Analysis," generally considered the first text to contain Kleinian ideas. We know from a note by Melanie Klein (1926, p. 129) that she had argued at Salzburg that children in the first phases of infantile sexuality understand and desire coitus as an oral act. But the three basic theories of 1926 were not all to be found here in their definitive form: the oedipus complex beginning immediately after weaning; introjection of the superego from the beginning of the oedipal conflict; and the existence of transference in the psychoanalysis of young children, with a comparable role to that played in adult analyses. Only the third of these was clearly formulated, as Rita's analysis had provided the opportunity for important technical considerations, while the importance of oral sadism was revealed by the analyses, all four begun in 1924, of Ruth, Trude, Peter and Erna (Klein, 1955), and perhaps by Melanie Klein's own psychoanalysis with Abraham, who was, as we know, interested in anything connected with this matter (see Abraham, 1924a). The account she gave at the Congress made a strong impression on Ernest Jones, president of the British Psycho-Analytical Society and chiefly responsible for the *International Journal of Psycho-Analysis*. He invited her to contribute to the review and to give a series of lectures in London the following year. Certain English psychoanalysts, notably Alix Strachey and Joan Riviere, had already sensed the importance of her work and supported her from the beginning, which was a great help.[3]

[3] Joan Riviere, whom we now know to have been one of the first and principal collaborators of Melanie Klein, was also one of the closest British disciples of Freud, by whom she had been analyzed, and with whom she corresponded regularly (Jones, 1957).

In 1924, while she was treating the four children we have just mentioned, she read several papers to the Berlin Psycho-Analytical Society. "The Effect on the Analysis of Children of Interruptions in Treatment" and "The Activity of Superego in the Fourth Year of a Child's Life" were both delivered May 6. On June 14, in collaboration with two colleagues, she gave interpretations of children's drawings. Erna's analysis was sufficiently far advanced in the autumn for Melanie Klein to report it under the title "Extract from the Analysis of an Obsessional Neurosis in a Six-Year-Old Child" in the course of a meeting of German psychoanalysts organized by Abraham at Würtzburg on eleventh and twelfth of October. After hearing this report Abraham declared, in the discussion which followed, "The future of psycho-analysis lies in the psycho-analysis of children." This declaration was a great surprise to Melanie Klein, who, unaware of the importance of her discoveries, considered herself a faithful disciple of Freud and Abraham. She felt that her approach was so natural and obvious that any pupil of Freud could have come to the same conclusion, and that the characteristic features of her ideas were the direct reflection of the young child's psychology. On November 11, 1924, she spoke on "Infantile Manifestations of the Sense of Guilt." Finally, on December 13, she read a paper titled "The Psychological Principles of Analysis in Childhood." This paper was either very long or theoretically important, as contrary to the Berlin custom of brief clinical papers, the entire evening was devoted to it. Very likely identical with the famous article, "The Psychological Principles of Early Analysis," which was not published until 1926 (*International Journal of Psycho-Analysis*, 8:25–37), it forms in retrospect a true manifesto of Kleinian ideas. By December 1924 Trude's analysis was finished; those of Peter and Ruth were very far advanced; Erna's had been going on for six months (and was to last eighteen months more). Melanie Klein now knew the connections between oral sadism and the initial phase of the oedipus complex, a central fact on which the 1926 article was based.

During 1925 she took little part in the discussions of the Berlin society. The only paper we know her to have read was a short one delivered in February: "An Analogy Between Certain Crimes and Children's Phantasies." In the same year she published "A Contribution to the Psychogenesis of Tics" in the *Internationale Zeitschrift für Psychoanalyse*, an article which did not yet contain any of the new ideas and was a direct continuation of the 1923 texts. She seems to have been completely absorbed in her analysis with Abraham in this period. But Abraham, who suffered from emphysema, went to give three lectures in Holland. He returned at the beginning of June with what he took to be bronchitis, and had to go to bed. Melanie Klein's analysis was thus broken off after fourteen months, never to be resumed. Abraham had in fact injured his pharynx by swallowing a fishbone in Holland. This had led to infectious bronchial pneumonia, then a pulmonary abscess, and finally a subphrenic abscess. Feverish attacks alternated with fever-free periods and euphoric states which gave him the illusion he would soon be cured. This lasted until January 1, 1926, when he died (Freud and Abraham, 1907–1926).

Shortly after her analysis was interrupted, Melanie Klein, expecting, like everyone else, that Abraham would soon recover, went to England to give the lectures Jones had requested the previous year. She stayed there for six weeks and gave six lectures to the members of the British Society of Psycho-Analysis. She received a warm welcome, and her ideas were generally accepted, a pleasant surprise for her; in Berlin only Abraham had really supported her. Ernest Jones invited her to settle in England for at least a year. Colleagues asked her to analyze their children.

Returning to Berlin, she followed the progress of Abraham's illness. When he died, her mourning was certainly long and painful; Melanie Klein, usually so active, read no papers and published no articles until the end of 1928, with the exception of "The Psychological Principles of Early Analysis," which appeared in 1926 but was probably written or at least begun early as 1924 (Freud and Abraham, 1907–1926). Besides the usual disturbing effects of this kind of situation, Melanie Klein lost with Abraham her main guarantor at a scientific level and her only real supporter in Berlin. As she could scarcely tolerate the Berlin society, the British proposals now appeared to her in a different light. She had not wanted to leave Berlin while Abraham was alive, and while, according to Maria Torok and Nicolas Abraham's introduction to the French edition of *Essays in Psycho-Analysis* (Klein, 1968), she hoped to use her couch to gain complete mastery of what she could already give to children. But after Abraham's death she accepted Jones's offer, terminated her current analyses, notably Erna's, and made arrangements to settle in London. She was now forty-four years old. With practically no ties left on the Continent, she was entering upon a new stage in her career, which was to make her the inspiration of the English school of psychoanalysis.

THE PSYCHOANALYTIC EDUCATION OF FRITZ-ERICH

1. The Identity of Little Fritz

Relating in 1955 the circumstances of her technique of psychoanalysis through play, Melanie Klein declared:

> My first patient was a five-year-old boy. I referred to him under the name 'Fritz' in my earliest published papers. To begin with I thought it would be sufficient to influence the mother's attitude. I suggested that she could encourage the child to discuss freely with her the many unspoken questions which were obviously at the back of his mind and were impeding his intellectual development. This had a good effect, but his neurotic difficulties were not sufficiently alleviated and it was soon decided that I should psycho-analyse him. (Klein, 1955, pp. 122–123)

In fact Fritz's case played a considerable part in Melanie Klein's earliest writings. "The Development of a Child," published in 1921 and, as we have seen, made up of two parts, one written in 1919 and the other in 1921, was devoted entirely to him. She took up the case again in two articles published in 1923: "The Role of the School in the Libidinal Development of the Child" and "Early Analysis."

In "The Development of a Child" Melanie Klein (1921) introduces the child in the following terms: "The child in question is a boy, little Fritz, the son of relations who live in my immediate neighbourhood. This gave me the opportunity to be often in the child's company without any restraint. Further, as his mother follows all my recommendations I am able to exercise a far-reaching influence on the child's upbringing" (p. 2). When Melanie Klein wrote these lines she was living in Slovakia, and we can deduce that the child too was living at Ruzomberok. But in "Early Analysis" she says she resumed the analysis of the boy when he was just under seven—that is to say, in 1921, at which time she was in Berlin. So either the child's family, by an extraordinary coincidence, had also moved to Berlin, or, which is hard to imagine, the child was sent to Berlin to continue his analysis. It occurred to us that this child was probably Melanie Klein's youngest son, Erich, born in 1914, whose age coincides exactly with that of little Fritz. It is thus understandable that the child should have gone to Germany with Melanie Klein, and that she should have been able to take advantage from the beginning of the mother's willingness to follow her advice and the influence she could thus exert on the boy's education.

We should note an inaccuracy in her statement that "The Development of a Child" was her first published article. Its first part was indeed the first paper that she had read in public, to the members of the Hungarian Psycho-Analytical Society. But it was not published until 1921, at the same time as the second part, under the title and in the form that we know at present. In 1920, meanwhile, the *Internationale Zeitschrift für Psychoanalyse* had published, in its regular section "Papers on Child Psychology," the article entitled "Der Familienroman in Statu Nascendi." This article, included by Lola Brook in the bibliography accompanying Essais de Psych-Analyse (1948, 1968), is one of the very rare Melanie Klein texts never to have been translated into English or reprinted. When we examine this text, we realize why it was left in oblivion: practically its entire content is found unchanged in The Development of a Child (Klein, 1921, p. 4) and is as follows: as Easter approached, the child had clearly been disappointed by his mother's explanations of the fact that

Bunny

the Easter Hare, supposed to bring toys and sweets and hide them in the garden on Easter morning, did not exist. He had shown some coldness after that, and had taken a fancy to the neighbors' children, who assured him that the Easter Hare was real. Meanwhile his mother took advantage of a conversation to teach the child about pregnancy and the birth of babies; the explanations were badly received, and two days later the boy proclaimed that he was going to change his parents and live with the neighbors. Melanie Klein describes the episode in detail, and connects this wish to change families with the formation of the family romance described by Freud (1909b). But the child in question, obviously identical with Fritz, is explicitly referred to in the 1920 article as Melanie Klein's son: "My son Erich, now aged five, is a healthy, vigorous child . . . it was just before Easter and he had heard a lot of nice things about the Easter Hare" (p. 154). It was probably this exact detail that caused the article to be omitted from collections published later.

The play technique for the psychoanalysis of children thus originated in the relationship of Melanie Klein with her son between the days before Easter 1919 and the end of this "analysis" in 1921. She herself draws our attention to the importance of this relationship for the continuation of her work:

> This analysis was the beginning of the psycho-analytic play technique, because from the start the child expressed his phantasies and anxieties mainly in play, and I consistently interpreted its meaning to him, with the result that additional material came up in his play. This is to say, I already used with this patient, in essence, the method of interpretation which became characteristic of my technique. [Klein, 1955, p. 123]

We cannot but compare the case of Erich and that of little Hans, whose treatment, the first psychoanalysis of a young child, was described by Freud (1909a).[4] In both cases the analysis was carried out by one of the child's parents. This procedure, which today strikes us as strange, then seemed the obvious thing

[4] Freud had treated older children by psychoanalysis before 1900. In *The Interpretation of Dreams* he mentions "one of these very young hysterics," aged twelve (Freud, 1900).

to do; it appeared in fact to be the very condition which made possible the analysis of a very young child: "It was only because the authority of a father and of a physician were united in a single person," wrote Freud (1909a), "and because in him both affectionate care and scientific interest were combined, that it was possible in this one instance to apply the method to a use to which it would not otherwise have lent itself" (p. 5). The parents of little Hans, both of whom were "closest adherents" to Freud and his ideas, were encouraged by him, as Melanie Klein was later by Ferenczi, to observe their child, then less than three years old, from a psychoanalytic point of view, in order to verify the hypotheses advanced a year earlier in *Three Essays on the Theory of Sexuality* (1905). Their observations grew in number, and Freud was regularly informed of them (1909a, p. 6).

The original intention of the parents was not only to study Hans's development but "that in bringing up their first child they would use no more coercion than might be absolutely necessary for maintaining good behaviour. And as the child developed into a cheerful, good-natured and lively little boy, the experiment of letting him grow up and express himself without being intimidated went on satisfactorily" (1909a, p. 6). But eighteen months after the beginning of their observations, they noticed the development of a phobic symptom, and the father decided to undertake an analysis of the child. Similarly, Melanie Klein's initial aim with Erich was purely educative. But education turns to analysis when it is revealed that the child does not derive from it the expected liberation but instead suffers the reinforcement of neurotic traits. We can therefore consider that in 1919 Melanie Klein started from the exact point from which Freud and the father of little Hans had started a dozen years earlier. But she could go further, thanks to her understanding of the symbolism of children's games. This enabled her to overcome the major obstacle noted by Freud in 1918—the child's inability to make verbal associations.[5]

[5] "An analysis which is conducted upon a neurotic child itself," Freud (1918) wrote, "must, as a matter of course, appear more trustworthy, but it cannot be very rich in material: too many words and too many thoughts have to be lent to the child, and even so, the deepest strata [of its psyche] may turn out to be impenetrable to consciousness" (pp. 8, 9).

2. Melanie Klein's First Educational Objectives

Melanie Klein's ambition was purely educational at the outset, but it was grandiose and bore a note of militant enthusiasm.
Her aim was not to cure neurotic disturbances, to care for the
child and readapt him to his surroundings, and to help him
return to normality, as was later the aim of Anna Freud. No,
her point of view was quite different: ordinary humanity is not
normal; it is sick without knowing it. The most widespread
disease is intellectual inhibition. Melanie Klein (1921, pp.
18–25) surveys its most common manifestations, always taking
as a basis the following postulate, which remains implicit but
is nevertheless obviously at work: the only true normality is an
intellectual activity which includes the capacity to cover the
whole field of interests and the capacity to penetrate in depth,
applied to the practical as well as to the scientific and speculative
fields, entirely subjected to the test of reality and liberated in
particular from the illusions of religion. All the forms of "principal injury . . . to intellectual capacity" (p. 22) which she described in July 1919 are based on suppression, under the effect
of repression, of one or another of the aptitudes which seemed
to her the rightful outcome of a natural development of the
individual's capacities. This belief is supported by the contrast,
frequently noted, between the spontaneity and intellectual vi-
vacity of the young child and the more restrained, to some
extent "deflated" nature of the intellectual interests of the
school-age child. The difference is explained by the repression
of sexual curiosity inherent in the oedipus complex.

The inventory of types of inhibition which she draws up
is worth considering for a moment. "A distaste for thorough
investigation in and for itself" (p. 20) is not a natural thing, but
comes directly from adult opposition to the child's sexual curiosity: if we look too deep, the child remaining in the adult fears
the discovery of things forbidden by his parents in the past.
Superficial curiosity, therefore, is all he can allow himself. In
other cases, intellectual curiosity remains possible, and may
even be brilliant, but in a merely sectorial way: the subject stops
short at the consequences his ideas might imply; in particular,
he is afraid of questioning the "ideas forced upon him by au-

thority as true" (p. 20). In a third type, that of the "researcher," the intellect suffers a reduction in scope; attracted by a single problem, the subject "can devote the labour of a lifetime to it without developing any particular interests outside the confined sphere which suits him" (p. 20). Another learned type does not suffer this restriction of his field of interest, but "fails utterly in regard to the greater or smaller realities of daily life" (p. 20). The hypothesis that a lack of interest in day-to-day realities is caused by exclusive preoccupation with abstract thought appears unacceptable to Melanie Klein: only repression of the knowledge of the concrete realities of sex in childhood can explain the failure of intelligence in practical matters. All these states of diminished intellectual capacity are to be blamed on the repressive nature of an education which forbids the manifestations of a child's sexual curiosity. But education also has a disturbing effect by refusing to grant free play to reality testing and by imposing ready-made ideas on a child without giving him a chance to work them out by his own efforts and to judge truth and falsehood for himself:

> Permanent submission to the authority principle, permanent greater or less intellectual dependency and limitation, are based on this first and most significant experience of authority, on the relationship between the parents and the little child. Its effect is strengthened and supported by the mass of ethical and moral ideas that are presented duly complete to the child and which form just so many barriers to the freedom of his thought. [p. 23]

However, the intellectual spontaneity of the child resists this intrusion of the adult world: "a more gifted childish intellect, whose capacity for resistance has been less damaged, can often wage a more or less successful battle against them" (p. 23). Perhaps the child would finally preserve his intellectual freedom if the adults did not have an absolute resource—the religious illusion: "The idea of an invisible, omnipotent and omniscient deity is overwhelming for the child . . ." (p. 23). This idea of God is particularly easy to introduce to the child because of his archaic experience of absolute dependence on his mother;

as Freud (1910) noted, when he grows up and "perceives how truly forlorn and weak he is when confronted with the great forces of life, . . . he attempts to deny his own despondency by a regressive revival of the forces which protected his infancy" (p. 123). The child invents the idea of a protecting God who will protect him from his helplessness vis-à-vis the world, just as the all-powerful mother protected the baby. Moreover, the child's belief in the omnipotence of thought provides a motive for the acceptance of the idea of God, which, in a cycle of causality, feeds the sentiment of omnipotence which contributed to its acceptance. The capacity to test reality is finally modified by the separation of a vast group of thoughts, of received ideas, of inculcated standards, before which personal judgment must bow. Education thus becomes the accomplice of infantile narcissism and the child's "innate tendency to repression" (p. 22). It achieves the socialization of the child at the price of such a mutilation of his intelligence that the simple exercise of independent thought may appear exceptional:

> We are apt to lay stress on the 'courage' of the thinker who, in opposition to usage and authority, succeeds in carrying out entirely original researches. It would not require so much 'courage' if it were not that children would need a quite peculiar spirit to think out for themselves, in opposition to the highest authorities, the ticklish subjects which are in part denied, in part forbidden. [p. 22]

The attitude of the educator who is anxious to apply psychoanalytic knowledge will therefore be simple: no religious education; abolition of the taboos concerned with the child's sexual curiosity; sex education; and struggle against belief in marvels and against the manifestations of the "almost incurable megalomania of mankind" (Ferenczi, 1913, p. 196) which is expressed by the sentiment of the omnipotence of thought.

This program incontestably bears the marks of Ferenczi's influence. The variety of his interests was such that we often forget that he made his entry into the circle of Freud's disciples by reading in 1908, at the Salzburg congress, a paper in which he asks the following question: "What then are the practical advantages education can derive from these [psychoanalytic] experiences?" (1908, p. 281). He lays stress on one of the most serious mistakes of education, "the repression of emotions and ideas. It might almost be said that education cultivates the negation of emotions and ideas." But, as Freud has shown, the repressed always comes back, and tendencies repressed by education can remain so only at the price of "the automatic action of powerful safety measures, a process which consumes much too much mental energy" (p. 287). Thus the conscious personality is weakened by its ceaseless struggle against the repressed:

> Moralising education based on repression calls forth a modicum of neurosis even in the healthy. Only in this way are such social circumstances possible in which behind the catchword of 'patriotism' obviously egotistic tendencies can hide themselves, where under the name of 'social reform' tyrannical suppression of the individual freedom is propagated, where religion receives homage partly as a drug against fear of death (i.e. a drug serving egotistical purposes) and partly as a permissible means of mutual intolerance. . . . Neurosis and hypocritical egotism are the ultimate effects of an education that is based on dogmas, and fails to pay attention to the true psychology of man. [p. 289]

The striking thing about Ferenczi's remarks is that in them the effects of repression are all related to educational influences, and that psychoanalysis is viewed as inspiring a remolding of pedagogical attitudes which should make it possible to prevent neuroses and the evils due to education: "A question arises spontaneously: what would be the therapeutic and pedagogic means of overcoming these evils?" And since, with Ferenczi, we never need to wait long for an answer, he wrote soon afterwards that education "is to psychology . . . as horticulture is to botany" (p. 281). Here we are very close to ideas expressed by Freud himself at this time: it is "civilized" sexual morality that oppresses the individual. The progress of education must involve the suppression of the idea of God and the introduction of sexual education:

> I think that the most significant contribution to progress in the education of the child is the fact that in France the State has

introduced in place of the Catechism an elementary book which gives the child his first instruction on his position as a citizen and on the moral duties which will fall to him one day. But this elementary instruction is regrettably incomplete in that it does not also include instruction on sexual life." [1908][6]

With Ferenczi as with Freud, the aim of any system of education inspired by psychoanalysis is the blossoming of the child's personality in all its dimensions; for Ferenczi in particular the accent is on the preservation and amplification of the capacity for pleasure; the evil he seeks to avoid is that education should make people "unable to find unselfconscious pleasure in the natural joys of life" (1908, p. 281). In 1919 this aim also played a part in the thought of Melanie Klein. But what she adds, and what is special to her, is the privilege granted to intelligence and intellectual autonomy. For her, at this period, the most disturbing symptom was the lack of intellectual spontaneity. The aim of the psychoanalytic education of little Erich was above all to liberate his curiosity by satisfying his sexual curiosity and avoiding repression.

3. Erich's Development Before 1919

Erich's psychoanalytic education began a few days before Easter 1919. The boy was then four years, nine months old. He was born around June 1914, and his father had been away for a year when Erich was between six and eighteen months of age. Around his twentieth month he showed an exaggerated love for his father. He did not begin to speak, his mother says, until he was two; Melitta and Hans had apparently been more precocious, and we can see in Melanie Klein's remark a sign of her anxious attention to the intellectual development of her chil-

---

[6] Note also the lines written by Freud in 1908: "In view of this we may well raise the question whether our 'civilised' sexual morality is worth the sacrifice which it imposes on us. . . . It is certainly not a physician's business to come forward with proposals for reform; but it seemed to me that I might support the urgency of such proposals if I were to amplify Von Ehrenfels's description of the injurious effects of our 'civilised' sexual morality . . ." (p. 204).

dren, as in fact the age at which Erich began to speak was perfectly normal. Between two and three years he was subject to night terrors. At two years and nine months he ran away, and was found in a nearby street staring attentively into the window of a watchmaker's shop. A certain tendency to run away persisted for six months. At three he saw his brother naked in the bath, and exclaimed with delight, "Karl [Hans] has a pipi too!" and said to him: "Please ask Lene [Melitta] if she has a pipi too". He expressed himself correctly at three and a half, but "even then especially remarkable sayings, such as one hears at a very early age sometimes from gifted children, were not observed. In spite of this he gave the impression both in looks and behaviour of an alert and intelligent child" (Klein, 1921, p. 2). According to the judgment of his ambitious mother, "he mastered a few individual ideas very slowly" (p. 2). He could not name colors until he was more than four years old. At four years, three months he began to ask questions, notably "What is a papa needed for?" and "What is a mamma needed for?" The deep significance of these questions was not understood, and the reply was that one needed parents to love and take care of one (p. 3). The child did not persist with these questions. At the age of four and a half he understood the notions of yesterday, today, and tomorrow. His mother thought him backward in practical matters; he did not understand why tradesmen should be paid, and was surprised that people who had so many things should not give them away. At the same period, the number of questions he asked increased considerably. The feeling of omnipotence was very firmly established: he stated, against all evidence, that he could cook, read, write, etc. One day he asked his mother to cook spinach so that it would turn into potatoes, which she interpreted as a belief in her omnipotence. Another day he asked her to give him, immediately, the town of B., where they were due to go the following summer. He showed a marked distaste for roads and streets. He was, however, extremely interested in vehicles, and was never tired of playing at coachman or chauffeur.

As we can see after collecting together the information, scattered through the four articles on his case between 1919 and 1923, which Melanie Klein gives on Erich's development before the beginning of his psychoanalytic education, the child made normal progress. What we should note is that his mother, on several occasions and without any real motive, was anxious about his intellectual development.

4. The First Period of Sexual Education

We must stress the extreme brevity of Melanie Klein's experience as set forth to the Psycho-Analytical Society of Budapest on July 13, 1919. Her observations at that time had lasted less than three months. The educational interventions fell into two short periods, one of three days, the other of four, separated by a brief interval, and the results were evaluated on the basis of the child's development over the following six weeks.

The process began by chance. We know that Erich had been asking more questions for about three months. When Melitta and Hans recalled in front of him events about which he knew nothing, it was explained to him that he was not yet born at the time. Erich appeared very disagreeably affected by the idea of not always having been there. He asked: "Where was I before I was born?" and, a little later: "How is a person made?" His mother explained to him how the child grows inside the mother's body, without mentioning the father's part in conception, in accordance with the rule she had made at the beginning: "We shall let the child acquire as much sexual information as the growth of its desire for knowledge requires . . ." (Klein, 1921, p. 1). This rule implies a positive aspect—the child's question is answered completely, without changing the subject until he changes it himself—and a limiting one: information is given only on the facts on which the question is based. Erich reacted to his mother's explanations by appearing distracted and embarrassed, but at first repeated the question every day. Then he asked Hans and the governess, who told him the fable of the stork, and repeated the same question several times. Then he went back to his mother after several days and repeated the question "How is a person made?" This time he reacted quite differently to the explanations; he told his mother the story of the stork, and her denial of it led to a

general review of childish beliefs: the Easter Hare, Father
Christmas, and angels did not exist. Locksmiths, by contrast,
were acknowledged to exist; the child was beginning to find
intellectual points of reference by which to test reality. However,
events occurred which bore witness to the child's difficulty in
assimilating sexual education. The main one is the episode reported in "Der Familienroman in Statu Nascendi" (Klein, 1920),
which is linked with the difficulties met in the setting up of the
test of reality. A few weeks before this episode, Melanie Klein
had contradicted the story of the Easter Hare told by the neighbors' children. As he liked this story very much, Erich had
received his mother's explanations with bad grace. He had reacted in the same way when she told him that the Devil, about
whom the the neighbors' children also spoke, did not exist. In
both cases he had tried to show his mother the Easter Hare and
the Devil; but it was only a rabbit and a foal glimpsed in a
meadow. The neighbors (the L.'s) were thus a milieu the influence of which ran counter to his mother's explanations. Two
days after the conversation on the origin of children, the Easter
Hare, Father Christmas, etc., Erich announced that he was
changing families. Henceforward he would be the brother of
the L. children. He held to this decision all day and refused to
obey Melanie Klein, whom he no longer considered his mother.
The neighbors had to be asked to send him home in the evening.
He made up with his mother and met her next morning with
the question: "Mamma, please, how did you come into the
world?" When Melanie Klein told Ferenczi about this incident,
she adopted the interpretation he suggested: Erich was very
embarrassed, because of his earlier repressions, by his mother's
explanations; he had wanted to choose a family in which people
were not born in such an unpleasant and common sort of way,
but in a way that was more poetic and more refined.

In any case, the return to his mother was accompanied by
the liberation of his curiosity. For some time he asked questions
about details of the growth of the fetus, and even the mechanism of this growth. One rainy day, chance led to the opening
of a discussion on the existence of God. Erich asked whether
God really knew how long it would rain. His mother replied
"that God did not make the rain but that the rain came from

the clouds, and explained the matter to him" (Klein, 1921, p. 6). Next day he brought up the three questions again: on the origin of babies, their growth, and the rain. He also asked, "But there really is God?" Melanie Klein thus found herself in an embarrassing position: she was an atheist, and had given her children no religious education. However, education at that time included religious instruction, and children were brought up to the idea of God. Arthur Klein, Melanie's husband, though not a practicing Christian, "held a pantheistic conception of the deity" (p. 7). But the question had not up to then been a problem, and they had not yet decided anything between them. After a moment's hesitation, she replied that God did not exist and added, in reply to an objection by Erich, that many grown-ups did not know exactly and could not really tell. This conversation led the little boy to try to master the relationship between existence and perception. What he saw existed, but why could he not see everything that existed—for example, his aunt's house, which he could not see at the moment? Was it the same for his mother as for him? Could she, or could she not, see this house, which was situated in another town? Then he asked her about the origin of the sun. As soon as his father came home in the evening, and before his mother could explain matters, Erich asked him whether God existed. He replied in the affirmative. His wife arrived while the child was beginning a discussion, and so he explained: "no one has ever seen God and some people believe that God exists and others believe that he doesn't. I believe that he does but your mamma believes that he doesn't" (p. 7). This reply had a cheering effect on Erich, who was very anxious at the beginning of the scene. After a few new questions, he took his mother's side: God did not exist, but things you could see, such as trams, did.

That day appears to have marked a decisive turning point. Erich had found a criterion for the existence of objects. At the same time he had observed a difference of opinion between his parents, and had to make his first intellectual choice. His mother's expectations were beginning to come true: the parents' authority, as a criterion of truth, had been shaken, and, as this point of reference was no longer available to him, he applied to the question of God a method of verification drawn from

personal experience. After that day, the child's questions pro-
liferated but took different directions.

The material collected by Melanie Klein during the next
six weeks can be classified along two major axes: liberation and
sublimation of sexual curiosity, and strengthening of the sense
of reality correlated with the decline of the feeling of omnipotence. As far as the first is concerned, questions relating to
birth changed their nature and referred now to the comparison
between humans and animals. Questions on the origin and formation of things applied to all the organs and parts of the
human body, to animals, to plants and their parts, and to in-
animate objects. The child's curiosity turned to the interior of
the body and its contents, urine, and feces. One day while helping to shell peas he made a remark which Melanie Klein (1921)
mentions only briefly (she was unable to interpret fantasies of
this type until after 1925): "He . . . said that he gave the pod
an enema, opened the popo and took out the kakis" (p. 10).
He was also interested in the internal mechanism of things: the
plumbing, a revolver, mechanical toys. In the same period questions emerged which showed that he was wondering about sex
differences. Had his mother always been a girl? Had he always
been a boy? These processes corresponded with a double liberation of his intellect, in breadth and in depth. For the first
time Melanie Klein was experiencing the fact she had postulated: that the lessening of repression brings with it a capacity
for sublimation. The description and explanation of this fact
were to be, three years later, central of her first original contributions.

As far as the second axis was concerned, the sense of reality
progressed rapidly in the boy. His practical adaptation improved. He admitted the necessities of trade; he became interested in money; he began to ask his sister to read him articles
about the Devil from the encyclopedia so that he could form
a definite opinion as to his existence. With great difficulty he
finally admitted that the neighbors' children, who had been ill-
treating him and lying to him for some time, were behaving
badly toward him. He stopped making excuses for them and
changed his playmates. He tested the omnipotence of his parents and progressively recognized the limits of their power,

being sometimes pleased about it (they were not much more powerful than he) and sometimes displeased (if they could not do certain things, then neither could he). He was learning to perceive the difference in meaning between wanting to and being able to. He undertook a systematic investigation on points more particularly concerning his relationship with his parents. What was he allowed to do? Why? What were his duties and rights? What were those of his parents? He wanted to know the precise motive behind prohibitions and argued pertinently if orders were imposed on him without a comprehensible reason. After six weeks he was capable of distinguishing for himself, in most cases, between "stories" which were beautiful but unreal, and "real things" which were not necessarily beautiful but really existed; and he formed a general idea of these two categories.

Melanie Klein (1921) sketched a dynamic and economical explanation of the phenomena she observed: the development of the conflict between sexual curiosity and the "tendency to repression" (p. 22) played a motive part in the conflict between belief in the omnipotence of thought (inspired by the pleasure principle) and the reality principle. The juxtaposition of sexual and intellectual interests enabled them to become stronger than the attachment to the illusion of omnipotence. At the origin of all these processes the, "tendency to repression" had been overcome because the support lent it by the relationship with the parents had disappeared; explanations of the birth process and the divergence of the parents on the existence of God had weakened its position.

Such were the facts and ideas that Melanie Klein presented in her first communication. She obtained from the psychoanalysts of Budapest the very favorable reception we have mentioned, and was elected a member of the society on the spot. In the course of the discussion Anton von Freund offered a criticism and a suggestion. He recognized the psychoanalytic character of her observations, but reproached her with the fact that her interventions were not at all psychoanalytic; she had not offered the child any interpretation and, more particularly, had taken into account only the direct questions of the child, his conscious curiosity. A truly psychoanalytic education, von Freund suggested, would take into account "unconscious questions" and reply to them. Melanie Klein defended her position at the time, but later recognized the soundness of this remark. In addition, von Freund (who clearly knew the identity of the young boy, which Melanie Klein did not likely conceal in her presentation) suggested that she distinguish the moment of "analysis" from other moments of the parental relationship by assigning a fixed time and place to this type of conversation—to explanations of sexuality and, where necessary, interpretations. This advice was received as was the other: at first rejected, then accepted.

5. The Second Period of Psychoanalytic Education

After the initial phase, Erich continued to ask many questions and to develop his practical sense for two or three months. Gradually it became clear that he was repeating indefinitely questions the answers to which he had known for a long time. Melanie Klein began to suspect the truth of von Freund's remark: repression was far from being eliminated; the questions which Erich did not ask and had never asked, about the father's part in conception and the sexual act, were troubling him unconsciously and were being expressed in questions without meaning for the conscious mind. However, Melanie Klein did not yet put into practice the advice given to her, and was content to observe. Things deteriorated rather quickly; during the next two months Erich asked scarcely any new questions, and compulsively repeated stereotyped questions; then followed in succession a withdrawn attitude and inhibition in play. Erich showed signs of boredom even when he was with his mother; he no longer showed any interest in the stories she told him. The inattention he had shown at the very beginning of his analytic education, when listening to the answers given to him, reappeared. He lost interest in other children and did not know what to do in their company. He had some feeding difficulties and in addition lost the taste for playing, even at coachman or chauffeur, which at one time could keep him busy for hours. The change was not a typical neurosis; the child slept well and was healthy, but Melanie Klein was experiencing her first failure, and it was probably a great disappointment. She had to agree with von Freund, and interpreted Erich's general inhibition as a victory for the tendency to repression: "After he had asked many and different questions as substitutes for those he had repressed, he had, in the further course of development, come to the point where he avoided questioning altogether and listening as well, as the latter might, unasked, provide him with what he refused to have" (Klein, 1921, p. 24). The evaluation of the period following the first phase of sexual explanations had to change: the emergence of questions, their number, their growing depth, were a sign of a diminution of repression, and of a greater intolerance of censorship of unconscious derivatives, but were not of final liberation. The child's sexual education had therefore to be undertaken for a second time, and he would be given complete information. In doing this Melanie Klein overcame her own resistances, which had up to this point been expressed in an optimistic philosophy and in the illusion that explanations which were as a whole very superficial would be enough. This deeper investigation, both personal and theoretical, enriched her way of working. She was about to meet play and fantasy, which were finally to become the centerpiece of her theory and technique, thanks to an approach which was also to become characteristic of her method; it consisted of going far beyond the child's obvious preoccupations.

From that point she watched for the first new manifestation of Erich's curiosity, which was to give her the chance to complete her earlier explanations. One day the boy asked how plants grew from seed, and his mother explained the process of fertilization; he scarcely listened to her explanations and quickly interrupted her. Another time he said that if a hen were to lay eggs, a cock was needed, but he very quickly left the subject, and his general attitude remained inhibited in all directions. Liberation came suddenly after a few days, when Melanie Klein gave him a sweet and told him a story which pleased him very much: the sweet, she said, had been waiting for him for a long time, and the sweet's adventures gave rise to a story which delighted Erich, and then to another. From this moment onward the child spontaneously told fantastic stories, richer and richer and longer and longer, with extraordinary verve. Melanie Klein then began cautiously to give him interpretations in order to break down the resistance which sometimes interrupted the stories, and thus discovered that interpretation could lead to a fresh start; this was finally to become very important in her psychoanalytic technique. After some time, Erich resumed his questioning regarding the origin and creation of things.

At the same time he reestablished contact with other children, and began again to play, alone or with friends. In his fantasies and play, oedipal impulses were now clearly recognizable: in his fantasies, two cows were walking together, when one jumped on the other's back and rode astride her. One morning he said to his mother: "I shall climb up on you; you are a mountain and I climb up you" (p. 31). He expressed a wish to see his mother naked and to see "the picture that was in her stomach" (p. 33)—that is to say, the place he was in before being born. In one of his games, two chess pieces were a soldier and a king. The soldier insulted the king and was then put in prison, where he died. But he came back to life, promised not to do it again, and was simply arrested. Two little figures of dogs were his father and himself; one was beautiful (himself) and the other dirty (his father). This emergence of oedipal fantasies was accompanied by a general change. He became more and more cheerful and talkative. In a very short time and with very little help he learned to read with such avidity "as almost to seem precocious" (p. 32). Remembering Melanie Klein's worry about her son's supposed backwardness, we can easily imagine how delighted she was at this development.

The decisive episode of this second phase of Erich's psychoanalytic education was a conversation coming after the reappearance in Erich's games and fantasies of the infantile sexual theory of the anal child, according to which children are made of food and are identical with the feces. He even declared when he was on his pot that the "kakis" were naughty children who would not come, or threatened to beat them because they were too hard or took too long to come.

One day Erich, sitting on his pot, explained to his mother that the "kakis" had run up onto the balcony (the stomach) again, and did not want to come down into the garden (the pot). She gave him an interpretation: "These are the children then that grow in the stomach?" (p. 33). Then, when the child reacted favorably, she continued with her explanations about the difference between feces and children, and recalled the explanations already given about the sexual act, the role of the sperm, and the ova. Erich expressed the wish to "see how a child is made inside like that" and, soon afterward, the wish to "do it to mamma" (p. 34). Melanie Klein then told him of the prohibition of incest; every man had only one wife; she was the wife of Erich's father, when he was big she would be old and he would marry a beautiful young girl. Erich was on the verge of tears, and made her promise that she would still live with him, then asked a string of questions about the growth of the fetus. Following this conversation, he actively assimilated at a conscious level the whole of the explanations he had received, largely gave up the theory of the anal child, and was much less interested in his stomach, about which he had formerly spoken a great deal. In the following days the oedipal fantasy became clearer and clearer, and his mother gave him explanations in a form that was already "Kleinian." Erich, starting from a dream, began a complicated story about a big motorcar and a little motorcar which went into a tramway, the little car running between the big one and the electric train. His mother explained "that the big motor is his papa, the electric car his mamma and the little motor himself, and that he has put himself between papa and mamma because he would so much like to put papa away altogether and to remain alone with his mamma and do with her what only papa is allowed to do" (p. 35). This inter-pretation led, after a brief hesitation, to the resumption of the story. More cars came on to the scene, two chauffeurs had a fight, and one of them was his grandfather. After a silence and an uneasy glance at his mother, he developed the story of the fight. Melanie Klein then asked him who the adversary was. He at once replied, "Me," and turned his story into more and more complicated warlike adventures. As fantasies and games of this type multiplied, his mother reduced the number of interpre-tations; she considered that "part of his complexes had become conscious or at least preconscious" (p. 39) and that that was enough.

This second phase of analytic intervention lasted about two months from the episode of the sweet which had started it. We cannot emphasize too greatly the importance we feel it has in the exploration of her relationship with Erich and for the future of the psychoanalytic play technique.

There were two transformations in this phase. One concerns the attitude of Melanie Klein herself: she became better at measuring the depth of the repression and of the unconscious fantasies. More especially, she seemed to have abandoned her initial objectives. She no longer brought the development of intellectual curiosity into the foreground; it seemed as though she were keeping her distance from her narcissistic desire to make Erich into a new edition of Emmanuel, a superior being on the intellectual plane. She had met with failure, which had led her to understand, after the event, the implications of von Freund's remarks. A comparison of the two periods of intevention yields the impression that on the first occasion the approach to the unconscious was only a means toward a project of elitist pedagogy in the context of an ideology very near to that of the *Aufklärung*, the rationalist philosophy of enlightenment, critical spirit, free thought, and the rejection of authority and religion. In Melanie Klein's real practice, this ideology served as the rationalization of a narcissistic approach to Erich. During the second period, on the other hand, the educational motives fell into the background, became less ideological, and were not so militantly proclaimed. For that reason they could succeed; when his mother changed her attitude, Erich could not only play and use his imagination, but learned to read in a few weeks and gave an impression of precocity. The second transformation lay in this response on Erich's part; now that his mother had partly given up projecting her narcissistic ideals onto him, he could express himself in his own way, through play and fantasies. There ensued, for a few weeks, an extraordinary communication in fantasy between mother and child, making possible a partial elucidation of the oedipus complex at the very moment it was reaching its maximum intensity. This two-month period brought Melanie Klein to an understanding of the equivalence of play, dreams, and fantasy as manifestations of the unconscious. It also gave her her first

experience of a sequence—explanations, apparent refusal, return to play showing that the explanation had been unconsciously accepted—which she was later to apply to the theory
of interpretation. This period, it may be argued, marked the
second stage of the Kleinian "detachment" which formed a
prelude to the formulation of the theories of 1923 (see Chapter
2).

This intensely rich period was interrupted by outside circumstances. Melanie Klein was ill for two months toward the
end of 1919 and could not devote much time to Erich. During
his mother's illness, the child was extremely anxious. He had
difficulty going to sleep. He was less good, was miserable, played
much less, showed an excessive zeal (which his mother could
now recognize as compulsive) for learning to read, and developed a slight phobia with regard to children met in the street.
When she was better, her first care was to fight against the
manifestations of anxiety in her child.

6. The Third Period and the First Analysis

This gave rise to a period of six weeks which Melanie Klein
called a period of "analysis" as opposed to the other phases,
which she called "psychoanalytic education". It appears that it
was during this period that she introduced the technical methods advised by von Freund: "I set a certain time—even if this
had occasionally to be changed—apart for the analysis, and
although owing to our close daily association I was much with
the child, this was steadfastly adhered to" (Klein, 1921, p. 50).
Melanie Klein tried to interpret Erich's dreams according to
the classic method described by Freud: separating out the elements of the manifest content, and tracing the associations stem-
ming from each of them. Here she came up against the
difficulty foreseen by Freud: the child is not capable of free
association on demand. She therefore partially gave up the
systematic exploration of dreams. Instead she founded her
interpretations on the comparison of dreams with each other,
and on symbolism.

This phase of "analysis" brought out homosexual components arising from the boy's negative oedipus complex. One of his anxiety dreams, in which he was pursued by men armed with sticks, guns, and bayonets, gave rise to an interpretation accompanied by fresh explanations. When Melanie Klein explained to him that the weapons represented his father's big penis, which he wanted, but of which he was afraid, the child objected that "the weapons were hard but the wiwi was soft" (p. 40), which led to his being reminded of the explanations about erections. The child, taking up the story again, explained that one of the men chasing him had stuck in the other "and there was only one man!" (p. 40). In other dreams and the fantasies which extended them, he was afraid of the Devil's tail, and described the stomach and the belly as a furnished interior (p. 41). But someone sits on a chair, puts his *head* on the *table* and the whole house falls down. In reply to a question from his mother, he said that the disastrous intrusion was a little stick which "came through the wiwi into the belly and into the stomach . . ." (p. 41). He wanted coitus with his father but dreaded it, fearing he would be destroyed. The fear of witches and poisoners also appeared, and Melanie Klein did not succeed in interpreting it to his satisfaction; she linked it partly with the old sexual theory of the anal child, made from food, and partly with the hostility which Erich felt against her because she had forbidden him to masturbate. However, she glimpsed for the first time the mechanism of splitting, the description of which was ultimately one of her major contributions to psychoanalytic theory (Klein, 1946): the figure of the witch is only the representation of an image obtained by the "division [*Abspaltung*] of the mother-imago" (Klein, 1921, p. 42). This disturbing imago had been "split off from his beloved mother, in order to maintain her as she was" (p. 42). This precursor of the split-off bad mother is the imago of the woman with a penis; one of its symbols is the cow, whose "penis" gives milk. This splitting shows Erich's ambivalence toward the female sex; he sometimes viewed little girls or grown-up women with an unreasonable antipathy. The interpretation of another dream shows us Melanie Klein's first sign of interest in the mechanism of projection. Erich dreamed that he was with an officer. They were coming out of a place, the yard of a warehouse, where he had seen little

wagons going in and out of the buildings. The officer threatened him and would not let him get up. The coming and going
of the wagons represented coitus with his mother. The child
wished to take part in the coitus of his parents. But instead of
interpreting the boy's anxiety in terms of fear of castration by
the father as a punishment for this forbidden wish, she interpreted it in a different way: the boy, frustrated in his incestuous
desires, wishes to attack his father, and projects his hostility
upon him, so that from that moment he fears to be destroyed
by him. This was the beginning of her personal theory of the
child's danger situation. As far as can be ascertained, Freud
never put forward the projection of the boy's parricidal hostility
onto the father to explain the origin of castration anxiety.

At the end of these six weeks of analysis, the manifestations
of anxiety had disappeared. The child went to bed without
trouble and slept without waking. His play regained all its richness, and contact with other children was reestablished. Only
the phobia about strange children remained, and even that in
a very attenuated form. At that moment—if our reconstruction
of the chronology is accurate, this was in June 1920—Melanie
Klein left her son and did not see him regularly for six months.
At any rate the psychoanalytic observation and interventions
were interrupted. We know that during this period Melanie
Klein was present at the congress at the Hague, where Ferenczi
introduced her to Abraham. Arthur Klein, for his part, settled
in Sweden in 1920. Perhaps his wife had joined him there. It
is certain that she returned to Erich at the end of 1920 and
took her children to Berlin, where they arrived in the first days
of 1921. On February 3 she read to the Berlin Society of Psycho-
Analysis the article "The Development of the Child," which was
published that year in *Imago*. During these six months the child
had not relapsed despite the separation, and had even undertaken to rid himself of his phobia by forcing himself to go out
into the street, first running with his eyes closed, and then more
calmly, of which he was very proud. However, at the end of
1920 he showed a marked aversion to analysis and to fairy tales,
the only point on which regression could be observed. At this
period Melanie Klein evaluated her experiment with moderate
but real optimism, in contrast to the enthusiastic comments with

which her 1919 paper had concluded. She considered that on the whole the neurotic troubles were almost overcome, and that the prognosis was favorable: "It may be hoped, therefore, that he will achieve his freedom from his mother by the proper path; that is, by the choice of an object resembling the mother-imago" (p. 50). But her earlier experience put her sufficiently on guard against the persistence of unconscious complexes for her optimism to be without illusions: "I should not like to assert that [the recourse to psychoanalysis] was ended at the point up to which I have here described it. The display of so active a resistance to analysis, and the unwillingness to listen to fairy-tales seem to me in themselves to render it probable that his further upbringing will afford occasion for analytic measures from time to time" (p. 44).

7. The Fourth Period and the Second Analysis

The analysis was in fact resumed once they were settled in Berlin. This time she "went very deep" (Klein, 1923a, p. 78). We can reconstruct its course by the numerous allusions made to it in two articles published in 1923: Early Analysis (1923a) and The Role of the School in the Libidinal Development of the Child (1923b). Sending Erich to school brought on a regular infantile neurosis, with a marked school phobia. This phobia quickly extended to the road leading to school and reactivated his old fear of walks in all its intensity. In all probability the analysis as first concerned with the movement phobia and the road to school, and explored only secondarily the significance for the child of the school background and work. In fact, as early as May 5, 1921, Melanie Klein read a paper entitled "The Disturbances of Orientation in Childhood," which we know from Lola Brook to have been one of three texts put together to make "Early Analysis." Almost all the clinical examples of orientation disturbances in the published article refer to the case of "Fritz." It was not until August 11, 1922, that she gave a talk entitled "The Analysis of a School Composition," which probably involved some of the material later used in "The Role of the School in the Development of the Child." We have already noted the speed with which Melanie Klein, early in her career, published her discoveries; from this can be deduced an hypothosis which we may apply in the case of Erich.

If it is correct, the analysis first aimed to identify the unconscious significance of Erich's dislike of the road to school, before bearing on the significance of school itself. As soon as the anxiety underlying this phobia became obvious, it appeared to be connected with the trees bordering the road and with a bridge—purely imaginary—over which the child was supposed to pass. Erich liked roads bordered by fields, along which he would often urinate. But he was afraid that the trees on the road to school might fall on him: "The tree stood to him for his father's large penis, which he wanted to cut off and therefore feared" (Klein, 1923a, p. 94).[7] The imaginary bridge had a hole in it through which he was afraid of falling. A piece of string dropped on the road frightened him because it looked like a snake. A witch met on the way to school emptied a jug of ink over him and over his satchel; this was an evocation of the split image of the mother-with-a-penis, the penis represented by the jug. At about the same time he hopped on one foot the whole way to school, saying that somebody had cut off his foot. Thus, castration anxiety appears to have been the cause of this phobia.

The fantasies which appeared in the course of analysis make it possible to delve into this more deeply. The child declared that he would like to go to school if he could avoid the walk, and imagined all sorts of ways of doing so: he could put a ladder between the window of his room and that of the schoolmistress, or stretch a rope, also from window to window. He went as far as to invent a machine to throw the rope into different parts of the town where he wanted to go. All this was obviously the elaboration of his infantile sexual theories, and of his fantasies representing the interior of the body as the interior of a house. This fantasy of identity was shown to apply equally to space as a whole. He described fantasies in which his body and his mother's body were towns with a complicated

---

[7] From this point onward Melanie Klein had no doubts about the origin of castration anxiety.

geography, then countries with people and animals in them. He described in great detail the railways on which "pipi-trains" and "kaki-trains" ran. The terminal and the platforms represented the mouth, the anus, the penis. Other stations and other platforms were the eyes, and the openings of the ears and nose. "Thus we found," wrote Melanie Klein (1923a), "that his sense of orientation, which had formerly been strongly inhibited but now developed in a marked manner, was determined by the desire to penetrate the mother's body and to investigate it inside, with the passages leading in and out and the processes of impregnation and birth" (p. 98). After a period of analysis this appeared in the clearest way in the child's play: one day Erich took one of his toys, a little dog which was often called the *son* in his games and fantasies, and slid it over his mother's body, talking about its journeys: the breasts were mountains, the genital region a big river. But the journey ended badly: other toys accused the little dog of committing a crime (for example, damaging his master's car) and it was beaten or killed.

So it was not only reluctance to take the road to school that was explained by castration anxiety. This symptom was simly the expression of a basic misunderstanding of relationships in space which had already appeared on several occasions in the child's earlier life. At the age of five he did not understand why, after leaving Budapest hours before, they were not still there. As noted above, he asked his mother to give him immediately the town where they were to spend next summer; later, as we know, he had felt distaste for going out into the street, and even abandoned his favorite game (playing coachman or chauffeur) before showing a phobia about boys met in the street, of which he cured himself by his own efforts during the last months of 1920. At school, he had difficulty learning geography. This general inhibition of the sense of orientation in space comes from the symbolic meaning of space related to what Melanie Klein (1923a) calls the "geography of the mother's body" (p. 98). The analysis then made it possible to bring out a powerful earlier interest in movement and the exploration of space. Erich had run away several times sround the age of three; he had showed at a very early age an interest in vehicles—horse-carts, automobiles, the trams of Budapest, wagons from his father's factory. The "geography of the mother's body" already underlay this interest, the repression of which corresponded to the repression of the primary wish expressed in it: walking was equivalent to coitus with his mother; observing the movement of vehicles was equivalent to observing the movement of the penis. The repression of the oedipus complex had extended to its symbolic derivatives and had transfomed primary pleasure into anxiety. The interpretation of castration anxiety, bringing the oedipal desires into the conscious mind, allowed a new blossoming of movement play and the exploration of space.

The analysis of fantasies relating to school life enabled the same fantasy network to be revealed. It seemed as though interpretations relating to the symbolic geography of the body preceded the systematic exploration of the unconscious meanings of school exercises, for the fantasies mentioned by Melanie Klein (1923b) have considerable richness and complexity. Erich had learned to read at Ruzomberok, his excessive zeal showing the compulsive nature of his learning. At school he now had to learn to write and count. Learning to write gave him a great deal of trouble; later he made a large number of repeated spelling mistakes, always concerned with the same groups of letters, and he had great difficulty with division.[8] From the very beginning it was clear that the schoolmistress represented the imago of the woman-with-a-penis, and that his homework symbolized coitus and masturbation. The good marks he might get represented the penis, returned to him by a castrating mother. More specific fantasies were attached to writing:

> the lines in his exercise book were roads, the book itself was the whole world and the letters rode into it on motor bicycles, *i.e.* on the pen. Again, the pen was a boat and the exercise book a lake. We found that Fritz's many mistakes (which for a time

[8] The fact that the fantasies reported by Melanie Klein are connected with spelling and division provides an additional argument in support of the supposition that the learning difficulties were analyzed after the disturbances of orientation. It is hard to imagine a child who could not yet write at the beginning of 1921 facing the difficulties of spelling and even more of division before at least six months to a year—thus before the school year 1921–1922. We know that the analysis of the orientation disturbances was already well advanced on May 5, 1921.

could not be overcome, until they were resolved in analysis, when they disappeared without any trouble) were determined by his many phantasies about the different letters which were friendly with one another or fought and had all sorts of experiences. In general he regarded the small letters as the children of the capital letters. The capital S he looked upon as the emperor of the long German s's; it had two hooks on the end of it to distinguish it from the empress, the terminal s, which had only one hook. [Klein, 1923a, p. 100]

Almost every letter or every figure had its particular mythology. The *i* and the *e* of the Latin alphabet were two inseparable friends who always rode on the same motorbike: they loved each other so much that they could hardly be distinguished. The corresponding letters of the Gothic alphabet rode on a motorbike of a different make. The Gothic *i*'s were skillful and intelligent, possessed weapons, lived in caves, etc. The *L*'s, by contrast, were dirty, clumsy, and repulsive; the streets of their town were full of rubbish; clearly they represented the feces. Erich had great difficulty in writing the German double *S* until the underlying fantasy became conscious: one of the *S*'s was his father, the other himself. They were to embark together on a lake on board a boat represented by the pen. The Erich *S* always outran the father *S* and left him on the land.

The general inhibition with regard to writing was based on a special inhibition with regard to *i*, the double movement of which—up and down—is repeated in all the other letters. The dot on the *i* represented a thrust of the penis, like full stops and semicolons; explaining that you had to press hard on this dot, he raised his pelvis, then dropped it. When he could express his fantasies, he could enjoy writing, fashioning more and more little scenes on the subject of letters.

The inhibition in doing division, which probably came later, happened in a period when Melanie Klein was beginning to glimpse the importance of anal sadism. Erich had understood perfectly the principle of division, but his operations were always wrong. His associations went back to fantasies relating to the bringing down of the figures of the dividend. They had to be violently pulled down and that could not be pleasant for them. Quite early he fantasized about a circus act in which a woman was sawn in pieces without being killed, and that led to his first cannibalistic fantasy: "He then related (also in connection with a previously elaborated phantasy) that actually every child wants to have a bit of his mother, who is to be cut in four pieces; he depicted quite exactly how she screamed and had paper stuffed in her mouth so that she could not scream, and what kind of faces she made. etc. A child took a very sharp knife, and he described how she was cut up" (Klein, 1923b, p. 70). After a long and detailed description of this fantasy, during which he showed signs of nervousness, he admitted that the pieces were eaten by the children: "It now appeared also that he always confused the remainder with the quotient in division, and always wrote it in the wrong place, because in his mind it was bleeding pieces of flesh with which he was unconsciously dealing. These interpretations completely removed his inhibition with regard to division" (p. 70). From the next day onward, Erich got all his divisions right, to the stupefaction of both the teacher and himself.

At that time Erich was probably almost eight, and his analysis does not seem to have been extended beyond that period. In fact, from 1921 onward, his mother's psychoanalytic activities broadened and occupied her more and more. She had new patients—other children but also, though more sporadically, adults. From 1922 she worked at the psychoanalytic polyclinic in Berlin, and she gave courses for people in charge of kindergartens. But most particularly it appears that the interpretations given to Erich in 1921 were effective and that he definitely overcame his infantile neurosis, the manifestations of which, though stubborn, were never serious. In any case, the child was cured of his school phobia and his difficulties with orientation in space.

8. The Lessons of Erich's Education and Analysis

The major gains made by Melanie Klein in the analysis of her son were essentially methodological. Erich showed none of the massive symptoms the understanding of which would lead to the building of truly Kleinian conceptions, but his difficult education made it possible progressively to forge the tools (technical methods and initial theoretical notions) which would enable his mother to tackle her first really difficult cases.

We will confine ourselves here to examining the technical aspects of Erich's psychoanalytic education, as the following chapter will be devoted to a lengthy examination of the theoretical notions which arose from it; we will see how they constitute the first pre-Kleinian system, the relationship of which to the Kleinian system proper deserves to be examined in detail. On the technical plane Melanie Klein learned, in her dealings with Erich, the insufficiency of the best educational methods, the depth of the sources of guilt and anxiety, the interrelation of play and unconscious fantasies, the slowness of the process of interpretation, and the necessity of interpreting unconscious anxiety, which was always the characteristic feature of her method.

The realization of the inadequacy of every educational method was a lesson, no doubt a bitter one, of her experience with Erich. We have seen the illusions Melanie Klein entertained when, after less than six months of psychoanalytic education, she appeared convinced that the revelation of the origin of children and Erich's rejection of the idea of God would protect him from intellectual inhibitions. This rationalist optimism rested on a lack of understanding of the depth of the repression of the child's sexual curiosity and the early age at which it begins. It implied in the second place a singularly ambitious and intellectualist definition of normality, behind which we may glimpse the influence of a narcissistic ideal. But this narcissistic attitude was exactly what motivated Melanie Klein's perseverance when it was revealed that the beneficial effects of the first phase of sexual education did not last more than three months. She thought she had achieved definitive success. She was to lose her illusions, but the progress made by Erich in those three months proved to her that the instrument was to some extent effective, and that it was enough to go back to work. In the course of the four increasingly psychoanalytic phases of her educative and psychotherapeutic relationship with Erich, objectives stated in specifically psychoanalytic terms—liberation of fantasy activity, liberation of play—replaced the pedagogical objectives with which she began. Melanie Klein understood the necessity for a detour through the exploration of the unconscious before any attempt at reeducation, and the truth of the paradox which, all her life, was to be her answer to the supporters of other schools of child analysis, and for which she was to obtain at least partial recognition: psychoanalysis can help education only by placing any educational motive in parentheses. The child's good social adaptation and success at school cannot be goals for the child analyst; they are at most secondary bonuses of psychoanalysis. This brings with it a far-reaching attitude, more basic even than the technical measures and ideas through which it is expressed: "normality" cannot be stated in terms of objective criteria, but in terms of liberty, fluidity, and variety in the creation of fantasies. Thus one essential element of her ideological presuppositions of 1919 had been retained: no reference to external criteria can be acceptable in psychoanalysis. It was in fact taken even further: after deploring her son's lack of precociousness, she became able to feel unease at his excessive zeal for learning to read; that is to say, she could see that intellectual behavior was not particularly privileged, and that its excessive reinforcement might be a pathological sign. Its meaning, she realized, could not be evaluated in isolation, but only in relation to the personality as a whole. She thus admitted to what Daniel Lagache (1964) has called "the category of the whole." At the same time, she found a way of making better-founded evaluations; she discovered the true "psycho-analytical objects," to use an expression of her disciple Wilfred Bion: organizations of fantasies, the description of which was to help her later to build new foundations for psychopathology as a whole. The first lesson of Erich's education may be stated in the following terms: the objectives of the analysis of children can be defined only in psychoanalytic terms. This may seem little more than sterile tautology or short-sighted "technicism," but at all events it was, within any technical or theoretical formula, an attitude she was the first person (and for a long time the only one) to hold toward child analysis; and it was a direct result of her experience with Erich.

The second deep-seated attitude which Melanie Klein drew

from it was her peculiar sensitivity to anxiety. We know that later she elaborated this attitude into a theory, scarcely acceptable from a strictly Freudian point of view, of unconscious anxiety,[9] and into a very particular interpretive technique. What is interesting here is that this reactivity to anxiety was acquired in her work with Erich. She certainly proceeded from unconscious insight. This insight seems to have already been present beneath the intellectualist rationalizations of 1919. When she said, as she did then, that every state of diminished intellectual achievement was a sign of unconscious suffering and the result of repression, she was preparing herself, seven years before Freud's "Inhibitions, Symptoms and Anxiety" (1926), to seek for the anxiety hidden behind outward inhibition or lack of interest. The bond, so firmly fixed in her, between pleasure and the exercise of intelligence, led her to detect the suffering of Erich as soon as he gave up his curiosity, and to bring this suffering to light. She thus arrived at a technical measure completely alien to the official analytic technique of the period, if not to Freud's practice. This measure consisted in activating the development of anxiety. We should remember here that such a step was incomprehensible from a metapsychological point of view before the revision, in 1926, of the psychoanalytic theory of anxiety. Melanie Klein was emotionally affected and even frightened by the intensity of the anxiety suffered by Erich during the final phase of his analysis. She herself tells how this spontaneous attitude became an analytic technique:

> I deviated from some of the rules so far established, for I interpreted what I thought to be most urgent in the material the child presented to me and found my interest focusing on his anxieties and the defences against them. This new approach soon confronted me with serious problems. The anxieties I encountered when analysing this first case were very acute, and although I was strengthened in the belief that I was working on the right lines by observing the alleviation of anxiety again and again produced by my interpretations, I was at times perturbed by the intensity of the fresh anxieties which were being brought

[9] Freud (1915, pp. 177–179) considered the notion of unconscious affect scarcely comprehensible.

into the open. On one such occasion I sought advice from Dr.
Karl Abraham. He replied that since my interpretations up to
then had often produced relief and the analysis was obviously
progressing, he saw no ground for changing the method of
approach. I felt encouraged by his support and, as it happened,
in the next few days the child's anxiety, which had come to a
head, greatly diminished, leading to further improvement. The
conviction gained in this analysis strongly influenced the whole
course of my analytic work. [1955, p. 123]

This intense need to bring out into the open the smallest sign
of anxiety seems inseparable from the other attitude, whereby
behavior is evaluated by the place it occupies in the dynamic
totality of the personality. Anxiety is in fact the immediate internal manifestation of psychological disturbance: the sign (in
the first psychoanalytic theory of anxiety) of the repression of
a quantity of libido which is blocked in a condition of stasis; the
signal and the precursor (in the second Freudian theory) which
proclaims the thrust of an impulse not in accordance with the
ego; and the coming into play of the defensive process, the sign
of the activity of the death impulse (in the definitive Kleinian
theory). It signals the critical points of the defensive conflict—that
is to say, what the interpretation must reach, at least finally. It
gives a strictly psychoanalytic criterion for the pertinence of the
analyst's intervention.

All the other lessons she drew from Erich's analysis can be
related to these two transformations of her attitude. The giving
up of constructing educational methods had very little influence, and the discovery of this revealed the depth of the origin
of the sources of repression by a simple deduction, for at the
time everyone, including Melanie Klein, considered anxiety to
be the result of repression (or, more exactly, the result of the
increase of internal stimuli caused by the accumulation of libido
frustrated as a result of repression). The revelation of the early
stage at which repression appears is the consequence of the
interpretation of very early inhibition (she finally interpreted
Erich's "backwardness" of speech as such) which proves the
existence of very early anxiety (which also appears in night

terrors) and thus the existence of a repression at exactly the same time.[10]

The interrelation of play and unconscious fantasies is explained according to Melanie Klein within the concrete dynamics of anxiety. It leads directly to the essential thesis of 1923, which we shall examine in the next chapter: that inhibition is the consequence of an "unconscious anxiety."

The discovery of the slowness—but the reality—of working through in the child is linked with the discovery of the depth of the sources of anxiety. From the beginning, Erich's mother was not discouraged by the child's inattention during her explanations, by his opposition, or by his attempts to change families. She saw in them a resistance to sexual education, arising from the "innate tendency to repression," the importance of which she underestimated at that time, though she recognized its existence. Once her beginner's optimism had been cooled by the fluctuations of Erich's attitude, an optimism based on experience developed. Even when the child was not listening, he in fact heard, and what he heard made its way into his unconscious. We know that Melanie Klein often described the characteristic attitude of the child faced with a "deep" interpretation: he is at first distracted and inattentive, often goes on to something else, and some time afterward a game or a drawing shows that the interpretation is accepted. It was Erich who showed her the fixity of this characteristic sequence, at essential moments the first and second phases of his sex education (but not in the two final phases of analysis).

These factors together led Melanie Klein, from the first phase of Erich's education (the first phase of analysis in 1920), to defend what was to become one of the foundations of Kleinian psychoanalysis, the idea of the universally beneficial nature of the psychoanalysis of children. This idea has a negative and in a way polemical aspect: generalizing from what Freud said about little Hans, Melanie Klein (1921) affirmed the absolute harmlessness of psychoanalysis applied to young children:

[10] Although the notion of anxiety independent of all repression (e.g., in actual neurosis) occurred in Freud's writings in this period, Melanie Klein never used it. Until she worked out her own theory of anxiety after 1927, she considered all anxiety as closely related to the process of repression.

"There is certainly no reason to fear a too far-reaching effect from early analysis . . ." (p. 48). As Freud had already observed, the elimination of repression brings, not the crude putting into practice of sexual and aggressive desires, but the enrichment of sublimation. The role of psychoanalysis, then, is not only curative—that too is a constant of the Kleinian attitude—but preventive and, if not educational, at least formative: "What early analysis can do is to afford protection from severe shocks and to overcome inhibitions. This will assist not only the health of the individual but culture as well, in that the overcoming of inhibitions will open up fresh possibilities of development" (p. 48). Because of this—and here she disagrees with Freud—the possibilities of application are unlimited.

For the moment she was considering only normal children: "I am of the opinion that no upbringing should be without analytic help, because analysis affords such valuable and, from the point of view of prophylaxis, as yet incalculable assistance" (p. 45). Since every normal childhood involves an early neurosis, psychoanalysis always has its place: "It would therefore be advisable with most children to pay attention to their dawning neurotic traits; if however we wish to get hold of and remove these traits, then the earliest possible intervention of analytic observation and occasionally of actual analysis becomes an absolute necessity (p. 52). In order to carry out such a project she thought of founding psychoanalytic kindergartens directed by women psychoanalysts, comparable to the one Vera Schmidt had organized in Leningrad: "There is no doubt that a woman analyst who has under her a few nurses trained by her can observe a whole crowd of children so as to recognize the suitability of analytic intervention and to carry it out forthwith" (p. 53). Later, when she had invented the play technique, she turned, by contrast, to the most serious pathological cases. From 1924 she analyzed prepsychotic children, and thirty years later her method enabled her pupil Emilio Rodrigué (1955) to carry out an amazing technical feat: the analysis of a mute psychotic child. But her affirmation remained the same from beginning to end: the field of application of child psychoanalysis is unlimited.

2

The Proto-Kleinian System

Immediately on arrival in Berlin, at the same time as she was carrying out Erich's second analysis, Melanie Klein began to practice the psychoanalysis of children. Her patients, few to begin with, became progressively more numerous. The texts published in 1923 and 1925 mention some of them: Felix, Ernst, and Grete were analyzed before 1923; Werner and Walter, both mentioned in 1925, had at that date only just begun their analyses. Felix's case is the most fully documented; it is cited in ten different passages, some of which are several pages long. His analysis, begun as early as 1921, consisted of 370 sessions. "As he came to analysis only three times a week," it lasted three years and three months, and so ended in the course of 1924 (Klein, 1925, p. 106). It was Melanie Klein's first long analysis—"deep" as was said at that period—to be successfully completed. It enabled her to fix her technique exactly, and to illustrate her first psychoanalytic notions, worked out in large measure while interpreting the neurotic difficulties of this patient.

1. The Psychoanalysis of Felix (1921–1924)

At the beginning of his analysis Felix was a child of thirteen, without characteristic symptoms, but showing to a remarkable degree the features of what Franz Alexander (1923) called the

49

neurotic character. He was rather unemotional, had no taste
for study despite real intelligence, and was not very sociable.
For some time before the beginning of his analysis he had had
a tic which had not worried either his family or himself. This
clinical picture, containing inhibitions, but no marked symptoms, corresponds exactly to Melanie Klein's theoretical interests during this period, so that Felix, at first together with Erich
and then alone, had a considerable place in the writings of 1923
and 1925. The two articles of 1923 contain long descriptions
of his fantasies. The article of 1925, "A Contribution to the
Psychogenesis of Tics," is devoted almost entirely to him.

From the beginning of his psychoanalysis, which was exactly contemporary with Erich's second "analysis," Melanie
Klein applied to him the same hypothesis as she did to Erich:
his distaste for school and lack of scholastic success amounted
to a neurotic inhibition. It was therefore necessary to interpret
the fantasies underlying school activities in order to bring out
the anxiety which prevented success. Unlike Erich's inhibitions,
Felix's had more to do with his relationship with the schoolmaster than with the special symbolic meaning of the exercises.
However, the role of this symbolic meaning remained clearly
discernible. He told how certain boys in his class copied their
Greek compositions from one another. This fact was the starting
point for a fantasy relating to what he might do in order to
have a better place in class. He imagined killing all those above
him, so only the schoolmaster, who was unassailable, would be
better than he. Behind this belief in the teacher's inviolability
Melanie Klein discovered a fantasy involving the wish to take
his place on the dais, to speak instead of him, and to reduce
him to silence. Various associations enabled this fantasy to be
analyzed. One day Felix imagined that the teacher, who was
standing in front of the class, leaning his back against his desk,
was going to fall over backward, break the desk, and hurt himself. This fantasy betrays the sadistic conception of coitus; the
teacher represents the father, the desk the mother. The wish
to take the father's place, arising from Felix's oedipus complex,
is expressed in the wish to supplant the teacher in class. The
homosexual desire arising from the inverted oedipus complex
was at work in the rivalry with his classmates; it was important

to come nearer the teacher. The two impulses occasioned castration anxiety: the schoomaster, attacked in fantasy, might well avenge himself; and, as an object of homosexual desire, he might castrate Felix in sadistic coitus. Anxiety thus prevented the boy from achieving scholastic success, which would represent the fulfillment of homosexual or patricidal wishes; as in Erich's case, this anxiety was at the root of the inhibition.

Melanie Klein found a second analogy with her son: we know that Erich, before suffering a general inhibition of the sense of orientation, had shown a real liking for movement and exploration (his running away at about three years, his interest in vehicles, his passion for playing at coachman and chauffeur). Similarly Felix, before losing his interest in schoolwork at the age of eleven, had been an excellent pupil. The inhibition, then, was not a deficiency pure and simple; it was caused by the repression of an interest. She learned that during the time Felix was successful in his schoolwork he was clumsy, showed signs of excessive physical agitation, could not keep his legs still in class, and had a great aversion to sport and gymnastics. The transformation took place when his father, who had been in the army, returned from the First World War. He threatened to punish his son for his fear of physical exercise, and in fact beat him and called him a coward. At the same time he discovered and put a stop to Felix's masturbation. The headmaster of the school died, and an illness of the boy at about this time necessitated a nasal examination which reactivated his castration anxiety (this he had associated with medical and surgical intervention ever since his circumcision, which was carried out at the age of three). Felix succeeded in conquering his fear, developed a passion for football, and also participated in gymnastics and swimming. He gave up masturbation, though not without difficulty. But when his father undertook to check his schoolwork, he lost the taste for study, and school became a torture. His inhibitions had not been resolved but merely altered. It seemed as if Felix could not be successful at school and in sport at the same time: failure in one of these activities had to compensate for success in the other. However, this observation did not satisfy Melanie Klein. Intrigued by the rather late development of the boy's interest in sport, she wondered where it came from and, more particularly, where it derived its energy. She thus took a step which seems decisive, as it presaged her first theoretical innovations: for the first time she had the idea of trying to bring out the unconscious significance of a normal and successful activity which did not comprise any regression in the level of functioning of the psychological system. The events which occurred after the father's return show that Felix had transferred his interest in schoolwork to sports. His father's threats and injunctions showed up the phenomenon insofar as they modified the factor of ego syntonicity. But do these events allow us to understand in full this exchange of the value of pleasure and unpleasure attached to schoolwork and sport? We have to suppose that the psychological energy attached to the former had been withdrawn from it and reinvested in the latter. The interpretation of learning difficulties made it possible to bring out the nature of the fantasies associated with school; they involved the infantile sexual theory of coitus as destructive, functioning as the expression and the stake of the conflict, and a compromise between active and passive oedipal impulses. Only an unconscious equivalence between sport and competition in schoolwork can explain Felix's change in tastes. The analysis therefore turned toward the exploration of the unconscious meanings of football.

From the very beginning this sport appears to have been linked in Felix's mind with masturbation. The only masturbatory fantasy that remained conscious in the first period of his psychoanalysis was the following: "He is playing with some little girls; he caresses their breasts and they play football together. In this game he is continually disturbed by a hut which can be seen behind the little girls" (Klein, 1925, p. 108). The hut was revealed as a lavoratory, leading to memories relating to Felix's mother. This enabled Melanie Klein to interpret the boy's anal fixation and his unconscious hostility toward his mother. Football, a game in which the ball has to be put into the goal, appears as a symbolic representation of coitus. The fact of playing football is for the unconscious the equivalent of masturbation, and serves to discharge surplus sexual tension. But the problem now is the earlier distaste for physical exercise in any form. Faithful to her general hypothesis, maintained since 1919, that all repugnance hides an inhibition, she considered the past clumsiness and cowardice of her patient as the effect of an early inhibition: his initial love of movement, associated from the start with sexual images, had been the object of a first repression which left him no other outlet but physical agitation in class. His schoolwork, which expressed the same unconscious fantasies, had escaped inhibition because here they showed themselves in a more disguised and ego-syntonic form. The same libidinal impulses could therefore be discharged between the ages of six and eleven years in the form both of pleasure in schoolwork and of anxiety regarding violent excercise. The father's return and his brutal intervention only modified the economy of this unstable balance by acting on the factor of ego syntonicity; the change of tastes which followed had taken a road already traced by unconscious links between sport and study as substitutes for masturbation and sexual interests.

As the analysis continued it brought out everything that was compulsive and reactionary in his interest in football. When Felix understood that the sport was for him, a none too satisfactory substitute for masturbation, his interest declined, while he showed a renewed interest in certain school subjects. At the same time he was progressively able to overcome his anxiety at touching his genital organs, and began again to masturbate when he was fourteen.

However, Felix could not yet allow himself an improvement in his condition without paying in one way or another. At the very moment he was making such progress, the tic, which up to then had appeared only at long intervals, began to dominate the clinical picture. This tic had three phases: it began with a feeling of tearing in the nape of the neck, which initiated first a movement of throwing back the head, then a rotation of the neck from right to left; it ended with a movement of the chin, which was pressed against the chest, accompanied by a sensation of drilling into something. This tic had appeared shortly before the analysis, when he had secretly been watching sexual relations between his parents. Melanie Klein linked the first phase of the tic with Felix's identification with his mother (a feeling of being brutally penetrated), the second with the boy's own movements when trying to see and hear the scene better, and

the third with his identification with his father in an active
sadistic role. The frequency of the tic decreased with deeper
exploration of Felix's homosexual wishes and the fantasies
bound up with the primal scene, experienced in very early
childhood and reactivated by the recent observation of parental
coitus.

During this period of the analysis the boy found a new
source of pleasure. He began to be interested in music, to go
to concerts, and to develop a passion for certain conductors and
musicians. It was easy to link this interest with the sublimation
of the homosexual impulses which had found an outlet in the
tic, and to realize that the taste for music was not appearing
then for the first time, but rather was reappearing after a long
period of inhibition. Comments on the grand piano which had
prevented him during a concert from meeting the feature so-
loist gave rise to screen memories: he remembered being afraid
at seeing his distorted reflection in the polished surface of the
piano in his parents' home. He called to mind the position of
his cot in relation to his parents' bed, when he used to sleep in
their room before he was six years old; the height of the big
bed prevented him from seeing what was happening in it, and
his observation of the primal scene had been essentially auditory. The audible signs of his father's genital exploits were thus
at the root of his early interest in noises and sounds. In his
third year Felix had liked to sing; in that way he was identifying
with his father. This pleasure was repressed after his circumcision at the age of three, but he had had time to become
interested in the motor and rhythmical elements of music. The
conductor appeared to him as the tolerant father who allowed
the musicians (his children) to take part in the concert (his
sexual relations with the mother), directing and guiding them.
When Felix's interest in music reappeared during analysis, passive admiration was accompanied by elements expressing
greater activity: the young music lover was fascinated by the
virtuosity of great conductors, and would have liked to know
how they made the musicians follow their beat with such precision. As he became conscious of the meaning of this interest,
the active elements developed. After a few homosexual episodes
he was able to feel passionate admiration for an actress and

thus to move on to the choice of a heterosexual object. He then had a vague relationship with a girl older than himself, which Melanie Klein asked him to break off at least temporarily in order not to bring down the wrath of his father against the treatment. When she ended the analysis, Felix, then aged sixteen, was a good pupil again, was interested in music and theater, and had become heterosexual. Both the compulsive love of sport and the tic had disappeared.

At the end of this psychoanalysis—the first she carried out under ordinary conditions—Melanie Klein was capable of linking the whole of her patient's development with the successive transformations of his masturbatory fantasies; these were seen to govern his inhibitions, his symptoms, and his sublimations as a whole. She could establish also that the variants of these fantasies organized Felix's object relations during successive periods, both in his development and in his analysis. When, in early childhood, he shared his parents' room, his masturbatory fantasies often involved a composite being, half old man, half child (half his father, half himself) coming down from a tree trunk. Later his fantasies involved the heads of Greek heroes. At puberty the heterosexual urge brought first the fantasy of the girls with whom he played football; then, in the course of the analysis, he fantasied a woman lying on him and, finally, under him. Progress in development and cure appeared not only in the abandonment, "condemnation," or "wearing out" pure and simple of the unconscious fantasies revealed by interpretation, but in the work out of these fantasies at a higher level, from the point of view both of libido and of the structure of the object relationship. Thus the psychoanalytic treatment of Felix made it possible to amplify the conclusions of Erich's psychoanalytic education and psychotherapy. It led Melanie Klein to work out a genetic theory of fantasy that served as a guide to interpretation and provided her first theory of cure.

2. The Implicit Theoretical Elements of Melanie Klein's Clinical Approach Before 1923

It is possible to reduce this conception of fantasies to a series of general statements which, though not always explicitly formulated by Melanie Klein, are shown by her clinical data and interpretations to admit of few exceptions.

●*Thesis 1. All behavior and all psychological activity are the realization or expression of unconscious or preconscious fantasies.*

This thesis was not generally formulated in the texts of the period 1921–1925. Nonetheless it may be said to exist as an implicit assumption, especially in light of the myriad activities and psychological forms Melanie Klein ascribes to fantasies, whether unconscious or preconscious.

Motor activity. This includes moving about, exploration of space, the sense of orientation, and the enjoyment of walks. Erich provides the prototypical illustration:

> I will give an instance of phantasies which occurred later on in the analysis, in which the original pleasurable significance of the road was evident. . . .
> His original pleasure in roads corresponded to the desire for coitus with the mother. . . . In this connection there were many phantasies which showed that he was under the influence of the mental image of the inside of his mother's body and, by identification with her, of his own body. [Klein, 1923a, pp. 95–96]

Food likes and dislikes. The example of Erich is equally characteristic in this respect. Melanie Klein (1921) compares his numerous fantasies relating to the stomach and his attitudes to food: "the stomach had a peculiar significance for this child. . . . He would sometimes too complain at meal-times, though not often, of 'cold in the stomach,' and declared it was from the cold water. He also displayed an active dislike for various cold dishes" (pp. 32–33). At another phase of Erich's education: "This represents impregnation through eating, and his disgust at certain kinds of food was determined by these phantasies" (1923a, p. 97).

Acuity of perception. "When he first came to analysis, Felix had a very pronounced tendency not to see the things that were nearest to him"; Melanie Klein explains this as "the repression of scoptophilia which was heightened by the primal scene" (1925, p. 111).

Body image. In Erich's case this is described as a representation elaborated through innumerable fantasies connected with bodily functions and with the identification with the mother. Recall here Erich's fantasies about the stomach and the womb considered as houses or flats, with their doors (the bodily orifices), their balconies, their furniture, etc.; his personifications of feces, urine, and the penis (the "Kaki-trains," "General Pipi"); and his identification of his mother's body with a town and, finally, with the entire universe (the "geography of the mother's body").

The voice, singing, and speaking. These are infiltrated with sexual fantasies. In Grete's analysis (Klein, 1923b), "the girl's stammering proved to be determined by the libidinal cathexis of speaking as well as of singing. The rise and fall of the voice and the movements of the tongue represented coitus" (p. 62). We know that "Felix had already in his third year revealed by his singing an identification with his father" (Klein, 1925, p. 109).

Physical activity and sport. These are attached to underlying fantasies not only in Felix's case. "This meaning of football, and indeed of all sorts of games with balls, I discovered from the analyses of both boys and girls to be typical" (Klein, 1923a, p. 90).

Concerts, theaters, the cinema. We have seen numerous illustrations in Felix's case, and Melanie Klein (1923a) provides others: "In a number of cases it became clear that theatres and concerts, in fact any performance where there is something to be seen or heard, always stand for parental coitus—listening and watching, standing for observation in fact or phantasy—while the falling curtain stands for objects which hinder observations, such as bedclothes, the side of the bed, etc." (pp. 101–102). In another passage she goes into greater detail: "In Mrs. H. I found that a marked artistic appreciation of colours, forms and pictures was similarly determined, with this difference, that in her the early infantile observations and phantasies were concerned with what was to be *seen*" (p. 102).

Scholastic and intellectual activities. Recall here the innumerable games and fantasies of Erich, to which may be added similar ones found with Lisa, Ernst, and Grete. They affected all school subjects: reading, writing, arithmetic, grammar, history, geography, and natural science.

> In reference to the analysis of sentences Grete spoke of an actual dismembering and dissection of a roast rabbit. . . .
>
> In Lisa's analysis I learnt that in studying history one had to transplant oneself into 'what people did in earlier times.' . . . of course the infantile phantasies of battles, slaughters etc., also played an important part, according to the sadistic conception of coitus. . . .
>
> . . . in connection with the repressed interest in the mother's womb . . . interest in the natural sciences is frequently also inhibited. [Klein, 1923b, pp. 71–72]

Neurotic symptoms. These, of course, are determined by underlying fantasies, and Melanie Klein shows herself to be a faithful disciple of Freud in everything concerning dreams, parapraxes, screen memories, etc.

Object relations. These are determined in their entirety by unconscious and preconscious fantasy.

The organization of the personality. This idea is expressed most particularly with regard to the case of Felix (Klein, 1925): "there was a close connection of the tic with the whole personality of the patient, with his sexuality as well as with his neurosis, with the fate of his sublimations, with the development of his character and with his social attitude. This connection was rooted in his masturbation phantasies . . ." (p. 118).

This list, which omits no type or level of behavior, shows the central place which from this period on was occupied by fantasy in Melanie Klein's overall attitude, even though she did not yet formulate the thesis explicitly.

Insistence on this point may seem surprising. The idea of the active presence of fantasy scenes is now common to a large number of psychoanalytic authors, especially in France and Great Britain, and the importance of this conception in the psychoanalytic study of limited groups is well known. Wilfred

Bion (1961) has distinguished three different forms of the "basic group," according to the unconscious fantasy activity common to its members: dependence, attack-flight, and coupling. From a more general point of view, Laplanche and Pontalis (1967) write,

> the psycho-analyst must endeavour in the course of the treatment to unearth the phantasies which lie behind such products of the unconscious as dreams, symptoms, acting out, repetitive behaviour, etc. As the investigation progresses, even aspects of behaviour that are far removed from imaginative activity, and which appear at first glance to be governed solely by the demands of reality, emerge as emanations, as 'derivatives' of unconscious phantasy. In the light of this evidence, it is the subject's life as a whole which is seen to be shaped and ordered by what might be called, in order to stress this structuring action, a phantasmatic *(une phantasmatique)*. [p. 317]

The fact remains, however, that there is no explicit mention of this idea in the writings of Freud. There are certainly plenty of references showing that he has considered some activity of pure thought or some apparently rational activity in practical life as the expression of a fantasy, but it is never the subject of a general affirmation. It may even be thought that certain Freudian conceptions are directly opposed to this idea. Freud in his later writings tended to view the oedipus complex as in certain cases not so much repressed as suppressed and passed over. The very idea of fantasy in Freud is closely connected with the idea of a regressive path of excitation, as opposed to a progressive path controlled (in the first instance, at least) by consciousness and perception. A text like "Formulations on the Two Principles of Mental Functioning" (Freud, 1911) clearly opposes hallucination—the prototype of fantasy—to reality testing. Numerous authors, notably those of the American school of ego psychology and of the British school of Anna Freud, believe that there are purely "rational" psychological activities which have nothing to do with fantasy, provided certain favorable conditions exist. Thus Anna Freud (1965) could write: "There is a long way to go before a child can control its feeding in an active and rational way, either at a quantitative or a qualitative level, depending on its own needs and appetite, without taking into account its relationship with the one who gives it this food, or its conscious or unconscious phantasies" (pp. 69–70). In another passage she admits that it is possible to find, by extraanalytic observation of very young children or predelinquent adolescents, "alternation between the two modes of functioning: during periods of calm, behaviour is governed by the secondary process, but each time an impulse is realised (by sexual satisfaction, an attack, or possession of an object) the primary process wins" (p. 23). In such a conception, fantasy, infiltrated by the primary process, whose mark it always bears, even in its most secondary-process forms, appears as an agent of disorganization rather than of organization as regards behavior.

There is reason therefore to think that if today we are accustomed to admit that fantasy shapes and organizes the whole of behavior, and that, as Daniel Lagache (1964) writes, "the representation of reality is infiltrated by fantasy" (p. 6), we owe this state of affairs to the specific influence of Kleinian ideas. Freud made no positive utterance on this point. It was Susan Isaacs (1943), Melanie Klein's friend and pupil, who explicitly said for the first time that fantasies are the principal contents of unconscious psychological processes. At the time the idea appeared new enough for Susan Isaacs to distinguish "fantasy," a daydream which could be either conscious or repressed, from "phantasy," a psychological activity preceding repression, and for Ernest Jones to make the following comment: "I am reminded of a similar situation years ago with the word 'sexuality'. The critics complained that Freud was changing the meaning of this word, and Freud himself once or twice seemed to assent to this way of putting it, but I always protested that he made no change in the meaning of the word itself; what he did was to extend the conception" (in Isaacs, 1943). Susan Isaacs was certainly moving toward an "extension" of the notion of fantasy; she was thus formulating theoretically an implicit orientation of Melanie Klein's practice, one which can be detected from 1923 on.

●*Thesis 2. All conscious fantasies are derivatives or variants
of conscious and unconscious masturbatory fantasies.*

This thesis must be advanced with the same proviso as the
preceding one: we do not find it formulated literally in these
general terms. Still, it is difficult to find in Melanie Klein's
writings, even before 1926, an example of a fantasy that is not
connected, directly or indirectly, with masturbatory activity.
Earlier we encountered a passage in which she links Felix's
"whole personality" with his tic. The passage goes on: "This
connection was rooted in his masturbation phantasies; and in
Felix's case it became particularly clear that these phantasies
materially influenced his sublimations, his neurosis and his personality" (Klein, 1925, p. 118). This idea had been no more
than glimpsed during Erich's psychoanalytic education. It is
Felix's analysis which seems to have imposed it on Melanie
Klein, and we know from her own statements (Klein, 1932, p.
9) that she stressed it in the unpublished talk she gave in 1924
to the Salzburg Congress.

●*Thesis 3. Masturbatory fantasies are themselves variants or
offshoots of the primal scene, real or fantasized.*

This thesis took shape from 1923, at the clinical level if not
the theoretical level. Here too Felix's psychoanalysis plays a
decisive part. "The analysis took us back to the earliest masturbation phantasies directly connected with his observation of
parental sexual intercourse" (Klein, 1925, pp. 115–116).

This thesis helps us understand the unconscious equivalence of all the sublimations which discharge the sexual tension
activated by observation of the primal scene. In particular,
Melanie Klein stresses how the form of masturbatory fantasies
is influenced by the actual conditions of the primal scene, fa-
voring a particular perception of a particular part of the body,
and the attitude—active or passive—taken by the subject: "In
Fritz it was the movement of the penis to which he was fixated,
in Felix the sounds which he heard, in others the colour-ef-

fects. . . . In fixation to the primal scene (or phantasies), *the degree of activity*, which is so important for sublimation itself, undoubtedly also determines whether the subject develops a talent for creation or reproduction" (Klein, 1923a, p. 103).

It is important to stress that in 1923 this idea had not yet been developed as it was in the theory formulated later. Its connection with psychoanalytic ideas as a whole had not yet been specified. In particular, the connection of masturbatory fantasies with autoerotism or object relations remained obscure. From a strictly Freudian point of view, autoerotic behavior is accompanied from the first by the hallucinatory representation of the breast, which thus appears as the precursor of masturbatory fantasies. It would therefore appear difficult to connect masturbatory fantasies with the original fantasy of the primal scene, which could not organize them until later, when the genital impulses have emerged. At no point during her writings of the period 1921–1925 does Melanie Klein consider this difficulty. We can nonetheless observe that the masturbation in the clinical cases on which she bases her work is always of a phallic nature, even if the fantasies accompanying it contain anal-sadistic and, more rarely, oral-sadistic elements. We should note also that from this period onward, though Melanie Klein sometimes used the classic concepts of autoerotism and narcissism, in her theoretical discussions she made practically no use of them.

●*Thesis 4. All undeveloped behavior or aptitudes are inhibited because of the anxiety caused by the repression of libidinal impulses which underlie them, through the intervention of a particular type of masturbatory fantasy.*

Two ideas meet to give rise to this thesis. One was present from the beginning of Erich's education: it originated in Melanie Klein's basic postulate that the normal state is not an average state but an optimal one comprising the full development of all aptitudes, a postulate initially accompanied by the illusion that an unrestrictive upbringing would be enough to permit full development of the child's creativity. In 1923 she gave up this illusion and, as we shall see, admitted the existence of normal inhibitions. Nevertheless she held with the greatest possible firmness to the attitude which made her suspect the work of repression behind the lack of any aptitude. But her accumulated experience led her to vary this position in accordance with the child's earlier history. Felix's psychoanalysis confirmed that her thesis was well-founded when it was revealed that the disgust and fear of sport and physical activity shown by the child between six and eleven went back to the early repression of a former interest. But the progressive awakening of the adolescent's love for music, while providing an argument in favor of the idea that his former lack of interest was due to anxiety, showed Melanie Klein that it was possible to speak of true inhibition only when an earlier aptitude had shown itself. The initial thesis was maintained, but now in a limited form. It was in this form, verified by clinical data, that it became an essential starting point of the theories built up in 1923.

●*Thesis 5. Progress in treatment and development rests upon the liberty to create fantasies. Psychoanalytic cure is the reeducation of the capacity to fantasize.*

This idea proceeds directly from the preceding theses. It was to remain to the very end one of the constants of the Kleinian approach in psychoanalysis. It arose from Melanie Klein's first objective, which was educational, and took the form in which we state it at the beginning of the second period of Erich's psychoanalytic education, at the end of 1919. It was then, in fact, that Melanie Klein realized that Erich's decrease in sexual curiosity was accompanied by a general inhibition of imagination and play; she also observed that the renewal of intellectual interests was preceded and caused by an extraordinary liberation of fantasies. It is highly probable that this thesis, though it springs logically from the others, in fact preceded them historically; starting from the experience, acquired with Erich, of the motive role of the liberation of fantasies, she was able to observe that all a child's activities are underlain by fantasies. It was in the course of Felix's psychoanalysis that theses 2 and 3 were imposed upon her, and that thesis 4 received its definitive form.

The psychoanalysis of children is conceived as a reeducation insofar as Melanie Klein started with an educational undertaking and found in her first patients only a fairly mild symptomatology, one dominated by school phobia and inhibition. These two factors contributed to her conception of the goal of the analytic process in terms of the redress of inhibitions and the preparation of children for success at school and for creativity. In short, we can allow that Melanie Klein's psychoanalytic approach in 1923 had a definite educational standpoint.

It is important, however, to stress the extreme originality, from 1923 onward, of her ideas concerning the relationship between psychoanalysis and pedagogy. We would be seriously mistaken if we thought that in the first years she shared the ideas of Hermine von Hug-Hellmuth, which were taken up later by Anna Freud. We know that H. von Hug-Hellmuth (1921) held that the child analyst had to play the simultaneous roles of psychoanalyst and pedagogue. She declared in 1920, at the congress at The Hague, that

> the *curative* and educative work of analysis does not consist only of releasing the young being from its suffering; it must also give it moral and aesthetic values. The object of this curative and educative treatment is not the mature man, capable, once liberated, of taking responsibility for his own actions: it is the child and the adolescent, that is to say human beings who are still in a phase of development, who must be reinforced by the educative direction of the analyst, in order to become adults, capable of having a strong will and definite goals. Anyone who is analyst and educator at the same time must never forget that the aim of the analysis of children is the analysis of character—in other words education. [p. 287]

Child analysts of the period all admitted that the child's unfulfilled developmental potential necessitated the introduction of technical modifications into analysis so that it could be used in that field. They saw psychoanalysis as auxiliary to education. Melanie Klein, on the contrary, from 1919 on saw their relationship in quite a different light. For her it was not a question of adding to the burden of educational demands on the child, but of lightening it. When she discovered the prevalence of fantasy in psychological activity, she found a clinical basis for her belief—at first purely ideological—in the child's own ca-

√ pacity to grow and develop intellectually, and began to differ radically from the reigning conception of the time. If the child's incapacity to tolerate educational measures made analysis necessary, some reeducation would be needed. But there should be no attempt to inculcate anything—standards, values, or knowledge. On the contrary, the work of repression must be destroyed in order to restore to the child its capacity to fantasize, on which all development rested. To use a modern expression, it was not a question of education but of training, in the sense in which the word is used in the psychosociology of limited groups. Training, as Kurt Lewin has shown, supposes a decrystallization of former habits and standards, permitting the autonomous formation of new standards and new decisions. Further, Melanie Klein considers that this dimension of reeducation is imposed on analysis only for practical reasons: no one thinks of taking a child to the analyst unless it is developing badly. She thinks psychoanalysis should in fact precede education, which would then have a clear field:

> It would be best, therefore, to reverse the process; first of all, an early analysis should remove the inhibitions more or less present in every child, and work at school should start on this foundation. When it has no longer to fritter away its forces in dispiriting attacks upon the childrens' complexes, the school will be able to achieve fruitful work significant for the development of the child. [Klein, 1923b, p. 76]

Insofar as this restitution to the child of its capacity to create fantasies is a precondition of success in all education, it is what we might call preeducation. We know that this thesis, with a few details revised, remained to the end a major element of Kleinian psychoanalysis and a subject of controversy with the school of Anna Freud.

3. The Place of Inhibition in the Defensive Process

Whereas the preceding theses are as a whole implicit in the works of the period 1921–1923, Melanie Klein formulated in

1923 an explicit and extremely precise theory of inhibition, sublimation, and symbolization, and of their relationships from a metapsychological point of view. This first Kleinian theory is generally not regarded very highly. It disconcerts Kleinian psychoanalysts who cannot find in it the concepts familiar to them—early oedipus complex, projection, introjection, oral sadism—and so consider that Melanie Klein had not yet found her own path. Outside the Kleinian school it has been ignored or rejected like the rest of Melanie Klein's work. It may be shown, however, that this metapsychology of sublimation is a coherent whole, perfectly adapted to explain the clinical material available to Melanie Klein at the time; that it played a major part in the invention of the play technique, which would not have been possible without it; and that it was never abandoned but rather became an integral part of Melanie Klein's mature thought. We might say that it occupies in Melanie Klein's work a place comparable to that of the 1895 Project in the work of Freud. This theory, partly set out in "The Role of the School" is developed in "Early Analysis."

Melanie Klein's starting point was the phenomenon of inhibition; her practice had shown her its importance, its frequency, and its relation to anxiety. The fact immediately apparent in her early analysis of children was the equivalence in her early analyses of children was the equivalence of anxiety and inhibition:

> Light was thrown to a remarkable degree upon this inner connection between anxiety and inhibition by the analysis of little Fritz. . . . the anxiety (which at one time was very considerable but gradually subsided after it had reached a certain point) so followed the course of the analysis that it was always an indication that inhibitions were about to be removed. Every time that the anxiety was resolved the analysis made a big step forward, and comparison with other analyses confirms my impression that the completeness of our success in removing inhibitions is in direct proportion to the clearness with which the anxiety manifests itself as such and can be resolved. [Klein, 1923a, p. 78]

When anxiety recedes, the inhibited activity develops and gives rise to sublimation. But from Felix's psychoanalysis onward

Melanie Klein was led to consider that every inhibition presupposes a repressed primitive interest, which she considers a sublimation. Thus in 1923 she was led to reflect on the relation of anxiety to repression. If the psychoanalysis of children, and in particular that of Felíx, makes it possible to recognize the major role of inhibitions in the young child's symptomatology, what is the nature of the relation between inhibitions and neurotic symptoms? If both phenomena stem from repression, what are the factors which cause repression to lead either to an inhibition or to a symptom? Also, Melanie Klein came to distinguish normal inhibitions from neurotic ones. Do the two differ in their mechanism? And in what case is the inhibition normal rather than neurotic? Finally, why do certain aptitudes develop freely while others are repressed? The answers to these questions, which would make it possible to construct a general theory of symptoms, inhibitions, and sublimation, depended on an examination of the process of repression and the appearance of anxiety.

In the first Freudian theory of anxiety, which remained in force until 1926, anxiety appeared in a single form, which was later given the name of automatic anxiety. Frued saw anxiety as the affective manifestation of a quantitative process: the increase in the sum of excitations within the psychic system. Thus, in his texts devoted to actual neuroses, Freud admits that in these disorders the unsatisfied libido is discharged in the form of diffuse somatic symptoms and anxiety. He isolates from the neurasthenia described by Beard a syndrome dominated by general anxiety, which he calls anxiety neurosis (Freud, 1895b). Among the manifestations of the tendency to anxiety he notes the existence, side by side with symptoms in which anxiety is accompanied by somatic disturbances or is connected in a more or less labile way with a representative content, of manifestations of pure anxiety: "Waking up at night in a fright (the *pavor nocturnus* of adults) which is usually combined with anxiety, dyspnoea, sweating and so on, is very often nothing else than a variant of the anxiety attack. . . . I have become convinced, moreover, that the *pavor nocturnus* of children, too, exhibits a form which belongs to anxiety neurosis" (p. 95). The idea dominating the Freudian conception of anxiety neurosis is that anx-

iety is free-floating and fixates more or less on certain situations
or certain representations, but that it is first as regards all the
other symptoms: "Either this fit of anxiety comprises only the
feeling of anxiety without any associated representation, or it
attaches to this feeling the nearest interpretation . . ." (p. 96).
This anxiety has nothing to do with repression; it is the immediate result of an increase in the quantity of excitations
caused by sexual abstinence, voluntary or forced, whatever the
psychological position of the subject in relation to this abstinence and in relation to sexuality, accepted and assumed, or
repressed. Freud thus describes virginal anxiety, the anxiety of
young couples unsatisfied by their first sexual intercourse, the
anxiety of women whose husbands suffer from premature eja-
culation or impotence, etc. Sexual frustration prevents sexual
excitation from being adequately discharged and is the direct
cause of the accumulation of tension which manifests itself as
anxiety. Freud kept to the end this conception of anxiety neurosis or actual neurosis.

The anxiety found in psychoneuroses is caused in the same
way, with the difference that sexual frustration is the product
of an intrapsychic process, repression. Repressed libidinal impulses cannot achieve discharge or satisfaction, so they accumulate within the psychical apparatus, where they increase the
number of excitations. In virtue of the general equivalence of
the constancy principle and the pleasure principle, this increased tension produces unpleasure, and when the tensions
in question are libidinal in character they produce anxiety.
Every manifestation of anxiety has this same etiology. Melanie
Klein's thoughts during 1923 fitted solidly into this Freudian
conception, except that she completely ignored the possibility
of a direct transformation of libido into anxiety in the context
of actual neurosis—an eventuality which in any case was considered by psychoanalysts, even as early as this period, to be an
abstract idea rather than a clinical reality.

She reaffirmed, then, Freud's statement (1916–1917) that
"discharge in the form of anxiety" is "the immediate fate of
libido meeting repression" (p. 402) and believed, as he did, that
neurotic symptoms are aimed at protecting the subject against
the development of anxiety, finding the confirmation in infan-

tile symptomatology: fits of anxiety which children often hide from their families, night terrors. Thus, "in children anxiety would invariably precede the formation of symptoms and would be the most primary neurotic manifestation, paving the way, so to speak, for the symptoms" (Klein, 1923a, p. 79). However, though anxiety is a general phenomenon in childhood, not every child has permanent recourse to neurotic symptoms to protect himself against the development of the anxiety which springs from the repressed libido. The appearance and consolidation of neurotic symptoms are signs of a failure of repression. Like every psychical process, repression obeys the pleasure principle, and its aim is to avoid the unpleasure connected with a dangerous impulse. When it can only exchange this unpleasure for anxiety it has not fulfilled its purpose, even if it has succeeded in banishing into the unconscious the "representative representations" of the impulse. But from a strictly economical point of view the success of repression is difficult to understand in the first Freudian theory. If it is true that the repressed libido is transformed into anxiety, what happens to this anxiety in the case of successful repression—that is to say, repression unaccompanied by anxiety? Here the originality of Melanie Klein's conception makes itself clear in two different ways.

1. She attempts, with a certain ambiguity of expression, a sign of considerable embarrassment, to reduce to the single eventuality of transformation into anxiety the three destinies of impulse at the end of the repression process: suppression pure and simple of the impulse, "so that no trace of it is found" (Klein, 1923a, p. 80); the appearance of an affect with a particular qualitative value; and transformation into anxiety. In such a case "anxiety would really be present unconsciously for a time" (p. 80). Here she comes up against the notion of unconscious affect which had already proved a stumbling block for Freud. We know that in Freud (1915b, pp. 177–179) had absolutely rejected the idea that affect could be unconscious or repressed. As affect is simply the conscious perception of a process of secretory or motor discharge, affect—or, more exactly, the quantum of affect associated with the impulse which is the object of repression—cannot be present in the psychical apparatus outside of consciousness; it is suppressed or inhib-

ited, except for the representation, which is preserved indefinitely as it is. As this is so, Freud admits that in practice
unconscious feelings are spoken of loosely. Although Melanie
Klein declares her concurrence with these views, she alters the
emphasis significantly; she asserts that Freud justifies the use
of the expression "unconscious affect" by accompanying this
use with theoretical reservations, and so admits the existence
of unconscious anxiety following the process of repression. We
can see here the first signs of the position she was to take later;
that all affects begin by being unconscious before reaching consciousness. But for the moment this is only an involved—and,
it must be admitted, very nearly erroneous—interpretation of
certain of Freud's writings.

2. She suggests an identification of the mechanism that
enables the repressed affect to be kept in a state of virtual
disposition with the mechanism that ends in inhibition. From
this point of view inhibition becomes the process that enables
the normal subject to inhibit anxiety and to avoid as far as
possible the formation of neurotic symptoms. Thanks to this
hypothesis, Melanie Klein could attach her clinical approach to
the phenomena of inhibition and the theoretical attitudes implicit in it to a global conception of the defensive process. Felix's
psychoanalysis showed that the inhibited activities were the object of a primal pleasure connected with the masturbatory fantasies underlying it. When repression of these fantasies takes
place, the activities they underlie are also repressed. The libido
that is added through masturbatory fantasies is transformed
into anxiety, and the activities themselves become anxiogenic.
At that point they are abandoned, and inasmuch as this allows
the avoidance of anxiety itself, inhibition may be said to have
made this possible.

Inhibitions and Sublimations

It is difficult not to compare this description of the process
of inhibition with Freud's description, in texts published in this
period, of the genesis of the phobic symptom of anxiety hysteria, notably in the case of little Hans. We know in fact that
in anxiety hysteria the phobia makes it possible to bind the

anxiety attached to repressed impulse fantasies by attaching it to an external object or situation. It is then sufficient, to avoid suffering, to avoid the object or the situation known to be phobogenic. When a subject has succeeded in displacing his anxiety externally, he needs do no more than cut short all occasions which might cause the development of anxiety, thanks to psychic barriers: precautions, inhibitions, prohibitions. These defensive structures appear to us in the form of phobias and constitute the essence of the illness. In this sense the mechanism of inhibition, as Melanie Klein describes it, is similar to that of a situation phobia; we might say that it is partly that of an activity phobia: the subject who has displaced the anxiety onto certain activities avoids them as the phobic avoids a phobogenic situation. This comparison makes it possible to understand the undeniably agoraphobic elements found in the most spectacular manifestations of little Erich's inhibition of the sense of orientation, and also in the typical "flight forward" which enabled him to overcome on his own, in his sixth year, his phobia of boys met in the street.

However, the analogy is not complete. Freud considers that the phobia comes from displacement onto an external situation, and the fixation to this situation of a quantity of libido already transformed into anxiety by repression. The investing of a situation with libido converted into anxiety comes later than repression, and is its consequence; if it were not repressed, the libido would find direct satisfaction in adequate discharge. Displacement thus appears as a process succeeding repression; it is a defensive process, pathological in nature, giving rise to a neurotic symptom. For Melanie Klein, by contrast, where it is a question of inhibition the displacement of anxiety onto an activity of the ego is simply a following of the path traced by an investing of the libido preceding this activity. When repression transforms the libido into anxiety, this transformation does not apply only to the libido which has remained attached to directly sexual aims; it extends also to those which have invested the activities of the ego. Any activity of the ego may then become anxiogenic. In this case we reach a phenomenon of general inhibition of interests and activities, of which Erich provided a striking example some months after the first attempt at psy-

choanalytic education. Anxiety proper is avoided at the expense
of a total restriction of psychic life. After this it is found only
in the form of boredom, various dislikes, clumsiness, and more
or less diffuse feelings of unpleasure which illustrate very well
the idea of anxiety "prevented from developing." But in most
cases anxiety is unequally distributed among the different activities of the ego, as the libido had been unequally distributed.
Behavior underlain by those of the fantasies which are the nearest offshoots of masturbatory fantasies is anxiogenic and so is
abandoned, and that accompanying more disguised fantasies
may be kept. Thus from six to eleven years Felix lost the taste
for sports and physical activities in which rhythmic movement
was linked with ill-disguised masturbatory fantasies, whereas he
could succeed in school activities with more displaced and disguised fantasies underlying them.

It is clear that the explanation which Melanie Klein suggests
for the inhibition mechanism can apply just as well to that of
phobia: the phobia of boys met in the street, then that of the
road to school, evinced by Erich, appeared to her as particular
cases of the inhibition of the sense of orientation which, in her
son, followed great pleasure in walking and exploring space.
In working out her conception of previous libidinal cathexis of
the inhibited activity, Melanie Klein appears to have been inspired by an article by Karl Abraham (1913) devoted to the
study of severe forms of agoraphobia. He stresses that in the
case of one of his patients walking was impossible because of
its significance as a substitute for coitus: "walking and dancing
offered him a substitute for sexual gratification which was otherwise denied him by his neurotic inhibitions" (p. 236). Thus
Abraham, who up to a point held to the most classical conception, admits the notion that the sexual cathexis of walking comes
later than the repression of his patient's incestuous impulses.
However, he goes beyond this conception on two points. First
of all he notes the relative frequency in neurotic persons of a
real compulsion to walk: "It is not seldom the case in neurotics
that the act of walking is accompanied by sexual excitation,
especially a genital one" (pp. 236–237). Having noted this, he
applied the following explanation to agoraphobia: "The 'negative' of this peculiar perversion, according to Freud's view in

his *Drei Abhandlungen zur Sexualtheorie* seems to be the neurosis which we know as 'street anxiety' " (p. 237). Thus he admits that the sexual pleasure in walking is denied in agoraphobia; that is to say that the condition implies a pleasure in walking before the appearance of the symptom. He stresses that the sexual significance of walking is "familiar to any psycho-analyst who has investigated a case of locomotor anxiety. Nevertheless, it is not sufficient merely to point out the symbolic meaning of walking: emphasis must be laid on the pleasure-value of walking itself" (p. 238). From then onward he was led to seek an explanation for the primal pleasure in walking, and invoked constitutional factors: "My investigation of the present case . . . led me to the conclusion that neurotics suffering from locomotor anxiety have to begin with a constitutionally over-strong pleasure in movement, and that neurotic inhibitions of bodily movement have arisen later from the failure of the repression of this tendency" (p. 238). This explanation is a very specific one; Abraham applies it only to agoraphobia. He mentions the constitution only when observing *excessive* pleasure in movement, and connects inhibitions of walking with a failure of repression caused by excess. As walking cannot be detached from its libidinal significance—which appears as a disturbing pathological element—repression prohibits both the activity of the ego and the sexual pleasure grafted on to it. Melanie Klein generalizes the explanation: it becomes applicable to all inhibitions and phobias. She abandons the notion of a pathological constitution and notes the displacement of the libido from sexual activities to ego activities via masturbatory fantasies, a process which is conceived no longer as intrinsically pathological, but as part of the normal development of aptitudes.

From this point of view no basic difference can be found between an inhibition and a sublimation so far as origin is concerned. Melanie Klein in fact believes not that sublimation is a special direction for an impulse to take, traceable only in the case of art or intellectual activity, but rather that there is sublimation every time a sexual impulse finds a substitute satisfaction after being displaced onto an ego activity. Such phenomena as walking, singing, and athletic activity thus appear as sublimations of sexual impulses, as shown by the masturbatory nature of the underlying fantasies. From then on there is a genetic equivalence between inhibition and sublimation. Melanie Klein goes even further, holding that *every inhibition presupposes a previous successful sublimation*; insofar as distaste for an activity is an attenuated form of the anxiety attached to it, this anxiety cannot attain the quantity needed for the appearance of the inhibition unless an equal quantity of libido has previously found satisfaction in the activity. Thus Erich developed a general inhibition of the sense of orientation only because he had previously taken considerable pleasure in the experience and exploration of space, a pleasure shown by his play and by the occasions on which he ran away around the age of three.

Inhibitions take on a neurotic character when they affect an essential function of physical or mental life—e.g., locomotion, orientation, learning. In normal cases they make it possible to reduce the anxiety caused by repression of the oedipus complex. They then affect previously successful sublimations which, however, the subject can relinquish without serious harm. Thus Felix, for whom the primal scene was essentially auditory, had from early childhood sublimated his oedipal impulses in singing. When his active impulses were repressed, their libidinal energy was tranformed into anxiety; singing then became an anxiogenic activity and was abandoned. But this abandonment, which enabled anxiety to be avoided, ensured at the same time the persistence of other sublimations in which pleasure could remain intact.

Thus, the theory of inhibition reduces in the last analysis to a theory of sublimation. The question of the origin of an inhibition reduces to the question of why one particular sublimation has to be abandoned rather than another. Melanie Klein's reply to this question involves taking into account quantitative and chronological factors closely bound up with each other. From a quantitative point of view, the number and variety of sublimations play a decisive part. The larger the number of sublimations, the more the libido is divided into quantities, which become smaller as the sublimations become more numerous. In extreme cases this process leads to the simultaneous existence in the same subject of tastes, interests, and activities each of which remains superficial. In normal cases the subject has numerous sublimations, but each is invested with a quantity of energy which enables it to develop. When the oedipus complex is repressed, anxiety can be bound by abandoning one or more sublimations abutting the repressed elements of the complex. It is then transformed into unpleasure connected with certain activities, distaste for certain foods, etc. It is clear that in this conception the degree of deformation of masturbatory fantasies plays an essential part: the more the subject has succeeded in transferring his libido onto objects, situations, and activities remote from the primal scene and the practice of masturbation, the more these sources of pleasure are likely to escape repression, the less is the quantity of libido attached to the forbidden desires, and the less, therefore, is the quantity of libido repressed. Consequently, anxiety is less. Sublimation in fact makes it possible to discharge sexual tensions and thus avoid anxiety. But the following point must be emphasized: what is important for the preservation of sublimation is not the objective distance between a given activity (sport, study, etc.) and the masturbatory fantasies linked with the primal scene; rather it is the degree of deformation, the variety, and the flexibility of the fantasies underlying this activity. When the movement of the hand in writing is immediately associated with the movements of coitus, writing is not as good a sublimation as, for example, sport, provided the fantasies relating to the movements of the ball, for instance, do not directly appear as movements of the penis.

It is therefore of the greatest importance that fantasies should be able to undergo numerous transformations, so that sublimation can progressively lose its initial connection with the primal scene. Such a transformation requires time. The later the repression and the earlier the investing of the ego activities with libido, the more likely is this investment to result in sublimations which are numerous and varied, and which do not call into consciousness the primal scene. In the last analysis, then, mental health depends on a race between sublimation and repression; the basic condition is the fantasy work which establishes sublimations.[1] When fantasy activity has played its part

---

[1] "If we equate the capacity to employ superfluous libido in a cathexis of ego-tendencies with the capacity to *sublimate*, we may probably assume that

before repression has taken place, "in proportion as the sublimations hitherto effected are quantitatively abundant and
qualitatively strong, so will the anxiety with which they are now
invested be completely and imperceptibly distributed amongst
them and thus discharged" (Klein, 1923a, p. 82). On this hypothesis, applicable to the most favorable cases, a quantitative
and qualitative optimum has been reached in such a way that
the anxiety brings no real inhibition and no abandonment of
an activity invested with libido, and shows itself in an attenuated
form: "The more perfectly the mechanism of successful repression accomplishes its work the less easy it is to recognize the
anxiety for what it is, even in the form of disinclination. In
people who are quite healthy and apparently quite free from
inhibitions it ultimately appears only in the form of weakened
or partly weakened inclinations" (p. 81). In most normal cases
anxiety is bound by a few inhibitions, which constitute the price
paid for normal health: "inhibition enters in a greater or lesser
degree into the development of every normal individual, while
here again it is only the quantitative factor which determines
whether he is to be called well or ill" (p. 80). The healthy man
is the one who has been able to "discharge in the form of
inhibitions that which in the neurotic has led to neurosis" (p.
80). As we move toward the pathological state we meet first
neurotic inhibitions, whose difference from those of the normal
person is purely quantitative, and then neurotic symptoms.
Considered as a whole, the phenomena of inhibition, both normal and pathological, represent intermediate degrees of a complementary series linking the neurotic symptom and a healthy
condition based on sublimation: "we should have to postulate
a complementary series between the formation of symptoms on
the one hand and successful sublimation on the other—these
series to include also possibilities of less successful sublimation"
(p. 89). But it appears that the fate of repression depends essentially on the degree of development reached by sublimations
at the moment when it operates. For this reason the processes
leading to health or illness all depend in the last analysis on the

the person who remains healthy succeeds in doing so on account of his greater
capacity for sublimating at a very early stage of his ego-development" (Klein,
1923a, p. 81).

early meeting between the first processes of repression and sublimation. It may be true that character, personality, habits, and inhibitions are formed as the oedipus complex and infantile neurosis fade, but all that is only the effect of earlier processes. The game is played much earlier; the effect of repression appears only after a delay.

Early Repression

Thus Melanie Klein, in extending her conception of inhibition and sublimation, arrives at the idea that the mechanism of repression acts at a much younger age than is generally thought. It can be traced in its characteristic effect, the development of anxiety, which can be observed in young children. In fact, as is usual with her, Melanie Klein does not for a moment consider the hypothesis that the anxiety of very young children might be an automatic process due simply to the accumulation of tensions following a lack of satisfaction. If she mentions birth trauma as a precursor of anxiety, she immediately stresses the renewal of this affect in the formation of the oedipus complex: "I have repeatedly in analysis discovered birth-anxiety to be castration-anxiety reviving earlier material and have found that resolving the castration-anxiety dissipated the birth-anxiety" (Klein, 1923a, pp. 81–82). All anxiety, then, is according to her the result of repression, and repression exists only in the oedipal conflict. So all infantile anxiety is the product and sign of the activity of repression, and thus of the *previous* existence of the oedipus complex. The most intense and spectacular manifestations of anxiety in young children are those of *pavor nocturnus*: "It seems no great step then to regard the *pavor nocturnus* which occurs at the age of two or three as the anxiety which is liberated in the first stage of repression of the Oedipus complex, the binding and discharge of which subsequently ensues in various ways" (p. 82). The theory of inhibition thus leads directly to the notion of an archaic oedipus complex, contemporary with the first night terrors; this notion was developed after 1926 and became one of Melanie Klein's most valuable contributions to psychoanalysis and to the social sciences in general. This hypothesis had been in existence since

1923. It appeared as the result of reasoning on the relationships between anxiety and repression. It had not yet been verified empirically, but its verification was to give rise to the formation of the Kleinian theory proper, which emerged from the "proto-Kleinian" conceptions of 1923: "It is clear (but the fact still requires verification) that, if it were possible to undertake an analysis of the child at the time of the *pavor nocturnus* or soon after it, and to resolve this anxiety, the ground would be cut away from under the neurosis and possibilities of sublimation would be opened out" (p. 82).

4. The Genesis of Primary Sublimations and the Proto-Kleinian System

But in 1923 Melanie Klein was not yet in possession of the clinical data which were ultimately to enable her to proceed in this direction. The whole of the proto-Kleinian conception of inhibition as repressed sublimation was directed toward bringing out the process of the first sublimations, and her conceptualization was entering that path. As Felix's analysis, like Erich's, established the existence of very early sublimations, how did they take place? To answer this question, Melanie Klein worked out a theory of *primary sublimation,* which makes it possible to account for later, secondary sublimations. This vast synthesis rests on the Freudian conception of primary narcissism and on various psychoanalytic works of Ferenczi, Jones, and Sperber. Its aim was to give a global psychoanalytic explanation of the origin of the libidinal investment of the outside world and of the activities springing from relational life.

The Problem of the Cathexis of External Reality

The proto-Kleinian theory of primary sublimation presupposes the Freudian conception of primary narcissism understood as an objectless state (Freud, 1916–1917, p. 413), a conception prefigured in two articles by Ferenczi (1913b, 1913c) which were a great source of inspiration to Melanie Klein. In the first phase of existence, marked by autoerotic sexuality,

libidinal instincts have no reason to turn toward the object because they find their satisfaction where they are, in the body
itself, in its erogenous zones, and they master the object in an
omnipotent way by an hallucinatory experience of satisfaction.
The first movement of the sexual instincts, when they distinguish themselves as such from the functions of self-preservation
on which they lean, is a movement by which they turn from the
primary object at which the self-preservative instincts are aimed
from the beginning—the mother's breast. We should therefore
distinguish two phases, coinciding with what Freud called respectively the initial ego-reality phase and the phase of purified
ego-pleasure. In the first, the sexual instincts are still confused
with the self-preservative instincts which show them the way to
reality. In the second, the libido, while still supported by the
ego instincts, is partly detached from them and is satisfied by
sucking at nothing, sucking the fingers, etc.—the first manifestations of autoerotism—and by the hallucinatory satisfaction
accompanying them. But Melanie Klein thought in 1923 that
this detachment was not complete:

> We know that at the narcissistic stage the ego-instincts and
> sexual instincts are still united because at the beginning the sex-
> ual instincts obtain a foothold on the territory of the self-pre-
> servative instincts. The study of the transference neuroses has
> taught us that they subsequently part company, operate as two
> separate forms of energy and develop differently. While we ac-
> cept as valid the differentiation between ego-instincts and sexual
> instincts, we know on the other hand from Freud that some part
> of the sexual instincts remains throughout life associated with
> the ego-instincts and furnishes·them with libidinal components.
> [1923a, pp. 84–85]

Departing from the usual dichotomy between primary narcissism and reality testing, we must acknowledge that the ego
impulses which permit the progressive establishment of a sensorimotor relationship with the external world are not "autonomous" or possess only their own energy; they are invested with
a libidinal energy which enables the subject to discover an interest in the external world. The development of the sense of
reality is subordinated to the progressive transport of quantities

of libidinal energy from the organism itself, which relates autoerotically to objects and people in the external world. This notion, which Melanie Klein generalized in 1923, was present in outline from her earliest writings; in 1919, observing Erich's oscillation between the sense of reality and the feeling of narcissistic omnipotence, she considered the rapid development of the sense of reality as a victory over repression. The fact that Erich's curiosity could be brought to bear on the general conditions of existence and perception, on the origin and formation of things, and on the definition of the possible and the real, the permitted and the forbidden, appeared to her a sign that through sexual curiosity, then in the process of sublimating via its extension to fields not directly sexual, the libido was cathecting the functions of perception and judgment. There is therefore a conflict in the young child between a part of the ego which produces repression, and a part of the ego cathected by the libido. The libidinal part is indispensable if the child is to pass from the stage of omnipotence of thought to reality testing. This is the opposite of Freud's classic conceptions (Freud, 1911):

> The supersession of the pleasure principle by the reality principle, with all the psychical consequences involved . . . is not accomplished all at once, nor does it take place simultaneously all along the line. For while this development is going on in the ego instincts, the sexual instincts become detached from them in a very significant way. . . . The sexual instinct is held up in its psychical development and remains far longer under the dominance of the pleasure principle, from which in many people it is never able to withdraw. In consequence of these conditions a closer connection arises on the one hand between the sexual instinct and phantasy and on the other hand between the ego-instincts and activities of consciousness. [p. 222][2]

For Melanie Klein, on the contrary, the sense of reality cannot win unless it is cathected by the libido. She was therefore

[2]The German word *Phantasie* means both imagination as a "faculty of the mind" and fantasy, the product of this faculty.

led to consider the ways and the stages by which this libidinal cathexis of reality takes place.

The Proto-Kleinian Conception of Symbolism

The process she describes includes the fact that the libidinal cathexis of reality is secondary to the libidinal cathexis of the body, a process which itself starts with the primary autoerotic cathexis of the erogenous zones. The means by which this evolution takes place coincide with the initial phases of *symbolism*, to use Melanie Klein's term, or *symbolization*, as we are more inclined to say today. The formation of the symbol and the libidinal cathexis of the body itself and then of the world are but two aspects of a single process leading to the formation of the *primary sublimations*.

The notion of a construction of the body image in the context of processes of libidinal cathexis orginated in Freud's description of the genesis of the hysterical symptom. We know that Freud considered Charcot's hysterogenic zones to be the result of a displacement of the erogenous zones. Ferenczi had taken up this idea and extended it far beyond the psychopathology of hysteria, making it the explanatory principle of the genesis of the symbols described by Freud. Insofar as such symbolization is considered by Freud to be an early mode of expression, certain authors had related it to a deficiency of discriminatory capacity in primitive man or in the young child. Symbolism would thus be a confusion, pure and simple, between objects similar in appearance. Ferenczi does not totally reject this conception, but insists that it is insufficient; apart from this negative condition, the formation of the symbol requires a positive condition, affective in nature. As long as he has no affective motive for interest in the external objects which are to become symbols of the body and parts of the body, the child neither sees them nor thinks of them:

> So long as the necessities of life do not compel them to adaptation and therewith to the knowledge of reality, children concern themselves to begin with only about the satisfaction of their instincts, *i.e.* about the parts of the body where this satis-

faction takes place, about the objects suited to evoke this, and about the actions that actually evoke the satisfaction. Of the sexually excitable parts of the body (erogenous zones), they are specially interested in the mouth, the anus, and the genitals. [Ferenczi, 1913b, p. 235]

We should recall here the psychoanalytic conceptions of "Stages in the Development of the Sense of Reality" (Ferenczi, 1913c). The child at the stage of purified ego pleasure knows no "good objective criterion" enabling him to distinguish the external from the internal. Everything that is pleasant is introjected, and everything that arouses unpleasure is thrown out. Thus the "objects suited to evoke" satisfaction (the mother's breasts, the mother herself as a real person) are objectively external but subjectively internal. We know that Jean Piaget (a member of the Swiss Psycho-Analytical Society up to the beginning of the 1930s) was later to describe this phenomenon from a cognitive point of view, showing that in the first stages of sensorimotor intelligence the object perceived is in the extension of the action itself. The purified ego pleasure, then, is at first a chaos of coexisting disorganized groups of sensations and motor impulses going back to the different erogenous zones. The first stage of development of the sense of reality passes, according to Ferenczi (1913b), through the locating of the parts of the body in relation to the erogenous zones:

> Similar analogies are formed also within the sphere of the bodily organs themselves: penis and tooth, anus and mouth, become equated. Perhaps the child finds an equivalent in the upper part of the body (expecially on the head and face) for every affectively important part of the lower half. . . .
>
> In this way also eyes become symbols of the genitalia, with which they had previously been identified—on the ground of extrinsic resemblance. There thus comes about a symbolic overemphasis of the upper half of the body in general, after interest in the lower half has been repressed. . . . [p. 236]

Alluding to this passage, Melanie Klein (1923a) supports Ferenczi's ideas and adds an explanation of this identification "on the ground of extrinsic resemblance" of the parts of the body with each other. Extending Ferenczi's ideas, she considers that as far as primary identification is concerned (that is to say, in the terminology she borrows from Ferenczi, double equivalence, first between the upper and lower parts of the body, then between parts of the body and objects in the external world) the basis of the comparison is to be found in the pleasure value common to two parts of the body, but unequal in quality: "According to Freud, the early orientation to the subject's own body is accompanied also by the discovery of fresh sources of pleasure. It may very well be this that makes possible the comparison between different organs and areas of the body" (p. 85). There is, then, a continuous process of investment of the body which begins with the emergence of sexuality by the libinal investment of the erogenous zones, and extends progressively from the fingers, extremities, face, etc. to the whole of the skin.

This idea, that the basis of the comparison is to be found in the equivalence of the pleasure value of the terms compared, seems to have been put forward by Ferenczi in 1913, in the texts we have cited. But the generalized form in which Melanie Klein used it in 1923 is the product of modifications to this hypothesis by Ernest Jones (1919) under the influence of an article by Sperber (1915). Investigating the origin of symbolism from an ontogenetic and phylogenetic point of view, Jones, while recognizing the part played by negative factors (the incapacity of the "primitive" mind to discriminate), stresses the direct and indirect role of the pleasure principle in the identification at the basis of symbolism. Initially the primitive mind is interested only in that which is a source of pleasure: "the primitive mind which is ruled by this principle [of pleasure] notices most what most interests it personally, what, therefore, is most pleasurable or most painful. It ignores distinctions between two ideas when they are indifferent to it, and notices only those that are interesting" (Jones, 1919, p. 149). Then, "when the primitive mind is presented with new experience, it seizes on the resemblance, however slight, between it and previous experiences. . . . this is governed by the pleasure-pain principle. . . . the association between ease and pleasure or between difficulty or labour and pain is a primordial one" (pp. 149–150). This conception of the prevalence of the pleasure principle is elaborated by Jones in the context of the psychogenesis of symbolism. The idea of applying this hypothesis to the comparison of the parts of the body with each other belongs properly to Melanie Klein, who could thus sketch the idea that the genesis of the body image is not a process of the cognitive functions of the ego, but rather rests on the movement of the libido governed by the pleasure principle.

Once the body image is thus constituted by the expedient of libidinal equivalence between its parts, the libido can cathect the images of the external world by sliding along equivalences comparable to those established within the body itself, between parts of the body and objects. Here we return to the ideas of Ferenczi. In light of the exclusive domination of the pleasure principle in the child's first stages of development, it is not surprising that his attention should in the first place be directed to things and processes of the external world which recall, even by a remote resemblance, his dearest experiences (Ferenczi, 1913c, pp. 181–203).

So proceeds the establishment of these deep symbolic relationships, persisting throughout life, between the human body and the world of objects. Although at this stage the child sees in the world only reproductions of his own body, he learns to represent through his body all the diversity of the external world. We know that this conception, which Ferenczi developed very little further, became from 1921 on one of the major features of Melanie Klein's practice; after 1927 it found a definitive place in her theory. Even as early as 1919, in fact, the second phase of Erich's education, and then his analysis, revealed that the external world and the body symbolize each other. We recall that during the period of liberation of fantasies which followed the beginning of the second phase of Erich's psychoanalytic education, the child was multiplying fantasies relating to the functions of excretion and to the stomach: sitting on his pot he complained that the "Kakis" were naughty children who would not come down into the garden (into the pot) and had already gone back onto the balcony (into the stomach). The fantasy identity of child and feces rests on this symbolic equivalence. It is found in Erich's numerous fantasies relating to the stomach, seen as the interior of a house furnished and equipped for the stay of the anal child. Later, in the child's complicated fantasies in which his own body and his mother's are represented as towns, then as countries with a complicated geography, crossed by a railway network bearing "Kaki-trains" and "Pipi-trains," Melanie Klein (1923a) recognized the effects of the same symbolism and connected Erich's disturbances of orientation with the repression of this "geography of the mother's body," inspired by incestuous libidinal interests (p. 93).

All this fantasy work on space and the mother's body is traversed in two directions. In clinical examples we see only the representation of the body by objects from the external world. The stomach is a house. The extremities and joints of the body are "frontiers." The orifices of the body are doors and windows. As Freud, Ferenczi, and Jones observed, in symbolism the erogenous parts of the body and the sexual processes are always designated by nonsexual objects or phenomena; according to them, the reverse never happens. The classic opinion is that of Ferenczi (1913b), who links this asymmetry of the symbolic relationship with the "symbolic over-investment" in objects in the external world and the upper parts of the body, "from the moment when repression has destroyed our interest in the lower part of the body" (p. 236). We should observe, however, that Freud (1916–1917) admits that the use of symbolism in the dream is not due to the intervention of the censor, but that it is inherent in the mode of representation of the unconscious. It is as though the symbols not only functioned as substitutes for the things, organs, erogenous zones, and sexual processes symbolized, but were invested with their own pleasure value on the one hand while on the other constituting the only mode of designation for these zones, processes, etc. that is completely satisfying (in the strictly libidinal sense of the term).

Here the following hypothesis may be advanced: at the same time that the libidinal cathexis of external objects gives them a pleasure value, it enables the child to represent to himself, through the expedient of these external objects which have become equivalent to the body and its parts, the interior of his body (which up to then he has known only by coenesthetic and kinesthetic feelings). In "primary identification" the symbolic equivalence comprises two reciprocal phenomena: (1) the representations of external things receive the libidinal investment of parts of the body on the basis of a similitude noted under the domination of the pleasure principle; (2) the visible parts and the invisible organs of the body, and their organization in a represented space, are thought out through images provided by objects belonging to the external world, above all by the mother's body, which the child explores, and the parts of which he relates to the parts of his own body. He can imagine how his own body is assembled and articulated only through that of his mother. Thus the objects of the external world, and first of all his mother's body, would draw their irreplaceable value from the fact that they give the child his only means of representing his own body. This idea does not appear as such in Melanie Klein's writings. It does not form part of the "proto-Kleinian" ideas of 1923 or of the later Kleinian ideas. But it is supported by the material Melanie Klein brings to bear on the subject of the sense of orientation and the "geography of the mother's body" as regards Erich. Above all, it is the only explanation of certain declarations of Melanie Klein which are both contra-dictory and contemporary, which means we cannot explain the divergence by the evolution of her thought. She writes about Erich in "Early Analysis" (Klein, 1923a): "there were many phantasies which showed that he was under the influence of the mental image of the inside of his mother's body and, by identification with her, of his own body. He pictured it as a town, often as a country, and later on as the world . . ." (p. 96). In this passage it is the mother's body which appears as the primal target of symbolism; Erich's body is simply identified with it. However, two pages further on she admits an idea which appears to be the exact opposite of the previous one:

> Abraham pointed out that the interest in orientation in re-lation to the body of the mother is preceded at a very early stage by the interest in orientation in relation to the subject's own body. This is certainly true, but this early orientation seems to share the fate of repression only when the interest in orientation in reference to the mother's body is repressed, of course because of the incestuous wishes bound up with that interest. [p. 98]

That Melanie Klein can affirm at the same time the genetic priority—suggested by Abraham in 1921 (Klein, 1923a, p. 98)—of understanding by comparison with the child's own body, and the predominance in the psychic conflict of the image of the mother's body over that of his own, is comprehensible only if we distinguish a genetic order of libidinal cathexis, going from the child's body to that of the mother, and a symbolic order of representations in which the body image can exist only by an "identification" with the mother's body. The hypothesis put forward above contains nothing more than this distinction.

The fact remains that although the symbolic order of representations is the only one provided by the fantasy material, interpretation *always* brings it back to the genetic order or segments thereof. Thus, the interpretations Melanie Klein offered Erich always related houses, towns, etc. to the fantasy representation of the stomach or body of the mother. The reverse, which in Melanie Klein's later theories was to become possible without leaving the genetic context, is absolutely not represented in the writings of 1923. It seems quite legitimate to think that this was because Melanie Klein did not yet possess the theoretical equipment (the notion of reintrojection) which, for example, would have enabled her to interpret Erich's representation of his own body by reference to his mother's without upsetting the genetic order, which was considered primordial. We should take as the essential point of her conception the notion that primary identification happens according to a libidinal movement which goes from the body itself to external objects, in agreement with Ferenczi's ideas; at an early stage of his development the child tries to rediscover his bodily organs and their activities in all the objects he meets.

Primary Sublimations

The process of the libidinal cathexis of the body, then of the external world, is accompanied by a process of cathexis of the activities of the ego and of the body proper. The first phases of this process are confused, pure and simple, with the cathexis of the body proper, starting from the displacement of the libido from the erogenous zones: the motor and vocal exercises of the

small baby arise from this sensorimotor appropriation of the
body itself under the ascendancy of the autoerotic libido. All
of Melanie Klein's attention was directed to the second phase
of this evolution, which implies that the object cathexis is, if not
finished, at least proceeding and partly carried out. At this
phase the libidinal cathexis of the activities of the ego begins,
affecting speech and movement first: "Speech and pleasure in
motion have always a libidinal cathexis which is also of a genital-
symbolic nature. . . . After the use made by the sexual instincts
of the self-preservative instincts in respect of the function of
nutrition, the next ego-activities to which they turn are those
of speech and pleasure in motion" (Klein, 1923a, p. 104). The
cathexis of speech and motion follows the same route as earlier
cathexes: that indicated by the equivalences, governed by the
pleasure principle, between the erogenous zones—especially
the genital zone—on the one hand, and voice and voluntary
movement, on the other. This is an extension of the primary
identification of the upper parts of the body with its lower parts.
But speech and motion, especially walking, have also the value
of a symbolic representation of the primal scene. During the
analysis of Grete, "the girl's stammering proved to be determined by the libidinal cathexis of speaking as well as of singing.
The rise and fall of the voice and the movements of the tongue
represented coitus" (Klein, 1923b, p. 62). For Erich, "the spoken
word was . . . identical with the written. The word stood for
the penis or the child, while the movement of the tongue and
the pen stood for coitus" (Klein, 1923a, p. 100). During his
third year, Felix had expressed by his love of singing his "original identification with his father, that is, the heterosexual phantasy of sexual intercourse with the mother" (Klein, 1925, p.
110). Speech, then, is generally speaking an activity of the ego
cathected by the libidinal impulses, essentially genital, and, to
a lesser degree, anal: "The significance of speaking as a genital
activity . . . I found at work in a greater or lesser degree in
every case. In my opinion both this and the anal determination
are typical" (Klein, 1923a, p. 101). The same applies to movement; in the case of Erich it is particularly clear that "his original
pleasure in roads corresponded to the desire for coitus with the
mother. . . . Similarly we see that, in close connection with this,
his love of exploring roads and streets (which formed the basis

of his sense of orientation) developed with the release of the sexual curiosity . . ." (p. 96). These activities, which allow the discharge of libido by the expedient of a sexual cathexis based on symbolism correspond exactly to the Kleinian definition of sublimation: "the capacity to employ surplus libido in a cathexis of ego-tendencies" (p. 81). They are thus defined by Melanie Klein (1923b) as *primary sublimations* (p. 73).

As such, they have the following attributes and functions:

1. The mechanism which gives rise to them is identical in nature to that of later sublimations; the primary sublimations result from the application to the ego tendencies of a libidinal overload, a process we have seen at work as the cathexis of the body proper caught in that of the external world. Melanie Klein explicitly attaches this process to the support given to the sexual instincts by the instincts of self-preservation.

2. The libidinal cathexis of the primary sublimations is contemporary with the appearance of symbolism—today we would say "symbolization"—which takes the place of "identification" (that is to say, the primal confusion, under the influence of the pleasure principle, of the thing symbolized and the symbol) at the very moment of the appearance of these primary sublimations:

> We see that *identification* is a stage preliminary not only to symbol-formation but at the same time to the evolution of speech and sublimation. The latter takes place by way of symbol-formation, libidinal phantasies becoming fixated in sexual-symbolic fashion upon particular objects, activities and interests. . . . The connecting link was probably pleasure in motion or rather organ-pleasure in itself. [Klein, 1923a, p. 86]

The primary sublimations represent a decisive stage in the development of the ego, as they alone are based on identification which postulates, each increment of libidinal pleasure, the existence of an earlier pleasure of a non-libidinal nature, one corresponding to the satisfaction of the ego instincts—organ pleasure *(Organlust)*.[3] Through this combination of organ pleas-

---

[3]This point is not absolutely certain. The hypothesis rests on the interpretation of the term *Organlust* as meaning a nonsexual pleasure. A host of quotations might be offered from Freud defining autoerotism as a quest for

ure and the libidinal pleasure built upon it, ego activity—speech and movement—is identified with libidinal satisfaction, while the first manifestations of repression, making the symbolized sexual images unconscious, transform *identification* into *symbol*. With the appearance of symbolism, the secondary sublimations can find the path of the ego activities without needing to be, as it were, called up by a previous organ pleasure. The libido can thus cathect, starting from movement and speech, activities which do not themselves generate any pleasure: "when repression begins to operate and the step from identification to symbol-formation is taken, it is this latter process which affords an opportunity for libido to be displaced on to other objects and activities of the self-preservative instincts, not originally possessing a pleasurable tone. Here we arrive at the mechanism of sublimation" (Klein, 1923a, p. 86). In this passage, of course, we must understand sublimation in the sense of secondary sublimation, as opposed to the primary sublimations which make this mechanism possible but do not derive from it.

Through identification, the precursor of symbolism, primary sublimations acquire the value of equivalents of the primal scene. The libidinal cathexis of speech and movement "is effected by means of the early identification of the penis with foot, hand, tongue, head and body, whence it proceeds to the activities of these members, which thus acquire the significance of coitus" (p. 104). The symbolic representations accompanying them are thus the first masturbatory fantasies directly connected with the primal scene. Thus, Melanie Klein (1925), working out the specific factors in the psychogenesis of Felix's tic, rejects the connection between masturbatory fantasies and the primal scene as one of the factors causing the tic, for the very reason of the general nature of this connection:

---

organ pleasure. However, the *Introductory Lectures,* Melanie Klein's favorite reference in her 1923 writings, define this term as meaning nonsexual satisfaction. But whatever the nature—libidinal or otherwise—which is attributed to organ pleasure, it is still essential in primary sublimations for sexual cathexis, essentially genital, to be preceded by a primary pleasure taken in the exercise of the function, a motor or vocal activity—a pleasure without which cathexis could not take place.

The masturbation phantasies underlying the tic are certainly not specific, for we know that they have the same importance for nearly every neurotic symptom and, as I have repeatedly attempted to show, for phantasy life and sublimations. But even the special content of masturbation phantasies which was common to my two cases—simultaneous identification with both father and mother while the self participates—does not seem in itself specific. This type of phantasy is certainly to be met with in many other patients who have no tic. [p. 124]

The primary sublimations fail to give complete satisfaction to the libidinal impulses invested in them. This partial failure is the origin of the mobility of the libido, which must be ceaselessly in search of new ways of satisfaction. It is this irremediable lack of satisfaction on the part of the libido that accounts for the continual formation of new symbols throughout development, and for the fact that the libido, by virtue of the dynamism which is natural to it, is the motive principle of all activity:

Freud demonstrates that that which seems to be an impulsion towards perfection in human beings is the result of the tension arising out of the disparity between man's desire for gratification (which is not to appeased by all possible kinds of reactive substitutive formations and of sublimations) and the gratification which in reality he obtains. I think that we may put down to this motive not only that which Groddeck calls the compulsion to make symbols but also a constant development of the symbols. [Klein, 1923a, p. 104]

The question of why the libido is irremediably unsatisfied was still open in 1923. Was it, as Freud and Abraham thought, essentially because a substitute satisfaction, the only one repression allows, does not enable the adequate discharge of libido, as the passage quoted seems to suggest? Or was it because the libido wants from the beginning a state of total and lasting satisfaction, which reality could never satisfy? Although Melanie Klein held the second position in her later work, the deliberately economic nature of the proto-Kleinian ideas leads us to think that her hypothesis at this time was the first one.

3. The primary sublimations are the basis for the ceaseless

development of the other sublimations, to which they give their energy. In the last analysis all sublimations are rooted in either speech or movement:

> starting from the point where the pre-conditions for the capacity for sublimation are given by libidinal fixations on the most primary sublimations—which I considered to be speech and the pleasure in movement—the constantly extending ego-activities and interests achieve libidinal cathexis by acquiring a sexual symbolic meaning, so that there are constantly new sublimations at different stages. [Klein, 1923b, p. 73]

4. The development of sublimations takes place according to a predetermined order corresponding both to the order of the stages of development of the libido and to the order of the stages of the sense of reality. It is by way of the primary sublimations that the instinctive components attain to sublimation under genital dominance. We can thus attempt to view Melanie Klein's conceptions through the image of an edifice of sublimations which would take the form of an irregular pyramid, the peak of which would not necessarily be on a straight line from the base passing through the intersection of the medians of this base, but the height of which could be altered according to the quantity of libido sublimated in the plan, and according to the dominant axis of the sublimations—the speech axis or the movement axis. The base would correspond to the primary sublimations common to all human beings (Fig. 1).

5. The first of the secondary sublimations is play. Play behavior holds a strategic place in development because it is the immediate result of the primary sublimations which it brings into play, and of which, in a way, it is merely the combination. At the same time, it gives the subject the opportunity for libidinal cathexis of activities and objects in the world of make-believe before facing them in reality. It thus plays a major adaptive role arising from its function in the discharge of tension. Play, corresponding to the first layer of sublimations, supports the following layer, which comprises the first schoolwork and sport. Sublimation at this second level cannot be successful

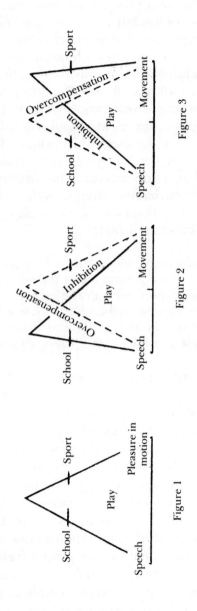

Figure 1

Figure 2

Figure 3

unless play has fulfilled its task of preliminary cathexis of these activities.

6. The structure of the edifice of sublimation accounts for the clinical aspect of inhibitions. In fact, every inhibition is based on an earlier repressed sublimation. Thus Felix, between six and eleven, suffered from an inhibition of sport and physical activity. The libidinal energy was totally absorbed in learning interests, which took on an aspect of overcompensation (Fig. 2). After his father's threats and mockery, the cathexes were exchanged (Fig. 3): success at school was inhibited, but sublimation in sport bore the mark of its origin: "It became increasingly clear to him in the course of the analysis that games were an unsuccessful over-compensation for anxiety, an unsuccessful substitute for masturbation" (Klein, 1925, p. 108).

Since all sublimations are based on play, all inhibitions are based on the inhibition of play:

> the foundations of later inhibitions—of vocational inhibition as well—are to be found, above all, in the frequently apparently evanescent ones concerned with the earliest studies. The inhibitions of these earliest studies, however, are built upon play-inhibitions, so significant for life and development, evolving from the earliest play-inhibitions. [Klein, 1923b, p. 73]

That is why the richness and spontaneity of the child's play—or, lacking that, its poverty and stereotyped nature—become a major diagnostic criterion. Insofar as play forms the first synthesis of the primary sublimations—pleasure in movement and speech—it is at the same time the chief means of development of sublimations, and thus the child's psychoanalytic treatment must bring the liberation of play. The psychoanalytic method is an investigative process and a treatment at the same time. As an investigative process it has to interpret the child's play by bringing out the masturbatory fantasies underlying every play activity and relating them to the primal scene, of which they are the elaboration. As treatment, it can attain its objective of reducing symptoms and restoring sublimations only by the interpretation of fantasy translated into play. The formal regression necessary for cure must relate to play, the inhibition of which marked the beginning of the formation of a neurotic symptom or the inhibition of an aptitude. The two dimensions—heuristic and therapeutic—of psychoanalytic technique applied to the child require that a privileged value be accorded to play as a diagnostic sign, as material to be interpreted, and as a means of developing the analytic process. In addition, both theoretical speculation regarding the notion of identification and the study of the precursors of symbolism and sublimation lead us to consider play as the immediate manifestation of the two primary sublimations. All the lines of force of the proto-Kleinian conceptions, it may be said, end by concentrating attention on the function of play. The invention of the psychoanalytic play technique thus appears to be the consequence of Melanie Klein's first psychoanalytic ideas. The scope, coherence, importance, and fertility of these ideas are not usually recognized; they have had to be reconstructed from theoretical passages and suggestions scattered through five texts published before 1926. But with the invention of the play technique, Melanie Klein could deal with very young children and with severe pathology of a sort she had not previously experienced. The new clinical data accumulated by this technique were later to give rise to the blossoming and the far-reaching modification of the proto-Kleinian system.

5. The Normal and the Pathological in the Proto-Kleinian System

We can now return to a question left incompletely answered at the end of section 2 above. The proto-Kleinian theories as a whole were aimed at the solution of a problem which, to paraphrase and generalize the Freudian idea of "choice of neurosis" (*Neurosenwahl*),[4] we might call "the choice of the method of discharge of anxiety": what are the specific differential factors governing the three types of evolution (sublimation, inhi-

[4] "The whole group of processes whereby the subject embarks upon the formation of one particular type of psychoneurosis as opposed to any other" (Laplanche and Pontalis, 1967, p. 69).

bition, neurosis) leading to health (based on repressed sublimations) or to the formation of neurotic symptom? The choice between sublimation and inhibition, as we have seen, always presupposes a preliminary phase of successful sublimation of the libido by a libidinal cathexis which has had time to develop and be enriched before repression sets in. This choice, then, comes later than the primary sublimations, and Melanie Klein was able to theorize about it as early as Erich's second analysis and the beginning of Felix's, in the first months of 1921. But the formation of the neurotic symptom—in fact she was thinking almost exclusively of the hysterical symptom—comes before the primary sublimations, or at least corresponds to an early intervention of repression which does not leave time for the primary sublimations and for play to develop. For this reason the anxiety caused by the repression of libido cannot be discharged through either sublimation or inhibition. As the libido has not yet been cathected in sufficient quantities on the ego activities—speech and movement—we find ourselves at the stage genetically preceding the primary identification. In the case of hysteria we are dealing with the first stage of this primary identification, that of construction of the body image by cathexis of the organs and parts of the upper half of the body: displacement and condensation, in accordance with the laws of the primary process governed by the pleasure principle, make them equivalent to the parts of the lower half of the body (according to Ferenczi's formula) or, more exactly, to the erogenous zones. The specific condition of the phenomenon of hysterial conversion, therefore, is the early supervention of repression at the first stage of primary identification—more precisely, at the end of this first stage, in the period of overlap between the process of cathexis of the upper half of the body and the process, already begun, of cathexis of external objects starting with their identification with the parts of the body.

This hypothesis enables us to account for the essential characteristics of conversion hysteria. The discharge of anxiety through somatic innervation refers back to fixation at the phase in which the parts of the body are equal in their value for libidinal pleasure; the displacement of the erogenous zones which gives rise to Charcot's hysterogenic zones is a survival of this. Under the conversion lies a fantasy which often translates an "identification by a single feature" (see Freud, 1921, p. 106); this goes back to the equivalence (the precursor of symbolism) between erogenous zones, the "upper" part of the body, and objects (including persons) of the external world. Melanie Klein (1923a) could thus write:

> we have in the symptomatology of hysteria a reproduction of the capacity for displacement of the erotogenic zones which is manifest in the child's early orientation and identification. Thus we see that identification is also a stage preliminary to hysterical symptom-formation, and it is this identification[5] which enables the hysteric to effect the characteristic displacement from below upwards. [p. 87]

The choice between the line of evolution which leads to hysteria and that which leads to sublimation and inhibition thus depends on an initial factor—the date of the appearance of repression and of the consequent release of anxiety. This date is estimated not only by reference to chronology, but by reference to the stage reached by libidinal cathexis. Melanie Klein makes no explicit statement on the causes of this early repression. She sometimes admits the importance of accidental factors: an example is the trauma of Felix's surgical operation, which gave substance excessively early to the castration threat. She often admits, particularly in Erich's case, the part played by an "innate tendency to repression." We should note, however, that her reticence on this point is easily explained: however early Felix's trauma and Erich's manifestation of this innate tendency may have appeared, they still came after the development of the primary sublimations, and these two children showed only slight neurotic symptoms in a symptomatology dominated by inhibitions. At this time Melanie Klein had not yet had any clinical experience of conversion hysteria, and her hypotheses were purely speculative. In summary, a fairly faithful idea of her thought is conveyed by the statement that she allows, between constitutional factors and external events, the complementary

---

[5] This is *primary identification* in Jones's sense—that is to say, the primitive form of the symbolic equation rather than identification in the usual sense.

series described by Freud; she refers to it in contexts which are similar but nonetheless different.

The second specific factor of the choice between the hysterical symptom and sublimation-inhibition is to be found in the constitution: in certain subjects the ego activities might have a constitutional capacity to receive libidinal cathexis: "On the other hand we might suppose that there is yet another factor of importance for the capacity of sublimating—one which might well form a very considerable part of the talent with which an individual is constitutionally endowed. I refer to the ease with which an ego activity or tendency takes on a libidinal cathexis and the extent to which it is thus receptive" (Klein, 1923a, p. 87). We might be tempted to compare this innate receptivity of the ego activities with organ pleasure (as Melanie Klein appears to understand it), or with the constitutional pleasure in walking which Karl Abraham described in 1913, and consider it a nonsexual functional pleasure. Melanie Klein (1923a) finds a symmetrical correspondence to it in the classic idea of "somatic compliance" as used in the theory of hysteria: "on the physical plane we have an analogy in the readiness with which a particular area of the body receives innervation and the importance of this factor in the development of hysterical symptoms" (p. 87). Subjects would thus be distributed along a continuum the two extremes of which would be somatic compliance, predisposing to hysteria, and what we might call "ego compliance" predisposing to sublimation and thus to health: "These factors, which might constitute what we understand by 'disposition,' would form a complementary series, like those with which we are familiar in the aetiology of the neuroses" (p. 87). Melanie Klein also admits a third factor, "the capacity for maintaining the libido in an undischarged state," which too would be constitutional. It is the precursor, in proto-Kleinian theory, of the "constitutional capacity to bear anxiety," which will be described later as one of the factors leading to the paranoid-schizoid position.

The interaction of these three factors enables us to account for the direction taken by development, toward hysterical symptoms or toward sublimations. This brings to a close the general inquiry opened by the proto-Kleinian theory on the psychogenesis of sublimation, inhibition, and symptoms. This conception, which assigns an extensive role to constitutional factors, nonetheless emphasizes the moment of the appearance of repression as the final differential factor, whatever the nature of its determinants (constitution or events). In the last analysis the decisive question is: when did repression transform the libido into anxiety? If at the stage of primary identification, we shall see the formation of hysterical symptoms. If at the stage of primary sublimations, there will be neurotic inhibitions. If at the stage of secondary sublimations, there will be those slight inhibitions which are the price the normal individual must pay for psychological health. Melanie Klein was thus led to consider the existence of very early manifestations of repression.

From the very beginning of her psychoanalytic activities, she held firmly to two basic preconceptions. First, she completely ignored Freud's idea of a true anxiety independent of repression. The second Freudian theory of anxiety, which maintained, under the name of automatic anxiety, the notion of anxiety previous to repression, had no influence on her, and she did not modify her attitude on this point until she had worked out her own theory of anxiety connected with the death impulse. Second, she did not mention defense mechanisms as existing before repression; she did not formulate a theory about them until after 1926, and even then retained the idea that repression always operates against oedipal impulses. Thus, extending her conceptions of 1923, she was led to admit the hypothesis that in certain children, at least, the oedipus complex is already present, and affected by repression, at the onset of night terrors, that is to say between two and three years. Clinical examples are already to be found in the 1923 texts: Erich spoke late, in his mother's judgment, because of the repression already acting against the voice, which was invested with libido according to genital symbolism. He ran away at the age of three because he was already sublimating his genital impulses in walking and the exploration of space, which symbolized the exploration of his mother's body, inspired by the incestuous impulses of the oedipus complex. Felix liked to sing during his third year because he could express in this way his identification with his father's active role in the primal scene. All this appeared only in scattered indications and was not yet the subject of an integrally and strictly formulated conception. Melanie Klein's attention nevertheless turned to the locating of early repression and the early oedipus complex. From this point of view the proto-Kleinian conceptions of 1923 are directly at the origin of two of the main Kleinian theories of 1926: the existence of an archaic oedipus complex and an archaic superego, which are not considered "early" phenomena. Although they come before a normal date, they are the normal initial forms of the oedipus complex and the "classical" superego, just as "archaic" Greek sculpture is the initial form of the "classical" sculpture of the era of Phidias.

6. The Place of the Proto-Kleinian System in Melanie Klein's Work

The proto-Kleinian conceptions of 1923 were essentially based on the analyses of Erich and Felix, which faced Melanie Klein with a symptomatology consisting mainly of inhibitions. These conceptions comprise a genetic theory based on normal psychology and psychopathic considerations arising from it. On the plane of description of normal development, Melanie Klein's originality is seen in her vast synthesis of the more fragmentary views of Ferenczi, Jones, and Abraham. Through it she succeeds in accounting for the development of the personality as a whole, and especially the functions of the ego, in terms of libidinal cathexis. She thus introduces the idea of a genetic continuity between autoerotism, formation of the body image, symbolization, and primary, then secondary sublimations.

As far as the defensive process is concerned, she links anxiety in all its forms to the repression of the oedipus complex. The ensuing psychopathology enables her to work out the psychogenesis of hysteria, inhibition, and sublimation, which forms a coherent system.

We know that Melanie Klein was to abandon these views after 1926. However, we have seen that a number of proto-Kleinian notions directly prefigure her later ideas. It thus seems possible to affirm that the proto-Kleinian system of 1923, far from representing a form of thought which Melanie Klein was later to reject in its entirety, contained all the essential elements of her later theories, except for the strictly clinical data yielded by the first analyses using the play technique.

In the proto-Kleinian system three groups of hypotheses may be distinguished.

1. Some of the proto-Kleinian ideas were purely and simply abandoned: chief among these, essential in 1923, is the attribution to the libido of the role of developmental prime mover. From 1926 onward, Melanie Klein recognized the importance of aggressive impulses, and in 1932, in *The Psycho-Analysis of Children*, she accepted Freud's idea of the death instinct. From 1927 the only function left the libido was the attempted attenuation of the action of aggressive cathexes, to which were assigned the motive role in the development of symbolism, sublimations, and relations with the external world.

The idea that all anxiety comes from repression of the libido was to suffer the same fate. In the later theories, anxiety was the affective mode of reaction of the ego faced with the internal activity of the death instinct. But the role and the importance of anxiety were to be recognized still more firmly.

These two ideas are the only ones in the system of 1923 which are not found in the later writings. It is true that they were basic concepts on which all the other hypotheses were based: the 1923 theory was at bottom a libidinal theory, and all the rest made sense in relation to this central idea, which provided a principle of systematic unity. When this idea was abandoned after the discovery of archaic sadism and the leading role of aggressive impulses, the proto-Kleinian views lost their systematic character and risked becoming a rhapsody of theoretical elements and clinical notions lacking any unity.

2. Some of the proto-Kleinian ideas were preserved, but at the cost of revision of the connection between them, and of partial transformation of their content. In the majority of cases the transposition was intended to reconcile an early hypothesis with the discovery of the primacy of oral sadism.

The theory of inhibition underwent considerable transformation: in the definitive Kleinian system inhibition presupposes an earlier cathexis but no longer a successful sublimation. The conditions of inhibition are found in the cathexis of certain activities by aggressive impulses, giving rise to retaliatory anxiety, which leads to abandonment of the dangerous activity. The link between anxiety and inhibition, the nucleus of the initial Kleinian hypothesis on inhibition, first formulated in 1921, was maintained. But after 1928 anxiety could not arise from repressed libido; only aggressive impulses could give birth to anxiety.

Similarly, the theory of sublimation underwent correlative modifications; the idea of the libidinal nature of sublimation was kept. As predominance passed from the libido to aggressive impulses having genetic priority, sublimation was no longer a primary mechanism, lying in the direct extension of the construction of an image of the body and of the world, but a secondary one in relation to aggressive cathexis. With the introduction in 1927 of the notion of a reparative mechanism, sublimation based on reparation is a path which opens at the same point as that of inhibition. After an initial aggressive cathexis of the object or the ego activity, either retaliatory anxiety causes inhibition of the function, or the libido, following the path traced by aggressive activities, cathects the same objects or the same ego activities, and attenuates the retaliatory anxiety by making reparation in fantasy to the objects hurt by archaic sadism (this reconciliation with the object is the basis of sublimation). Sublimation and inhibition are thus two divergent and contemporary paths corresponding to two types of defense against anxiety, one effective and the other injurious to the self.

The general outline of the genesis of symbolism was retained in its entirety, but at the cost of a radical modification in perspective: the entire process was attributed to the activity of the death instinct. From 1932 onward the death instinct was used to account for both anxiety and the process of development of the life of relation: "the destructive instinct is directed against the organism itself and must therefore be regarded by the ego as a danger. I believe that it is this danger which is felt by the individual as anxiety" (Klein, 1932, p. 106). From this point of view the whole of development appears to be governed by the demands of the struggle against endogenous anxiety. The primal defense mechanism, which is the deflection of the death instinct to the exterior—that is to say, the projection of the internal danger onto objects which thus become imaginary persecutors—leads to an early interest in these objects, which have to be watched so that a defense can be mounted against them. The modification of perspective is thus quite radical. Even so, it is important to stress that although the train has been coupled to another engine, the order of the coaches remains the same. The order in which the death instinct cathects the organs and parts of the mother's body as a whole, and then, on the basis of symbolism and the "geography of the mother's body," the objects of the external world, this order remains exactly the same as that described in the writings of 1923.

The theory of fantasy outlined in 1923 was submitted to a less radical revision. Although amplified and considerably enriched by the discovery of oral-sadistic and anal-sadistic fantasies from 1924 onward, nothing essential was changed, save that the fantasies were no longer viewed as attached to the libido alone; sadistic fantasies and fantasies arising from the compromise between sadistic and libidinal impulses were now described. The function of fantasy as related to impulse—whether libidinal or sadistic—was described with growing finesse and became the subject of an increasingly explicit theory, but Melanie Klein's definitive conception was still directly descended from the theory of 1923.

The idea that all fantasies are masturbatory fantasies elaborated on the basis of the primal scene began to take shape in 1934 (Klein, 1935b) with the introduction of the notion of psychotic states, but remained in force in the later period and notably, in 1932, in the vast theoretical synthesis of *The Psycho-Analysis of Children*. It was never totally abandoned, as it always applied to fantasies accompanying oedipal conflict.

Finally, although the explicit educational aims which could still be detected in the 1923 writings were abandoned, Melanie Klein's ideas in this regard may be seen as evolving in the direction of already present in the early system. Thus she arrived at the notion of psychoanalytic treatment as the actual reeducation of the capacity to fantasize, which, when applied to very young children, may be considered preeducation. More than that, the initial psychopedagogical ideas reappeared at another

level, much more archaic, and the Kleinian doctrines of 1934
became the basis of pediatric ideas (e.g., those of D.W. Winnicott) and a normative theory of mothering and early education in which the prophylactic aims of the first writings
reappeared in force (Klein, 1935a).

3. Certain ideas, relatively secondary in the proto-Kleinian
system, became fundamental in the definitive Kleinian conception. First, the importance of play as the first secondary sublimation and the source of all the others, already recognized in
1923, was considerably increased by the introduction, in the
second half of that year, of the psychoanalytic play technique,
the technical basis of all Kleinian psychoanalysis. Second, the
early appearance of the oedipus complex no longer appeared
as an exceptional or pathological phenomenon, but as a regular
fact: the theory of the archaic oedipus complex became Melanie
Klein's essential idea up to the discovery, in 1934, of the depressive state. Third, the early appearance of anxiety released
by the repression of the oedipus complex, an idea already
strongly emphasized in 1923, was extended from 1926 onward
in what was to be the second great idea of Kleinian psycho-
analysis: the theory of the archaic superego. Finally, the mechanism of splitting, a conception mentioned sporadically from
1921 on (see Klein, 1921, p. 42) but only glimpsed then though
it already had a name, progressively took on the function of an
actual organizer of mental life and became a central idea in the
definitive Kleinian system.

We should note that in contrast to what happened with the
first three ideas, as regards the fourth, the definitive theory
was not limited to the accentuation of an hypothesis already
firmly stated. In the case of splitting, the definitive theory lent
a breadth, which could not possibly have been foreseen in the
early work, to what before 1923 was still but a clinical intuition.
By contrast, the analysis of play and of the archaic stages of the
oedipus complex and the superego were quite extensively prefigured in the proto-Kleinian system. They do not, however,
appear as basic theories but as hypotheses awaiting verification.
It must be emphasized that these hypotheses depend strictly on
the principles of the libidinal theory of 1923, without which
their formulation would certainly have been impossible. Mel-

anie Klein assigned play the value of a sublimation capable òf creating further sublimations because she was able to conceptualize her clinical intuition of the strategic position of play in the treatment of anxiety within a theory that links it definitely with the primary sublimations and with symbolism. Without the contribution of this conceptualization, and despite the fact that it was later abandoned, her intuition would have remained blind. We can make the same observation regarding the oedipus complex and the archaic superego. Only unlimited confidence in the Freudian ideas—though later she was to go beyond them—of the transformation of libido into anxiety as a result of repression, and of the nonexistence of repression outside the castration complex (and thus the oedipus complex), enabled her to deduce, purely theoretically, that the anxiety of the earliest night terrors was already the product of repression, proving that oedipal conflict already existed.

We can say, then, that the proto-Kleinian system, far from being the clumsy effort of a largely self-taught beginner, already contained three of the major inspirations of her work, directly anticipating the great discoveries of the period 1923–1926. In addition, six essential elements—the theories of inhibition, sublimation, identification, and anxiety, the idea of a primary identification of the parts of the body with each other and with objects, and a conception of masturbatory fantasies and their link with the primal scene—were partially integrated into the system of 1932 and were taken over, though with new transformations and limitations, into the final Kleinian system. The nature of their insertion into the final theory might best be coveyed via an architectural metaphor. These elements have been *underpinned*, as we might a building we wish to preserve but whose foundation is weak. We support it with a temporary structure, demolish the old foundation, and replace it with a more solid base, which must then be exactly joined to the old parts of the building so that they may rest on it with perfect stability. After 1926 Melanie Klein felt that her libido theory was weak and could no longer provide her ideas the unity, coherence, and stability they required. She therefore gave up this theory, replacing it with a new one, that of the primacy of the destructive instincts, which now supported the ancient building at the cost of a few modifications in its structure.

As for the abandoned libidinal theory, it belonged from then on to that vast graveyard of hypotheses which, in the words of Henri Poincaré, is the history of science. But, its death registered, we would be wrong to consign it to oblivion in the Registrar General's files. Though scientifically obsolete, this theory retains an essential historical and epistemological interest. Just as Newtonian physics made possible the invention by Michelson and Morley, of the experimental setup that yielded the data disproving Newton's theories, so the libidinal theory of 1923, bringing out the role of play in the formation of sublimations, enabled Melanie Klein to invent, at the end of the same year, the psychoanalytic play technique, which in turn was to bring out clinical facts unobservable within a metapsychology based on libidinal cathexis alone.

3

The Discovery of the Play Technique and Its Consequences

1. The New Style of Melanie Klein's Creativity

The proto-Kleinian conceptions quite naturally led toward the idea that an analysis undertaken very early offered the child the possibility of developing harmoniously from then onward:

> It is clear (but the fact still requires verification) that, if it were possible to undertake an analysis of the child at the time of the *pavor nocturnus* or soon after it, and to resolve this anxiety, the ground would be cut away from under the neurosis and possibilities of sublimation would be opened out. My own observations lead me to believe that analytic investigation is not impossible with children of this age. [Klein, 1923a, p. 82]

In the middle of 1923 Melanie Klein had the opportunity to verify her hypothesis: she was asked to psychoanalyze a little girl less than three years old, whom she calls Rita. The analysis lasted 83 sessions, which corresponds, taking into account the practice of daily sessions to which the Kleinian school has held up to now, to a duration of three to four months. The treatment was broken off prematurely because the family left to live abroad, but these few weeks were enough to reveal to Melanie Klein the universe of early fantasies, which she never ceased to explore. This analysis marks the third stage in Melanie Klein's "take-off"; it lies at the root of the considerable clinical and theoretical work which blossomed in her writings from 1926 onward. We know that Karl Abraham made no mistake about this; he proclaimed to Freud the exploits of his protégée:

> I have something pleasant to report in the scientific field. In my work on melancholia, of which Rank has the manuscript, I have assumed the presence of an early depression (*Ur-Verstimmung*) in infancy as a prototype for later melancholia. In the last few months Mrs. Klein has skillfully conducted the psycho-analysis of a child of three with good therapeutic results. This child presented a true picture of the basic depression (*Ur-Melancholie*) which I postulated in close combination with oral erotism. The case offers amazing insight into the infantile instinctual life. [Freud and Abraham, 1907–1926 p. 339]

We must note, however, that Abraham was partly unaware of the nature of the information Melanie Klein had obtained from this experience, and tended to consider it a simple confirmation of his own ideas. It is also probable that at this time her own opinion was not very different, and that she considered herself primarily a pupil of Abraham; she was waiting to begin her analysis with him, which she did in February or March 1924. In April of that year she read to the Salzburg Psycho-Analytical Congress a paper which is today still unpublished: "The Technique of Analysis of Very Young Children." We know something of the contents of this work, which very probably was the first version of "The Psychological Principles of Early Analysis" (Klein, 1926), through indications given by Melanie Klein (1932) herself:

> In a paper read before the Salzburg Congress in 1924, I put forward the thesis that behind every form of play-activity lies a process of discharge of masturbatory phantasies, operating in the form of a continuous motive for play; that this process, acting as a repetition-compulsion, constitutes a fundamental mechanism in children's play and in all their subsequent sublimations; and that inhibitions in play and work spring from an unduly strong repression of those phantasies, and with them, of the whole imaginative life of the child. Linked to these masturbatory

phantasies of the child are its sexual experiences, which along with them, find representation and abreaction in its play. Among such re-enacted experiences, the primal scene plays a very important part and generally occupies the foreground of the picture in early analysis. It is, as a rule, only after a good deal of analysis has been done, and both the primal scene and the child's genital trends have been to some extent uncovered, that we reach representations of its pre-genital experiences and phantasies." [pp. 9–10]

In a note to the 1926 text she alluded to the same presentation: "In the paper which I read at the Salzburg Congress in April, 1924, I gave examples to show that children at first conceive of, and desire, coitus as an oral act" (p. 129). It was upon hearing this presentation that Ernest Jones invited her to London to give a series of lectures on the psychoanalysis of children, an invitation she took up in the summer of 1925. During 1924 she carried out, by means of the play technique, which she had just perfected, the analysis of Trude (three years, three months) and began those of Ruth (four years, three months) and Peter (three years, nine months). She finished these in the course of 1925, as well beginning the analysis of Erna (six years old), which continued into 1926. She read papers on some points of detail to the Berlin society, before presenting, on December 13, 1924, a paper entitled, like the text published in 1926, "The Psychological Principles of Early Analysis"; it very likely represented a transition between the Salzburg paper and the final text. In October 1925, at a meeting of German psychoanalysts organized at Würzburg by Abraham, she gave a talk on the case of Erna, which the *International Journal of Psycho-Analysis* (1925, Volume 5) reviewed as follows: "In a paper entitled *From the analysis of an obsessional neurosis in a six-year-old*, Mrs. Klein (Berlin) traced the pathological manifestations to the child's abnormal instinctual life and threw some light on the technique and results of the treatment" (p. 100). It was in the course of the discussion which followed this communication that Abraham declared, as we have noted, that "the future of psycho-analysis lies in the psycho-analysis of children." Melanie Klein, not yet clearly aware of the importance of her discoveries, was astonished.

However, she did not publish Erna's case until 1932, in *The Psycho-Analysis of Children*. In fact, she published very little during the period in which the great Kleinian theories were being worked out, and waited much longer before publishing her ideas than she had in the preceding period. In 1924 she was forty-two years old; she was at the end of a crisis period marked especially by her divorce, and was beginning her analysis with Abraham. During this midlife crisis she passed from the type of youthful creativity described by Elliott Jaques (1974) to a "sculptured" creativity. In 1919–1920 she had waited less than three months to report to the Budapest society, and to publish partially (Klein, 1920), the experiment in sexual education attempted with her son, not even taking the trouble to hide the child's identity. In 1921 she gave information on Erich which had been collected at the very moment she was writing her article. In 1923 she described in published articles the case of Felix, two years before finishing his analysis. Between the ages of thirty-seven and forty-one she published a total of five articles containing ideas formed at the very moment when she was writing them down. We can apply to her method then the description given by Jaques (1974) of the work of creative people in their youth:

> the characteristic of creativity is that it is burning. It is intense, spontaneous, the work is finished straight away. The spontaneous effusions of Mozart, Keats, Shelley, and Rimbaud are the prototype. The greater part of the work seems to be done unconsciously. The conscious production is rapid, the speed of creation is often limited only by the artist's capacity to give material representation to the words or music which are his mode of expression. [pp. 240–241]

After 1923, however, Melanie Klein was much slower and more cautious. She published only two articles in three years. One, the longer (Klein, 1925), is linked by its content to the preceding period; it describes Felix's case and, despite its publication date, contains none of the new ideas she clearly had been formulating for over a year. The other (Klein, 1926), consisting of ten close-textured pages, was withheld from publication for two years and, as we have seen, was rewritten at least twice before its appearance in print. The group of articles—all short and concise—which followed until 1932 returned tirelessly to the study of the same four or five cases—Rita, Trude, Ruth, Peter, Erna—delving ever deeper into the concept. Thus, the synthesis of all this, *The Psycho-Analysis of Children*, may be viewed as the culmination of eight years' work. There again the ideas of Jaques (1974) are strikingly pertinent:

> creativity around forty is 'sculptured.' The inspiration may be burning and intense. The work of the unconscious is no less than before. But a great distance separates the first spark of inspiration from the finished, created product. Inspiration itself may come more slowly. Even if there are sudden flashes of inspiration, that is only the beginning of the process of creation of the work. The initial inspiration must first be externalized in its raw state. Then begins a process of formation and fashioning of the external product, by successive modeling and remodeling of the material. I use the term 'sculptured' because the nature of the sculptor's material—I am thinking of the sculptor in stone—compels the artist to carry on this type of relationship with the product of his creative imagination. There appears a whole interaction between on the one hand the unconscious, intuitive work, inspiration, and on the other hand the attentive perception of the external product being created and the reaction to it. . . . This process of externalization is the very essence of creative work at the age of the mature adult. . . . [p. 241]

We can also find these characteristics of mature creativity in the way in which Melanie Klein, bitterly disappointed by the interruption of her analysis and then struck with sorrow at the death of Abraham on New Year's Day, 1926, reacted to this loss: mourning deeply, she decided after mature reflection to go to London, temporarily at first, then to settle there definitively. She took up her scientific activity again in the autumn of 1926, after a silence of almost a year. "Resigned but not beaten" (Jaques, 1974 p. 260), she began the second stage of her life, that of final maturity, which was to make of her the true leader of a school.[1]

---

[1] At the beginning of the 1930s, the group of English psychoanalysts who shared Melanie Klein's ideas—that is to say, at that time almost all the members

2. The Psychoanalysis of Rita

The third stage of Melanie Klein's development began with the analysis of Rita and the almost simultaneous invention of the play technique. When Melanie Klein was asked to psychoanalyze Rita, in the spring of 1923, the child, who was then not yet three, had been suffering serious neurotic disturbances for a year. Although she seemed very intelligent, she showed an almost complete inhibition in play. She was very difficult to bring up, and her parents were constantly disconcerted by her oscillations between excessive goodness and unbounded naughtiness. Against a general background of anxiety, she was subject to intermittent moodiness, similar in all points to adult melancholic states—a condition of which Karl Abraham had been very aware. Rita, incapable of bearing frustration, reacted to the slightest deprivation with bursts of anger or deep depression. She often cried for no apparent reason, and would not say why when questioned. She pursued her mother with anxious questions—"Am I good?"; "Do you love me?"—but might immediately afterward turn defiant in answer to a slight reprimand. She was capricious, had eating difficulties, and often had no appetite. To all that was added a characteristic and fully formed obsessional symptom consisting of a bedtime ritual the demands of which had for several months been becoming more and more minute and imperative. The essential—and initial—point was as follows: she had to be tightly wrapped in the blankets, and the same had to be done with her doll. Otherwise, she said, a mouse or a *Bützen* (a word of her own, meaning the genital organs) would get into her room and bite off her own *Bützen* (Klein, 1945, p. 402).

Rita's mother herself suffered from severe obsessional neurosis, and was extremely ambivalent toward her little girl. She had breast-fed her daughter—who was her first-born—for some months. The first bottles had been very badly received, and the same thing happened when she was put on solid food.

---

of the British society, from Jones to Glover—was known as the English School of Psychoanalysis, in opposition to the Viennese school, which supported the ideas of Freud and Anna Freud on feminine sexuality and early development.

Attempts to wean her from her last bottle at night had to be given up; she was still taking it when she began her analysis, and every effort to stop it had plunged the child into such distress that her parents were horrified. Rita had been continent since the beginning of her second year, and her mother seemed to have put much anxious effort into the little girl's toilet training.

The child had clearly preferred her mother to her father until the end of her first year. She then showed a marked preference for her father and appeared very jealous of her mother. At the age of about fifteen months, when she was already speaking sufficiently well to make herself understood, she had several times climbed onto her father's knees and conveyed very clearly that she wanted her mother to go out of the room and leave them alone. From birth until the age of two she had shared her parents' room and on several occasions had witnessed their sexual intercourse. Her mother became pregnant when Rita was fifteen months old. At the age of eighteen months the child's behavior changed completely. Once more she preferred her mother, but Rita's relationship with her was still extremely ambivalent. She often expressed violent hate for her, and at the same time clung to her and would not let her out of her sight, even for an instant. As for her father, she now showed open aversion to him (Klein, 1945, p. 400).

At the same time, she had intense night terrors and a phobia for various animals; she was particularly afraid of dogs. Her neurosis was triggered by the birth of her brother when she was two years old. Then her play narrowed in scope, becoming inhibited, stereotyped, and compulsive. She spent hours dressing and undressing her doll, with no element of imagination. At the same time, the bedtime ceremonial appeared and then developed, accompanied by all the difficulties we have described.

Taking into account the age of the little patient and her difficulty in separating from her mother, Melanie Klein undertook the analysis in the parents' home, in the child's bedroom, under the anxious supervision of the family, who wondered how Rita would behave once she was alone with the

psychoanalyst. Melanie Klein (1955) later described the first
session in Rita's treatment:

> I was very doubtful about how to tackle this case since the analysis
> of so young a child was an entirely new experiment. The first
> session seemed to confirm my misgivings. Rita, when left alone
> with me in her nursery, at once showed signs of what I took to
> be a negative transference: she was anxious and silent and very
> soon asked to go out into the garden. I agreed and went with
> her—I may add, under the watchful eyes of her mother and
> aunt, who took this as a sign of failure. They were very surprised
> to see that Rita was quite friendly towards me when we returned
> to the nursery some ten to fifteen minutes later. The explanation
> of this change was that while we were outside I had been inter-
> preting her negative transference (this again being against the
> usual practice). From a few things she said, and the fact that she
> was less frightened when we were in the open, I concluded that
> she was particularly afraid of something which I might do to her
> when she was alone with me in the room. I interpreted this and,
> referring to her night terrors, I linked her suspicion of me as
> a hostile stranger with her fear that a bad woman would attack
> her when she was by herself at night. When, a few minutes after
> this interpretation, I suggested that we should return to the
> nursery, she readily agreed. [p. 124]

Nevertheless, the ice had not been broken. At the beginning of the analysis, the child tolerated Melanie Klein's presence
but did little more than carry on with her usual behavior: weak
stereotyped play with her doll, accompanied from time to time
by the assertion that this doll was not her baby. The analyst was
able to explain to the child that she was afraid to be the mother
of her doll because she was afraid to take from her mother her
real baby, the little brother who was born when Rita was two
years old. A detail which was occasionally added to the bedtime
ritual could then be interpreted. Rita sometimes insisted that
a furry elephant should be put beside her bed and that of her
doll. The elephant had to stop the doll from getting up in the
night and going into her parents' room to hurt them or take
something. Rita sometimes punished her doll for having such
sinister intentions in such a way that "the reactions of rage and

anxiety which took place when the 'child' was punished in these games showed that in her own mind Rita was enacting both parts: that of the authorities who inflicted punishment and that of the child who received it" (Klein, 1929b, p. 202). In this game the elephant represented the father who was preventing the little girl from getting close to him, from supplanting the mother and destroying her. It was the fear of the real father in his function of forbidder of incest which made it possible to understand, with the elephant game, an episode which the little girl had remembered; when she was two she had burst into tears when her father, for a joke, had threatened a bear in a picture book. Rita had identified with this bear, the significance of which was to appear later. This material as a whole revealed the fear Rita had of being cruelly punished for the unconscious wish she had had, all through her mother's pregnancy, to steal the baby she was carrying, and to kill her and take her place with her father. At this stage in her analysis her play lost a little of its stereotyped nature and its lack of relation to reality. But in a second stage it always turned to the advantage of those who were strict, avenging, and punishing. Rita showed in her play "the tendency to recognize reality only insofar as it related to the frustrations which she had undergone but had never got over" (Klein, 1929b, p. 206). The little patient was still showing her negative transference by speaking in a way that was deliberately incomprehensible. She often wanted to leave the room, but the renewal of the interpretation given the first day was generally enough to change her mind.

Once her play had become more free and flexible, it often turned around the theme of a journey Rita had to make with her teddy bear. They had to visit a nice lady who was going to give them presents. This "journey game," in its various forms, from then onward held the central place in the analysis. At the beginning, the journey always ended badly. A nasty woman came and disturbed it. Sometimes Rita wanted to drive the train herself; she got rid of the driver, but he came back and threatened her. When she arrived at her destination, she often found a bad woman instead of the good one she was expecting. The driver appeared in the analysis as playing the part of the father; the teddy bear was often, in the game, an object of dispute between the passenger and the driver: "the bear represented the father's penis, and her rivalry with her father was expressed by this fight over the penis" (Klein, 1945, p. 401). This rivalry originated in hatred of the father, the "preventer" of incestuous wishes, but also of the wish for a penis in order to satisfy the mother, which appeared during the period of night terrors, following the repression of the oedipus complex. As the analysis explored unconscious meanings, Rita's play developed, the "journey" could go on without hindrance, and other games appeared which clearly alluded to the primal scene.

Thus, one day she took a piece from a construction set, declaring that it was a "little woman." She put it beside the cardboard box containing the construction set and took another, longer piece which she called a little hammer, with which she hit the box hard enough to make a hole in it, making the following comment: "When the hammer hit hard, the little woman was *so* frightened" (Klein, 1945, p. 401). The hammer, says Melanie Klein, represented the father's penis, the box the mother, the "little woman" Rita herself, "and the whole situation represented her witnessing the primal scene" (p. 401). In the final phase of the analysis, the anxiety arising from the double rivalry—with the father in the male position of the inverted oedipus complex, and with the mother in the female position of the positive complex—was sufficiently attenuated for the ritual to fade out and for plainly libidinal elements to overcome and replace the aggressive elements. She then showed in her play truly maternal feelings for her bear and her doll. Shortly before the treatment was broken off, she declared one day, cuddling and kissing her bear: "I'm not a bit unhappy any more because now I've got such a dear little baby" (Klein, 1945, p. 406). The bear had lost its significance as a stake in her rivalry with her father. Rita had returned to the female oedipal position, which she had been unable to maintain at the age of eighteen months because of her terror of being punished by her mother. The analysis had enabled her to overcome this anxiety, which had appeared in night terrors and in the entirety of the little girl's behavior, and made possible the return to a normal oedipal situation which could lead on to a less disturbed development.

The analysis was broken off early in the fall of 1923, after three or four months, because the family relocated abroad. But for a long time Melanie Klein had news of Rita and was able to evaluate the long-term results of the treatment. The obsessional symptoms did not reappear. The anxiety had lessened, as had the depressive symptoms and the incapacity to bear frustration. Relationships with her father and her brother became good. Her relationship with her mother, though it remained ambivalent, improved enough to lead to a change of attitude on the part of the mother herself, who became less ambivalent with her daughter. The treatment thus had results that were lasting but partial. Some years later Melanie Klein (1932) wrote:

> I was able to convince myself at first hand of the lasting nature of the results of her analysis. . . . I found then that she had entered upon the latency period in a satisfactory manner, and that her intellectual and characterological development were satisfactory. Nevertheless, when I saw her again I got the impression that it would have been advisable to have continued her analysis somewhat further. Her whole character and nature showed unmistakable traces of an obsessional disposition. [p. 4]

In 1930, seven years after the end of treatment, Melanie Klein had news of Rita from her mother, assuring her "that she continued to develop satisfactorily" (p. 4).

This picture of Rita'a treatment is probably inaccurate in certain points, and certainly very incomplete and full of gaps. There are doubts particularly with regard to the chronological order of certain details, and even more to their connection with certain facts not yet mentioned. One reason for this situation is the scattered and fragmentary nature of the passages in Melanie Klein's work which are devoted to Rita. But the essential reason for our difficulties is the exceptional importance for Melanie Klein of Rita's case. During the twenty years following this analysis she referred to it constantly in her writings, sometimes disclosing certain details for the sole purpose of illustrating concepts she had just worked out. Only rarely in her work do we find later ideas, even very late ones, which are not illustrated at least once by the example of Rita. In this sense Rita, the first beneficiary of Kleinian psychoanalytic treatment, can be looked at side by side with Richard, who was probably one of the last children whom Melanie Klein analyzed herself, and on whose treatment—also very short and prematurely terminated—she pondered for more than twenty years, up to the time of her death (Klein, 1961). It is significant that when she decided, after working out her theory of the depressive and paranoid-schizoid characters, to discuss the question of the oedipus complex and to knit together her earlier descriptions and her new hypotheses, she chose the case of Richard to illustrate a boy's development, and Rita's to illustrate that of a girl. So the most complete account we have of Rita's analysis dates from 1945—twenty-two years after the end of her treatment—and the factual data are accompanied by interpretations referring to schizoid mechanisms, reparation, etc., which Melanie Klein could not have made in 1923.

This justifies any reservations we might have regarding certain aspects of the material mentioned in her writings after 1926, and particularly the oral reports which struck Abraham so forcibly. In his letter to Freud of the October 7, 1923, Abraham noted that Rita's "primal melancholy" was "closely connected with oral erotism" (Freud and Abraham, 1907–1926, p. 339). There are indeed many elements tending in this direction in Melanie Klein's statements: Rita had not given up her last bottle at the beginning of her treatment, and the effect of the "weaning trauma" is obvious in her later intolerance of any frustration, particularly the frustration of her oedipal desires inflicted by her father. Rita's analysis was probably behind the theory put forward by Melanie Klein at Salzburg in 1924, according to which children "conceive and desire coitus at first as an oral act." It is hard to see where this idea could have come from apart from Rita's treatment, as at that time she had just begun the analyses of Trude, Ruth, Peter, and Erna. But she offered no theoretical comments on these weaning difficulties before 1932, and it was not until 1936 that she chose to explain the circumstances of Rita's weaning in detail (Klein, 1936). It should be stressed, however, that when Abraham speaks of oral erotism, he means a stage in the development of the libido, ambivalent in its second stage (the oral-sadistic stage of biting) but having essentially a relation of *partial love* with its object. When Melanie Klein speaks of Rita's oralism, she does so under the heading of oral sadism caused by weaning, of hate and terror of the mother, and, in even later texts, of greed and envy. In these conditions we must give up all hope of determining at what moment of the analysis Rita's oral erotism was interpreted to her, because we do not in fact know if this was done at all. It is perfectly possible that Melanie Klein discovered interpretations relating to oralism only after the end of the treatment. We know, for example, from her own statements that she did not realize the importance of oral *sadism* until 1924–1925, in the course of the analyses of Ruth and Peter, and we shall see that when making immediate theoretical use of Rita's case in 1926 she insisted almost exclusively on the play technique and on the "early appearance" of the oedipus complex and the superego. As far as oralism is concerned, the only point which remains highly probably is this: in 1924 Melanie Klein had formulated her theory that the oedipus complex is triggered by the oral frustration of weaning, which brings with it a change of object, a conversion from the mother's breast to the father's penis, with the aim of oral incorporation. This theory was without doubt inspired by Rita's analysis. But in a more general way, Melanie Klein needed several years to "carve out" the ideas which came to her through her little patient.

3. The Discovery of the Play Technique

The play technique itself was not applied to Rita in a systematic, concerted way. To a certain extent it was imposed by the child and the circumstances. The treatment took place in the little girl's room, among her familiar possessions and her toys. Rita spent all the sessions in play, partly because she could not verbalize her emotions and fantasies completely, and at her age it was easier to act them out, and partly because play enabled her to avoid too direct a confrontation with the psychoanalyst. Melanie Klein had certainly no intention of giving play priority over any other mode of expression, but her earlier experience

with Erich had accustomed her to understanding the significance of play, and the proto-Kleinian theories of 1923 had
armed her with a clearly formulated conception of its role in
the origin of sublimation; she could thus be on a level with her
little patient, and consider play the equivalent of the adult's
free associations. But during Rita's treatment her analyst remained passive in this field, and limited herself to accepting the
child's play and interpreting it. We might compare—*mutatis
mutandis*—the parts played respectively by Erich and then Rita,
on the one hand, and by Melanie Klein on the other, with the
parts played in the invention of adult psychoanalytic technique
by Anna O.–Bertha Pappenheim and Emmy von N., on the one
hand, and by Breuer, then Freud, on the other. In the same
way that Bertha Pappenheim had imposed on the attentive and
benevolent Breuer her secondary states and self-hypnotic hy-
permnesia, Erich had communicated with his mother through
his play and the fantasies acted out in it. But the analogy is not
complete, as Freud had already transformed into a studied
technique the "talking cure" of Bertha Pappenheim when
Emmy von N. told him one day that he was disturbing the
course of her associations with his incessant questions, a criticism he took to heart. Melanie Klein, by contrast, did not make
a systematic technique of psychoanalysis through play—thus
reproducing the step Freud had taken after receiving Breuer's
confidences regarding Bertha Pappenheim—until Rita had imposed on her a treatment centered exclusively on play.

The play technique suggested by Rita was not really invented by Melanie Klein; that is to say, it was not used on the
analyst's deliberate initiative until after the end of Rita's analysis,
or at least at a time when her treatment was almost ended.
Melanie Klein described this invention in 1955 in "The Psycho-
Analytic Play Technique." In the second half of 1923 she had
undertaken the treatment of a little girl who could be considered normal, despite a marked aversion to school. Rita's analysis
had taught Melanie Klein the difficulties of a psychoanalysis
carried out in the parents' home, and she had decided from
then on to analyze children in her own office. The first sessions
were dull and monotonous. The child spoke with difficulty and
had produced only commonplace information on her school

life. A few interpretations had led to the emergence of new stories, scarcely richer than the preceding ones. In short, the psychoanalytic process was not taking off: "my impression was," Melanie Klein (1955) wrote:

> that I should not get much further in that way. In a session in which I again found the child unresponsive and withdrawn I left her, saying that I would return in a moment. I went into my own children's nursery, collected a few toys, cars, little figures, a few bricks, and a train, put them into a box and returned to the patient. The child, who had not taken to drawing or other activities, was interested in the small toys and at once began to play. From this play I gathered that two of the toy figures represented herself and a little boy, a school-mate about whom I had heard before. It appeared that there was something secret about the behaviour of these two figures and that other toy people were resented as interfering or watching and were put aside. The activities of the two toys led to catastrophes, such as their falling down or colliding with cars. This was repeated with signs of mounting anxiety. At this point I interpreted, with reference to the details of her play, that some sexual activity seemed to have occurred between herself and her friend, and that this had made her very frightened of being found out and therefore distrustful of other people. I pointed out that while playing she had become anxious and seemed on the point of stopping her play. I reminded her that she disliked school, and that this might be connected with the fear that the teacher would find out about her relation with her school-mate and punish her. Above all she was frightened and therefore distrustful of her mother, and now she might feel the same way about me. The effect of this interpretation on the child was striking: her anxiety and distrust first increased, but very soon gave way to obvious relief. Her facial expression changed, and although she neither admitted nor denied what I had interpreted, she subsequently showed her agreement by producing new material and by becoming much freer in her play and speech: also her attitude towards me became much more friendly and less suspicious. [pp. 125–126]

From then on, the psychoanalytic process had begun, and the analysis could carry on successfully, bringing the disappearance of the inhibitions and an improved relationship with the mother. This little girl can be identified as Inge, about whom Melanie Klein speaks on three occasions in *The Psycho-Analysis of Children*. Both cases are concerned with a little girl of seven, normal except for a fear of school, whose analysis was prophylactic rather than therapeutic. The dates also agree: "Inge's analysis, which occupied 375 hours in all, was in the nature of a prophylactic treatment. Her main trouble was an inhibition in regard to school. . . . In the seven years that have elapsed since the end of her treatment, she has developed very satisfactorily and has successfully entered the age of puberty" (Klein, 1932, p. 61). This text was written in 1931: Inge's analysis, then, ended in 1924, having lasted about eight months (175 sessions at five or six sessions a week), and everything leads to the conclusion that the invention of the play technique described in the quotation above should be placed at the beginning of Inge's analysis.

4. A Precursor of the Kleinian Conception of Play: Sigmund Pfeifer

When she made her first technical invention in 1923, Melanie Klein was neither the first nor the only one to use play as a technique in the psychoanalysis of children. Although she had little sympathy for the personality and methods of Hermine von Hug-Hellmuth, she always recognized the priority of her forerunner, who had begun to psychoanalyze children as early as 1917. Strangely, however, she never mentions the work of Sigmund Pfeifer, a Budapest psychoanalyst whom she had very probably met, and who had published, in 1919, a long and well-documented article based on observations of children made in a psychoanalytic spirit (rather than on material collected in the course of the treatment of children, which the author, it appears, did not practice) and entitled: Manifestations of Infantile Erotic Impulses in Play: The Position of Psychoanalysis with Regard to the Principal Theories of Play. Coming six years after Sandor Ferenczi's purely descriptive and purely psychopathological article on little Arpad (1913), this article, which has never been translated or even reissued, is as far as can be determined the first text to present not only descriptions but a complete theory of the play of normal children. It contains some very interesting hypotheses directly anticipating certain Kleinian ideas. For the first time ever, Pfeifer established that play belongs to the formations of the unconscious described by Freud, and gave it a place among dreams, fantasies, parapraxes, screen memories, word presentations, etc. He argued that the processes of elaboration of play are identical with those of dreamwork. In play as in dreams, the psychoanalyst, observing, finds condensation, displacement, and symbolization. Like dreams, play is in the service of imaginary wish-fulfillment, expressed in symbolic acts rather than in images. Pfeifer cites the example of a normal child whose favorite game, between the ages of four and six, was that of "stuck pig." He had taken a large piece of wood to represent the pig, and sat on it, grunting. The putting to death of the pig represented the murder of the father, while the grunts uttered by the child expressed identification with the father-pig and the wish to take his place. In this latter aspect, the game was overdetermined: the piece of wood, on which the child had fixed a horse's saddle, represented the mother undergoing the sadistic coitus of the father, with whom the boy was identifying. There is a striking analogy here with the future theories of Melanie Klein: release of the fantasies underlying the play, and relation of these fantasies to the primal scene.

There is a second astonishing analogy. Pfeifer describes, under the name of splitting-with-identification or dissociation-with-identification (*Abspaltung mit Identifikation*), the mechanism he considers characteristic of play, and assigns to it the functions of division of the libido among persons and the distribution of identifications. This double function rests on the symbolic value of play: "I will add," he writes,

> that this mechanism, the action of which I have seen in play, has a particular significance. . . . it enables the playing child to exteriorize his position with regard to the complexes of incest and anal erotism—to give only the most important—which, as we know, are prototypes for the development of every individual's character; it opens the way to their transference, and typically

to the transference operated upon playmates, brothers and sisters, and later fellow-men, society, the law—in a word, all forms of authority.

Splitting and the separation of the child's various positions—active and passive, genital and pregenital—lead to the distribution (*Verteilung*) of the split identifications among his playmates (p. 256). If we add to Pfeifer's conceptions the idea, peculiar to Melanie Klein, that these split identifications are distributed also among the personifications in games the child plays alone—and we have seen in the example of the "stuck pig" game that this reality does not escape Pfeifer's clinical sense, even though he does not state the theory—we have exactly the Kleinian theories advanced in the paper on personification (Klein, 1929). After reviewing and criticizing from a psychoanalytic point of view the "psychobiological" theories of play (Schiller, Spencer, Lazarus, and Wundt), the article ends with an original idea: in the oedipal stage, play is the direct expression of the child's sexuality; after the repression of the "incest complex" and entry into latency, play becomes in normal children the only possibility for the motor discharge of sexual impulses: "at the moment of the latency period, the child's sexuality, which has not disappeared, can manifest itself only through play" (Pfeifer, 1919, p. 281). This is a direct anticipation of another important idea of Melanie Klein: play serves to discharge masturbatory fantasies. It puts into action the primal scene, provides splitting-with-identification, distributes the split identifications among the characters in the game, and discharges autoerotic sexuality; this prefigures almost the whole of the Kleinian concept. But Pfeifer remained an observer of the child, and never considered analyzing children through play. His was a theory which never led to practice.

5. The Use of Play in the Educative and Curative Treatment of Hermine von Hug-Hellmuth

In Hermine von Hug-Hellmuth, by contrast, we meet practice without theory. Her main contribution, a paper to the congress at the Hague in 1920 (Hug-Hellmuth, 1921) which Melanie Klein had heard her read, is a veritable catalogue of the reasons why it is impossible to psychoanalyze a child, and which justify the use of an educative and curative treatment based on psychoanalysis. The child, she argues, is in a situation very different from that of the adult seeking analysis: "The child does not come of his own accord to the analyst . . . the child is in the midst of the very experiences which are causing his illness. . . . The child, unlike the adult, has no desire at all to change himself or to give up his present attitude towards his external surroundings" (p. 287–288). It is therefore particularly difficult to make him understand the object of the treatment; half of Hug-Hellmuth's article consists of the description of procedures and "ruses" intended to "break the ice." From this point of view the child must be analyzed at home, so that things will be easier for him, and so that he cannot play truant if the parents are tired of taking him to the analyst. Compulsion is accompanied by seductive maneuvers justified by the fact that "the first hour in treatment is of the utmost importance; it gives the opportunity for establishing a *rapport* with the young creature and for 'breaking the ice'. . . . Sometimes, in the case of those patients who obstinately shut themselves up, a ruse is helpful" (p. 293). Here is the story of one such ruse:

> a nine-year-old boy with suicidal impulses during the first hour took not the slightest notice of me, but simply laid his head on the table and made no response to any remark. A fly passing close to his face suggested to me the idea of pretending that I had got something in my eye. At once the boy, who always wished to be in the limelight, jumped up, saying: 'Please let me see; I will get it out, but you must not rub your eye'. Thus with his proffered help the ice was broken, because he felt himself of use to me. Every time after this, when a strong resistance made him retire into silence, I had only to ask for his advice or his help, and the analysis once more progressed favourably. [p. 294]

It is under this heading of procedures intended to break the ice that Hermine von Hug-Hellmuth mentions the use of play: "When dealing with children of seven or eight years of age, the analyst can often pave the way by sharing in the play

activities, and thus he can recognise several symptoms, peculiar
habits and character traits, and in the case of these very young
patients very often play will enact an important part throughout
the whole treatment" (pp. 294–295). But the use she makes of
play, and recommends, has very little in common with what
Melanie Klein did with it. Hermine von Hug-Hellmuth made
up games and stories to interest the child in the treatment and
make him react. Thus, her technique was not unlike Moreno's
psychodrama, invented in about the same period, in which the
therapist decided on the scenario, depending on what he knew
of the personality of the volunteer actors, and prescribed for
them their inner attitude.

This is how Hermine von Hug-Hellmuth obtained the par-
ticipation of Hans, a child who would not speak and whom she
"suspected" of having observed the sexual life of his parents:

> In one of the first treatment hours, I told him about a little boy
> who would not go to sleep at night, and made such a noise that
> his parents could not sleep either. I told also how little Rudi
> made a noise too in the afternoons, when his father wanted to
> rest; so his father became angry and Rudi was whipped (little
> Hans' reaction to this was to run to the sideboard and take down
> a 'krampus'[2] and to beat me on the arm saying 'you are
> naughty!') . . . Actually, his father, an officer of high rank, was
> on active service throughout the war, and had only returned to
> his family in Vienna on short leave. . . . The next day his death-
> wishes towards his father showed themselves more clearly. He
> was playing with his toy motor-car and several times ran over
> the chauffeur whom I had made out to be little Rudi's father.
> I pretended to telephone the news of his father's accident to the
> little boy. Rudi was supposed to weep bitterly at the news, and
> then I said that although Rudi had formerly wished his strict
> father away, now he felt very sad, because in spite of this wish
> he really loved his father very much. The reaction of little Hans
> was very characteristic: he listened to me lying on the floor,
> asking me eagerly now and then: 'What does little Rudi do next?'
> [p. 285]

---

[2] This is a small figurine, representing a character in Austrian folklore,
which often served as a stand for the whips used to punish children.

In this example play still has its function of breaking the ice. But this time there is no question of seduction. Although there is a dimension of reassurance (after all, Rudi is a good little boy), play is used essentially to cause a reaction in the child by penetrating his unconscious. Three peculiarities of this approach should particularly be noted: (1) the analyst realizes perfectly that the game is unconsciously or even consciously understood by the child and that the boy's reaction is provoked by the "latent content" of the game—the oedipal aggression of Hans against his father; (2) the analyst uses play as a language she does not hesitate to speak herself, and as a figurative mode of expression particularly appropriate to communication with the child's unconscious; (3) the analyst considers this language sufficient, and it is here that her practice finally becomes attached to a concept: the child's analysis should stop at making unconscious content preconscious. The analyst can alter the unconscious pathogenic elements without necessarily passing through language and consciousness:

> Whereas in the analysis of the adult, we aim at bringing about full insight into unconscious impulses and feelings, in the case of a child this kind of avowal expressed, without words, in a symbolic act is quite sufficient. We learn, indeed, from the analysis of the child that in him the psychic events take place in quite different layers from those of the grown-up, that they may be more closely or more remotely connected with each other and that in the child many impressions leave clearly-marked traces in spite of never having reached the threshold of consciousness. Even analysis does not make conscious thse fragmentary memories of primordial scenes, the blending of of new impressions with these former ones takes place, perhaps in the preconscious, and it is left to later experience at a higher stage of development to bring them into consciousness. [p. 296]

Thus, Hermine von Hug-Hellmuth's technique does not aim at a specifically psychoanalytic effect—that of the classical psychoanalytic cure—but rather is based on the principle of what, in the field of shamanism, the anthropologist Claude Levi-Strauss (1961) has called "symbolic efficacy." In this sense, her play technique seems to anticipate the psychoanalytic psychodrama as described by Didier Anzieu (1957) rather than Melanie Klein's psychoanalytic play technique.

6. The Originality of Melanie Klein's Play Technique

Pfeifer was interested in play from a purely scientific point of view, as an expression of the unconscious. Hermine von Hug-Hellmuth saw in it a process making it possible to change consciousness. The Kleinian play technique synthesizes these two conceptions, but adds interpretation, the only method that can produce specifically psychoanalytic effects. However, Melanie Klein in fact owed very little to her two forerunners. As far as Pfeifer is concerned, we are confined to guesses based on what we know of the personality and attitude of the creator of the play technique. Up to 1926, Melanie Klein laid no claim to originality. She considered herself a disciple of Freud and a pupil of Ferenczi and Abraham, whose advice she frequently sought. As often as she could, she linked her own ideas with those of her predecessors, referring to them very often in her published articles: Abraham, Alexander, Boehm, Mary Chadwick, Ferenczi, Anton von Freund, Groddeck, H. von Hug-Hellmuth herself, Jones, van Ophuijsen, Rank, Reik, Roheim, Sadger, Sperber, Spielrein, Stärck, and Steckel, not to mention Freud himself, are all referred to several times in her first five articles, and often Melanie Klein uses their real or supposed authority to support her hypotheses. Freud's jealous and supercilious attitude concerning the paternity of his ideas, which sometimes led him into quarrels over priority, is never found in her. Melanie Klein often entered into polemics, but never insisted on her priority, and as often as she could she found a precursor; thus, she linked the idea of the paranoid-schizoid character—which was entirely her own—with a suggestion by Fairbairn, and that of envy with Karl Abraham, though he had only glimpsed this clinical reality. As far as play is concerned she always referred scrupulously to the priority of Hermine von Hug-Hellmuth. It is tempting, therefore, to assume that she was not consciously influenced by Pfeifer, as it is almost certain that had she been, she would have quoted him many times; as it is, she does not even mention the existence of his article. And yet it is difficult to believe it was unknown to her. It is possible that she may have read the article when it appeared, without being greatly struck by it; in 1919 she was just beginning Erich's sexual education, and she did not realize the importance of play until 1920. It is likely she then herself rediscovered most of Pfeifer's ideas, during a period up to 1923—and even up to 1929, as it was not until then that she rediscovered his idea of splitting-with-identification. We know that such cryptomnesic phenomena played a certain part in Freud's discovery of psychoanalysis, and also in the invention of psychodiagnostics by Hermann Rorschach (Anzieu, 1973, pp. 40–44). Closer to Melanie Klein, Sandor Ferenczi had been asked in 1900 to review Freud's *Interpretation of Dreams*, and had refused, after skimming through the book, on the grounds that it was not worth his trouble. It was Jung's association test which, some years later, was to awaken his interest in psychoanalysis and lead him to an attentive reading of Freud's works. A similar phenomenon may well have occurred in the case of Melanie Klein; she could understand Pfeifer's ideas only by relating them to her personal experience, having forgotten that she had read his article at an earlier date, probably rather hastily.

As for any influence from Hermine von Hug-Hellmuth, the facts are much clearer; it may be said without hesitation that any such influence is very slight. The paper by the Viennese child analyst was read at the 1920 congress and published in 1921. We have seen that from the beginning of 1920 Melanie Klein was practicing a type of provocation of fantasy very comparable to that Hermine von Hug-Hellmuth was to describe eight or nine months later; the second phase of Erich's psychoanalytic sexual education had in fact begun with the episode of the sweet; it had been waiting for him a long time, Melanie Klein told her son, and she told him a story that delighted him and released his fantasies and his play (Klein, 1921, pp. 30–31). From this period on she practiced the procedure along the lines defined by Hermine von Hug-Hellmuth: the invention of the theme of the game by the "analyst"; communication in this way with the child's unconscious; and cautious abstention from any interpretation, coupled with a confidence in unconscious modification of the fantasies with very little conscious verbalization. At the beginning of 1920, in Erich's first "analysis," Melanie Klein went beyond this procedure. Here we can see the second phase of her "take-off." It was at this stage that the distinctly Kleinian attitude took shape. By 1923 there was a world of difference between the psychoanalytic play technique and the procedure recommended by Hermine von Hug-Hellmuth.

In the "educative and curative treatment" of the Viennese psychoanalyst, play was only one of many methods for breaking the ice and establishing contact. The introduction of play into the treatment was the result of a decision by the analyst, from a rather manipulative point of view and as a last resort, made necessary by the fact that the child of seven or eight could not well adapt to the standard analytic situation. In the gradual development of the Kleinian technique, by contrast, play was imposed by the children, and Melanie Klein accepted it with no preconceived ideas. It was only because Rita played in her treatment from beginning to end that this spontaneous process became, with Inge, a deliberate technique.

Hermine von Hug-Hellmuth did not hesitate to take a very "active" attitude and lead the play, fixing theme, characters, and course. Melanie Klein, by contrast, was absolutely neutral; for her, play was a language spoken by the child, not the psychoanalyst, whose role was to understand and interpret verbally. On this view, play is considered not a language in the narrow sense of the term, which would then have to be seen as operating at the level of the child's incomplete intellectual development, and which would have to be used to communicate with the child in a sort of "baby talk," but rather a distorted translation of fantasies expressed in symbolic acts, as the dream expresses in distorted images latent thoughts that are clear, ordered, and logical. In truly pathological cases the distortion is such that it prevents any free association at all; the "resonance of fantasy" does not occur, but must be reestablished by psychoanalytic interpretation. The Kleinian technique is aimed at restoring, in specifically psychoanalytic ways, the capacity for symbolic understanding which Hermine von Hug-Hellmuth took as a given, and on which she founded a type of psychotherapy that would enable her as far as possible to avoid communicating interpretations verbally to the little patient.

This technical divergence is based on a fundamental theoretical divergence. For Hermine von Hug-Hellmuth, as later for Anna Freud, who took most of her ideas from her, the child of seven or eight is scarcely capable of guilt feelings. He fears the real punishment inflicted by his parents much more than he feels moral anxiety, a sentiment corresponding with an intersystemic conflict between the ego and what in 1920 was still called the ego-ideal. At this age, it is argued, the relation to authority is just beginning to be interiorized. Melanie Klein, on the contrary, allows that night terrors correspond already to the repression—and not the suppression by the environment—of the first stages of the oedipus complex, and are the first manifestation of guilt. To her, anxiety is always the result of repression, and the distortion of play must be attributed to a crushing guilt. Thanks to the proto-Kleinian ideas of 1921–1923, she knew that play is the immediate carrying into effect of primary sublimations, and that all neurotic children suffer from an inhibition of play and, because of guilt feelings, have lost their capacity for resonance of fantasy.

On Melanie Klein's view, then, simple reassurance is not enough. When Hermine von Hug-Hellmuth's little Hans hears that Rudi has desired the death of his father, but that basically he loves his father, and on condition that he loves him enough to repress his death wishes without forming neurotic symptoms; this is to suppose that his hate is moderate and that his personality is within normal limits, or in any case that he is not seriously neurotic. But if Hans does not love his father at all, or if while loving him he also detests him intensely, he cannot feel understood by the intervention of the psychotherapist who denies or minimizes the aggression which is terrifying him inside. Only interpretation can bring real reassurance, for it alone will show that the psychoanalyst has measured the depth of the child's hate, and is not horrified by it. Although this conception of the effect of interpretation has been worked out only recently by the British psychoanalyst Wilfred Bion, Melanie Klein's pupil and continuator, who based his ideas on the late Kleinian concept of projective identification, we see that in fact it has been

at work since Rita's analysis, and that it underlies, though remaining implicit, the first interpretation given to Inge within
the play technique "invented" a few minutes earlier. What produces the striking effect of the interpretation is that the analyst
understood and said what Inge wanted to hide, and remained
perfectly neutral. In the conception of Hermine von Hug-Hellmuth, on the contrary, the child is not yet "civilized," his impulses meet no internal opposition, and such an attitude on the
part of the analyst would risk being understood as permission
to be "naughty" or as acceptance of a harmful complicity. "The
curative and educative treatment must furnish the child with
moral and aesthetic values" (Hug-Hellmuth, 1921, p. 287).

7. The Originality of Melanie Klein's Interpretive Technique

In order to devise the psychoanalytic play technique, Melanie Klein had to analyze Rita. But to analyze her she had to
know, to begin with, that the three-year-old child suffered from
a crushing guilt anxiety. This presupposes two conditions on
the analyst's part. The first is a hypersensitivity to anxiety, a
capacity for insight in this area, which was almost certainly a
trait in Melanie Klein's personality. The effect of this trait was
increased even further by a capacity to identify with children
based initially on the projection of maternal narcissism onto
Erich. This capacity for insight, present from the very beginning of her psychoanalytic work, governed her overall attitude
and lent her work its particular style. The second condition is
the possession of a coherent theoretical system capable of in-
tegrating the fact of early anxiety and guilt; as has been noted,
the play technique could not have been devised without the
previous building-up of the proto-Kleinian system. Thus, Melanie Klein's attention to the manifestations of anxiety is the
issue of a deep-seated attitude and a theoretically deduced hypothesis. It is this, as much as the play itself, which defines the
Kleinian psychoanalytic technique.

This was stressed earlier in Chapter 1. But now let us compare briefly the Kleinian technique as it appeared at the end

of 1923 with standard psychoanalytic technique as adapted by the schools of child analysis inspired by Hermine von Hug-Hellmuth. It is generally admitted in the psychoanalysis of adults that interpretations must be exact, opportune, concise, of moderate frequency, and repetitive. To be opportune means to have two dimensions: what is sometimes called the role of superficiality, the interpretation of elements which rise to the surface of consciousness, is applied in order that one may "plunge" progressively into the deepest layers of the unconscious. Respect for a certain unity and pertinence of fantasy is a corollary of this rule: in a given period of the analysis not everything is interpreted at once, but only elements which have a natural connection with each other in the unconscious network of fantasy. There is also a rule that a given type of defense must be analyzed before the interpretation is applied to the impulse which is its object; finally, as transference is a resistance even while it is a motive power of the cure, it arises from the previous rule that all behavior which is archaic in origin must be interpreted in the transference before being linked with its archaic prototypes. Conciseness and sparing use of interpretations are quite recent in origin, or at least are defined today much more strictly than in Freud's time. Repetition of interpretations in various forms is intended to promote working through.

In the educative and curative treatment as conceived by Hermine von Hug-Hellmuth, interpretation was only partially exact; the accent was placed on its opportune character in two registers only, the rule of superficiality and that of vigilance with regard to the pertinence of fantasy. Conciseness and relative infrequency were cultivated no more than they generally were at that time in the analysis of adults. As far as exactitude of interpretation is concerned, we know that Hermine von Hug-Hellmuth was content with partial exactitude because she thought it inopportune to bring to consciousness the meaning of manifestations of the oedipus complex. The question of being opportune was defined in so restrictive a way that in certain cases abstention from any interpretation was the rule. Such caution avoided taking even the slightest risk of breaking the rule of not confusing the registers of fantasy, as she deliberately remained on a superficial level. There could be no question of interpreting resistances; they had to be overcome by confidence-gaining procedures. As for transference, its interpretation had a minor role. She in fact recognized the existence of transferences (in the plural, as it was commonly used at the time; see Freud, 1909, p. 193) but not a *transference neurosis* because it was thought that "the child is in the midst of the very experiences which are causing his illness . . ." (Hug-Hellmuth, 1921, p. 288). However, her position was less rigid and more open than, for example, that of Anna Freud six years later. In fact she does not appear to have had a clearly formulated theory on this point, and while admitting the existence of a certain transference, she formally advises against its interpretation: "Discussion [with the child] about this latter, even when it [the transference] is quite clearly recognised, demands special caution in formulating it, because at bottom the child is unwilling to exchange his own parents for any stranger, even when there is every good reason for so doing" (p. 300). It is for the analyst who is practicing "curative and educative" treatment to double the part of the parents, to "furnish the child with moral and aesthetic values" (p. 287) by playing on the positive transference, but without interpreting it.

The Kleinian technique of 1923 stood in contrast to both that of the educative psychotherapy of the Viennese School and that of adult psychoanalysis. Based on the interpretation of the oedipus complex in the transference, it is distinguished from the first by the demand for complete exactitude of interpretations, and the recognition of the child's capacity to produce a complete transference, which must be interpreted. It depends on a method of interpretation of the child's deep anxiety, and is thus distinguished from the classic technique for adults. In comparison with the usual norms, the role of superficiality is, if not neglected, at least modified in most of its aspects: if anxiety is the consequence of the repression of the unconscious impulse, it is logical that the Kleinian technique should begin with the interpretation of unconscious anxiety, be extended to that of the defenses causing it, and then follow the usual order. The first interpretation given Rita is both the first example and a good illustration of the characteristics of the Kleinian technique of the period. In a rather long explanation, Melanie Klein (1955) first interprets the fear she inspired in Rita: "she was particularly afraid of something which I might do to her when she was alone with me in the room" (p. 124). Anxiety is thus designated first of all. The second phase of interpretation stresses the transferential character of this anxiety, linking it with its prototype: "referring to her night terrors, I linked her suspicion of me as a hostile stranger with her fear that a bad woman would attack her when she was by herself at night" (p. 124). It is particularly interesting to note that the anxiety was not connected with a real danger (some sort of punishment from the real parents) but with a fantasy, and that the inter- pretation was enough to calm Rita's fears and allow the session to continue in its designated place. This is a characteristic pro- cedure; all the examples of the beginning of an analysis given by Melanie Klein follow this rule.

The originality of the Kleinian technique appears, then, from this first interpretation; here it is reduced to its two initial, but principal elements—the interpretation of the *anxiety* which manifests itself in the *negative transference*—which had therefore been acquired by the middle of 1923. During Rita's analysis, the third characteristic aspect took shape: the complete inter- pretation of anxiety in its connections with hostile impulses against the mother and the father, arising from the positive and negative forms of the oedipus complex. This presupposes a fourth element, present already in the analyses of Erich and Felix but still implicit: the aggressive impulse, not the libidinal one, gives rise to anxiety. We have seen this in the analysis of Erich, whose castration anxiety was directly linked with the fact that the aggression aimed at the father was turned back against himself, without any mention of a part played by the father's threats or reprimands. We come across it again in the article on tics (Klein, 1925), again in a clinical context. There was no formulation in general terms until 1932, in *The Psycho-Analysis of Children*. We must, however, take into account the opinion of Melanie Klein (1932), who declared that she had held this idea since 1926: "In the paper upon which this chapter is based ('The Psychological Principles of Early Analysis,' 1926) I had already put forward the view that hatred and aggressive trends are the deepest cause and foundation of feelings of guilt" (p. 5).[3] It thus seems legitimate to assume that the four essential elements of the Kleinian technique—the stress laid on anxiety, the interpretation of the transference, "deep" interpretation going back as far as the oedipus complex, and the idea that aggressive impulses are at the root of anxiety—were acquired at the end of Rita's analysis, and were about to give rise to a theoretical reflection.

8. The Appearance of the Kleinian Theory of Transference

The Polemic with Anna Freud and the Question of Transference Neurosis

With regard to Melanie Klein's position on transference, it is important to dispel two very common ambiguities. The first concerns Melanie Klein's own declarations: she regularly describes her technique, stressing the fact that she includes the analysis, not only of positive transference, but also of negative transference. It is often said, as she herself does, that this is a mark of her originality. But here a demurrer should be entered. It is true that the Kleinian technique is thus distinguished from that of Anna Freud, who continued the work of Hermine von Hug-Hellmuth, for Anna Freud always underestimated the phenomena of negative transference: she wrote in 1926 when criticizing the conceptions of Melanie Klein:

> She believes that when a child shows hostility to her in the first hour, repulsing or even beginning to strike her, one may see in that proof of the child's ambivalent attitude toward his mother, the hostile component of this being displaced on to the analyst. But I believe the truth of the matter is different. The more tenderly a little child is attached to his own mother, the fewer

---

[3] She does say, "Children's games enable us to form certain special conclusions about the very early sense of guilt" (Klein, 1926, p. 132), but she goes on only to give examples of the relation between anxiety and sadism, and the conclusions are never explicitly formulated.

friendly impulses he has toward strangers. [A. Freud, 1926, p. 45]

According to Anna Freud, the child's hostility toward the analyst is to be explained by its indifference, in agreement with Freud's view that the first opposition to love is not hate but complete indifference. Being indifferent to the analyst, the child reacts aggressively to the frustration suffered—the absence of its mother. The first mention by Melanie Klein of the need to interpret negative transference appears in a text of 1927, a reply to Anna Freud's criticism. Earlier she had not particularly stressed this point, and had simply given illustrations. On this subject there was no fundamental divergence from Hermine von Hug-Hellmuth (1921), who also interpreted negative transference and who in fact considered it easier to analyze than positive transference: "we can find a way of explanation concerning the transference, which is generally much more readily accepted than the idea of the positive transference" (p. 300). It can be argued, then, that insistence on the technique of interpreting the negative transference is not a central element of Kleinian technique as such. Melanie Klein's many pronouncements on this subject are nothing more than a lively defense of an aspect of her method which is emphasized only in the context of her polemic with Anna Freud.

The more general question of the Kleinian theory of transference is much more delicate. Here the difficulties come from two sources: on the one hand the question has been obscured by the repeated criticisms of Anna Freud and her disciples; on the other, the true conceptions of Melanie Klein are very subtle and are linked with a central and generally ill-understood point in her psychoanalytic theory: the notion of the internal object. It is generally accepted that the background of the debate is this: the child psychoanalysts of the school of Hermine von Hug-Hellmuth and Anna Freud admit the existence of limited transferences, but are strongly opposed to the Kleinian idea that children are capable of developing a true transference neurosis. If we examine Anna Freud's argument, the following points emerge. (1) She questions the value of the interpretations given by Melanie Klein of the child analysand's actions "in relation to the objects in the treatment room and to her own person" (A. Freud, 1926–1927, p. 40). (2) Nevertheless she recognizes the existence of certain transference mechanisms: "this affectionate attachment, i.e., the positive transference to the analyst, becomes the prerequisite for all later analytic work"; but as examples of transference she gives only positive phenomena, the strictly transferential quality of which is, in our opinion, questionable: "You remember from my first lecture that I take great pains to establish in the child a strong attachment to myself, and to bring him into a relationship of dependence on me. I would not try so hard to do this, if I thought the analysis of children could be carried out outside a relationship of this kind" (p. 40). (3) She offers theoretical arguments that transference cannot be of any great importance: "Unlike the adult, the child is not ready to produce a new edition of his love relationships, because, as one might say, the old edition is not yet exhausted. His original objects, the parents, are still real and present as love objects—not only in fantasy as with the adult neurotic" (p. 44). (4) She concludes: "The child does enter into the liveliest relations with the analyst; he expresses a multitude of reactions which he has acquired in the relationship with his parents . . . but he forms no transference neurosis" (pp. 43–44).

Vigorously attacked, Melanie Klein replied with passionate ardor, and remarked twenty years later that Anna Freud came progressively closer to her views. Nonetheless, the debate lacks clarity. Melanie Klein's choice of a target in Anna Freud's ideas for counterattack is rather strange. Melanie Klein shows that the difficulty of locating the transference in the Viennese technique is caused by the educative role taken by the therapist, a stance that sacrifices analytic neutrality. She could quite easily characterize the situation using Anna Freud's own declarations (1926–1927): "the child knows very well just what seems desirable or undesirable to the analyst, and what he sanctions or disapproves of. And such a well-defined and in many respects novel person is unfortunately a poor transference object" (p. 46). In the Kleinian technique, by contrast, the analyst remains neutral and can thus see in the child the presence of a genuine capacity for transference. But it is clear that for Melanie Klein the debate is not between Anna Freud's recognition of the trans-

ference, but not the transference neurosis, and her own recognition of both; rather, for her the debate is over underesti-
mation or correct evaluation of the child's capacity for
transference. But she does not take the trouble to change the
subject of discussion explicitly, and so tends to cloud the issue.
Moreover, in replying she takes up views directly opposed to
Anna Freud's and, instead of simply correcting certain inex-
actitudes in her interlocutor's criticisms, ends up defending
theories attributed to her but which she has never before supported. "I must," she wrote (Klein, 1927), ". . . contest Anna
Freud's conclusion no less than her premises. In my experience
a full transference-neurosis does occur in children, in a manner
analogous to that in which it arises with adults" (p. 152). This
is the only appearance, in all her work, of the term "transference
neurosis." It is impossible to find it in any other published work
before or after 1927. Had we not this explicit declaration —
isolated, and advanced in a polemical context—we would have
reason to think that the very idea of a transference neurosis is
alien to Melanie Klein's conceptions. Apart from this single,
exceptional instance, on every occasion when another psychoanalyst might use this term, Melanie Klein uses the expression
"transference situation." It is thus important to clarify the debate, and first of all to situate Melanie Klein's theory of transference in relation to the classical descriptions.

Laplanche and Pontalis (1967) define transference thus:

> For psycho-analysis, a process of actualisation of uncon-
> scious wishes. Transference uses specific objects and operates in
> the framework of a specific relationship established with these
> objects. Its context *par excellence* is the analytic situation.
>
> In the transference, infantile prototypes re-emerge and are
> experienced with a strong sensation of immediacy.
>
> As a rule what psycho-analysts mean by the unqualified use
> of the term 'transference' is *transference during treatment*. [p. 455]

From their commentary on this definition we can extract
the following elements. (1) Transference is often narrowly defined as regards its field of manifestation (there is no transference outside psychoanalytic treatment), but widely as regards

its actual nature (everything that happens in treatment is considered transferential). (2) To this conception they oppose that of Freud: transference phenomena occur outside treatment as well, and everything that happens in treatment is not transferential. They quote a phrase from the case of Dora (Freud, 1905): "What are transferences? They are new editions or facsimiles of the impulses and phantasies which are aroused and made conscious during the progress of the analysis; but they have this peculiarity, which is characteristic for their species, that they replace some earlier person by the person of the physician" (p. 116). Their comment on this is as follows: "Freud remarks that these transferences (note the plural) do not differ in nature whether they are directed towards the analyst or towards some other person, and further that they do not constitute aids to cure except insofar as they are explicated and 'destroyed' one by one" (Laplanche and Pontalis, 1967, p. 457). (3) The development of Freud's conceptions of transference led to the notion of transference neurosis: "Freud reveals how it is the subject's relationship to parental figures that is once again lived out in the transference. . . . This extension of the notion of transference so that it becomes a process structuring the whole treatment around prototypical infantile conflict culminates with Freud's introduction of a new concept—that of transference neurosis (p. 458).

As far as transference neurosis is concerned, let us put aside the nosological sense of the term (essentially indicating hysteria and obsessional neurosis, distinguished, among the psychoneuroses, from "narcissistic neuroses," or melancholia) and consider only the sense applicable to our problem. Laplanche and Pontalis give this definition: "In the theory of the psychoanalytic cure, this term refers to an artificial neurosis into which the manifestations of the transference tend to become organised. It is built around the relationship with the analyst and it is a new edition of the clinical neurosis; its elucidation leads to the uncovering of the infantile neurosis" (p. 462). Freud, in fact, writes: "Provided only that the patient shows compliance enough to respect the necessary conditions of the analysis, we regularly succeed in giving all the symptoms of the illness a new transference meaning and in replacing his

ordinary neurosis by a 'transference-neurosis' of which he can
be cured by the therapeutic work" (1914, p. 154). According
to Laplanche and Pontalis, "the difference between transference reactions and transference neurosis proper is that in such
a neurosis the whole of the patient's pathological behaviour
comes to be re-oriented around his relationship to the analyst";
from this standpoint, they go on, "the following pattern of
development consitutes the ideal model of the course of the
cure: the clinical neurosis is transformed into a transference
neurosis, whose elucidation leads to the uncovering of the infantile neurosis" (p. 463).

It is clear that these definitions present transference neurosis as the result of an organization of "transferences" which
replaces the clinical neurosis of the adult. Adult clinical neurosis
and adult transference neurosis are two "new editions" of early
neurosis. In this sense Anna Freud is right in saying that the
child does not develop a transference neurosis because it is not
ready for a "new edition" of its relationship with its parents,
and we can see in Melanie Klein's ideas no element directly
opposed to this point. It might even be said that of Melanie
Klein and Anna Freud it is the latter who most nearly envisages
the possibility of a transference neurosis (in the usual sense) in
the child: "But there are ways and means of bringing about in
the child a situation which approximates the more favourourable
one of adult analysis with its transference neurosis. This may
come into play when we are dealing with a severe neurotic
illness in a child whose environment is hostile either to analysis
or to the child. In such an instance, the child may have to be
removed from his family and be placed in a suitable institution"
(A. Freud, 1926–1927, p. 47). In these conditions she believes
that the child would become detached from its family, would
attach itself to the psychoanalyst, and that the "re-enactment
of the pathology would be a genuine transference neurosis in
the sense in which we use this term in relation to adults, with
the analyst as focal object" (p. 48).

For Melanie Klein, this new phase of neurosis cannot be
isolated from the ensemble of pathological manifestations sub-
sumed under the name of transference neurosis, first because
this attachment of the child to the analyst would not be a trans-

ference in the strict sense, and then because she has a radically different conception of transference. For both Melanie Klein and Anna Freud, the child's relationship with its real objects (the parents) and his relationship with the analyst have the same intrinsic nature. But the real divergence lies here: for Anna Freud both relationships are "real" ones; the relationship of the child with the analyst reproduces the first but is equally "real." That is why the treatment must be, as Hermine von Hug-Hell-muth said, "educative and curative" at the same time; the analyst is a real object, and emotional attitudes and behavior are di-rected toward him; he "shares" this with the parents but is not "substituted" for them. He will thus choose to share their ed-ucative attitude.

Transference and Introjected Objects

For Melanie Klein, things appear in quite a different light: Erich's analysis, and more especially Rita's, gave her the idea, already stressed by Freud, that transference acts not only in the cure, but also in the "real" relationships of daily life, whether friendly and loving, or hostile. Her originality shows itself in the extension of this idea to young children: when the child comes for analysis, its "real" relationships with real objects are already, in a sense, transference relationships. By this we mean that the attitude of the three-year-old to its parents is not de-termined by the reality of their attitude, but by an internal imago, an imaginary and distorted representation of the par-ents. Erich had already shown this phenomenon for the first time: at the time of his school phobia, he was afraid that a witch might poison him (Klein, 1921, p. 41). A year later he imagined that a witch might pour a jug of ink over him on the way to school; this witch is "a figure . . . he had . . . obtained by di-vision of the mother-imago" (p. 42), and this splitting justifies the *real* aversion Erich felt toward certain women. At the cost of an anachronism it might be said say, in much later Kleinian terminology, that relationships with the real mother and with real hated women are governed respectively by splitting and by the projection of the "good" and "bad" mothers. What was still very fleeting in Erich's case became, with Rita's psychoanalysis, a central inspiration of Kleinian theories. Melanie Klein (1926) discovered that Rita had two types of interaction with her parents. In the one type she perceived them as they really were; in the other she saw in them fantastically distorted imagos. When Rita cried because her father threatened the bear in her picture book, "what determined her identification with the bear was her fear of blame from her *real* father" (p. 132). From this type of fear the following must be distinguished:

> Analysis showed that she did not *dare* to play at being the mother because the baby-doll stood for her amongst other things for the little brother whom she had wanted to take away from her mother, even during the pregnancy. But here the prohibition of the childish wish no longer emanated from the *real* mother, but from an introjected mother, whose role she enacted for me in many ways and who exercised a harsher and more cruel influence upon her than her real mother had ever done. [p. 132]

This introjected mother, of course, has as its prototype the real mother, distorted by the child's fantasies, but the fear she inspires is—although Melanie Klein does not use the word—transferred onto the real mother at a very early stage of development. The transference observed in the psychoanalysis of children is not a displacement of the relationship with the real parents onto the relationship with the analyst, but an application to a new object of the same type of relationship as with the parents, the transference to real objects of sentiments felt toward introjected objects. Three remarks will suffice for us to understand fully the declarations Melanie Klein made at this period on the psychoanalytic technique applicable to children.

1. As we shall see later, it was in the field of interpretation of anxiety that she first recognized the existence of the anxiogenic efficacy of introjected objects. It was not until 1932 that she recognized, side by side with introjected bad objects, that of the "good" mother.

2. In the relationship with the parents, attitudes toward "real" parents coexist and constantly intermingle with attitudes toward introjected objects. The real mother's reprimands oc-

casion the transference onto her of feelings of hate and terror called up by the imago of the bad mother (though later Melanie Klein would speak of projection in such a context, she had not begun using the concept during the period of Rita's analysis). Even maternal caresses and expressions of love have an effect opposite to that intended. The young child's neurosis, then, contains important transference elements but is not entirely a transference relationship, as the parents' real attitudes continue to be introjected, and particularly as the *real* parents are the *real* prototypes of introjected objects built up by distortion of the *real* being. In later Kleinian theory it is this interplay of real and introjected parents that allows the reduction of the unreal character of introjected objects and their progressive adjustment to the reality of the parents.

3. The technique of child analysis consists of the suppression of this interplay, achieved by the neutrality of the analyst, who replies to the child's words and actions only with interpretations, orders and forbids practically nothing, and neither praises nor blames anything. In these conditions the child transfers to the analyst its introjected objects—neither more nor less than it does with its parents—and the absence of any "real" response on the part of the analyst simply allows the manifestation in its pure state of the capacity for transference which the child possesses at every moment and in every field of its existence. It is from this point of view that we must understand the pronouncements made by Melanie Klein in 1927 on the presence of a complete transference neurosis in the child. Transference is present everywhere, including in "clinical neurosis," but only the strictly psychoanalytic situation brought into being by the play technique enables it to emerge and show itself in its pure state in the form of what at this stage she called "transference neurosis" according to the classical usage suggested to her by Anna Freud's criticisms.

However, since up to 1929 introjected objects were regarded by Melanie Klein as essentially bad objects, we can understand why she laid such stress on the negative transference in her clinical examples and in her argument with Anna Freud. She saw transference as a new edition, with real objects, of feelings toward the introjected object.[4] Up to 1927 she saw introjected objects as more menacing, more severe, and more anxiogenic than real objects. Temporarily, then, her conceptual equipment allowed her to deal theoretically with transference only in its negative form. But it did enable her to see transference as the true lever of the cure, as interpretation rapidly allows the institution of a new type of interplay between the introjected objects and the analyst in his reality as an interpreting partner in the play. The task of the analytic process, then, is to reduce pathogenic emotions in and through transference; the child develops a full transference neurosis, in the sense in which Melanie Klein understands the term, a usage which does not coincide exactly with its classical meaning.

9. The Theoretical Lessons of Rita's Analysis: From Anxiety to Oedipal Guilt

Rita's analysis not only gave Melanie Klein the idea of the play technique and inspired in her a theory of this technique which governed her use of it (by reference to a revision of the classical concept of transference); the analysis also provided information which was at the origin of the thoroughgoing transformation Melanie Klein made in the psychoanalytic conception of child psychology and its development. Rita's treatment gave rise to the three major ideas that defined Kleinian theory from 1923 to 1927: the early appearance of the initial stages of the oedipus complex, the early formation of the superego by introjection of the parental objects, and the infiltration by extreme

[4] This also explains Melanie Klein's total silence on the notion of countertransference. This is the transference by the analyst of his introjected imagos onto his patient, a transference "called up" by the particular modalities of the patient's transference. But for the analyst to mention the nature of his countertransference in the history of a case would be equivalent to the publication of his self-analysis. It is probably for this reason that Melanie Klein mentions her countertransference only twice in all her work—in the case of Richard in *Narrative of a Child Analysis* (Klein, 1961)—and then simply to say that it was positive and strong. As for the theory of countertransference, Melanie Klein never tackled this question.

sadism of the first stages of the oedipus complex and the formation of the superego.

Even before Rita's analysis, Melanie Klein had already formed the hypothesis that the night terrors of the third year were a manifestation of the anxiety caused by the first repression of the oedipus complex. She had then only to verify the hypothesis. Rita's example gave her the verification she was seeking. After preferring her mother during her first year, Rita gave, from the age of fifteen months, all the signs of an oedipus complex already in place: her preference for her father was clear, and her jealousy toward her mother and the wish to exclude her were equally marked, so much so that her parents had noticed it and informed the analyst even before treatment began.

Rita's analysis had also brought out the role of oral frustration and its incidence in the appearance of the oedipus complex. Weaning the child had been extremely difficult; she had found it very hard to adapt to the bottle, then to solid food. It had never been possible to wean her from the last bottle of the day and to make her take milk from a cup in the evening. In 1923 Melanie Klein had not yet seen oral sadism as clearly as one might think. The only allusion to cannibalistic urges found in the proto-Kleinian writings relates to a fantasy of dismembering and devouring which she found at work in Erich's inhibition when he was faced with the arithmetical operation of division (Klein, 1923b, pp. 69–70). We also know that Abraham, telling Freud about the end of Rita's analysis, insisted on the fact that it had revealed, in agreement with his views, the role of oral erotism and the existence of the primal melancholia he had postulated. It was quite without reference to oral sadism that Melanie Klein, starting from this analysis, built up the idea that the conversion toward the father with which the female oedipus complex begins is a consequence of the frustration of weaning, which weakened the ties with the mother. Thus, the initial stage of the oedipus complex begins toward the end of the first year and reaches its peak about the middle of the second.

The conception of anxiety was enriched by a new dimension. It appeared, following Rita's analysis, to be at once marked by a significance of guilt. This transformation is easy to locate by means of a quantitative analysis of the vocabulary of Melanie Klein's early writings. The word "anxiety" is used dozens of times in the 127 pages of the English edition occupied by texts published before 1926. In stark contrast we find in these pages only three instances of the word "guilt," the most significant being found in a discussion of a text of Freud on the question of the legitimacy of the use of the expression "unconscious guilt feeling"—a discussion in which Melanie Klein has in mind the notion of unconscious anxiety much more than that of guilt feelings. If we now turn to the ten pages of "The Psychological Principles of Early Analysis," published in 1926, we find two instances of the word "fear," five of the word "anxiety" (one in the expression "her anxiety and guilt"), and eleven of the word "guilt." This reversal of the frequency with which the words are used (the frequency of the word guilt is suddenly multiplied by 46) expresses one of the essential consequences of Rita's analysis: early anxiety is now understood in terms of guilt in the full sense of the word; that is to say, anxiety is linked no longer with a direct transformation of the libido into an unpleasant emotion, but rather with an intrapsychic tension between the ego and a severe and threatening *internal* demand. The introjected objects—the study of which we began when examining the theory of the play technique—constitute the first form of the superego, which is thus present from the first phases of the oedipus complex and will henceforward account for all the manifestations of anxiety and their consequences, especially inhibition and the disturbance of sublimations. From now on, anxiety appears independent of repression (it no longer represents the quantity of affect of the repressed impulse, though the connection between them is not yet specified; Melanie Klein abandoned the first Fruedian theory of anxiety at the very moment Freud abandoned it himself. But whereas in 1926 Freud immediately replaced his earlier theory with one distinguishing signal anxiety, the instrument and condition of repression, from automatic anxiety, Melanie Klein gives only glimpses, in a few clinical notes, of a theory of anxiety which was to remain incomplete for several years. The concept clearly given her by Rita's analysis is that the anxiety of night terrors is an anxiety

of the ego in the face of the superego; this idea was advanced
by Freud, and Melanie Klein adopted it almost at once.[5]

Nevertheless, the relationship between the superego and
the child's hostile impulses, which was later to become one of
the central elements of Kleinian theory, is already clearly indicated in the first passages mentioning Rita's analysis. If Rita
did not dare to be the doll's mother at the beginning of her
analysis, it was because of the prohibition from "an introjected
mother . . . who exercised a harsher and more cruel influence
upon her than her real mother had ever done" (Klein, 1926,
p. 132). Though the mechanism which makes it possible to pass
from hate to guilt is not yet clearly thematized, the relationship
of this guilt with the hostile wishes of the little girl directed
against her mother is clearly indicated in the clinical material.
Melanie Klein notes, without special comment, that in the
course of her play Rita was "inwardly playing both parts: that
of the authorities who sit in judgement and that of the child
who is punished" (p. 132) and that in the "journey games" the
threat of the introjected father appears in the form of a threatening return and an attempt at vengeance by the train driver,
whose place Rita has taken.

Again, Rita inspired the first version of Melanie Klein's
description of a child's aggression against the mother, and the
prototype the conceptions relating to sadistic attacks against the
mother's body. Rita did not dare to play at being the mother
of her doll because it represented the child she wanted to take
from her pregnant mother. Guilt is thus linked, as soon as it
appears in the conceptual field of Kleinian theory, with an
aggressive wish/fantasy aimed against the unborn child within
the mother's body, which the little girl wants to tear out and
destroy. This kind of interpretation of the girl's oedipal hostility, applied for the first time to Rita, opened the way for the
later description of sadism and the modifications of the theory
of the oedipus complex which followed from it, and which were
concerned not only with the *date of appearance* of the complex

---

[5] On June 5, 1924, she read an unpublished paper entitled "Activity of
the Superego in the Fourth Year of a Child's Life."

and the *cause* which triggered it, but also with the *content* of the wishes, fantasies, and sexual theories which built it up.

If we attach so much importance to Rita's analysis, it is not simply because it set Melanie Klein on the road to discovering the play technique, the "primary" transference, the initial stages of the oedipus complex and the superego, and the sadism of the child. Other cases besides that of Rita were to be the occasion of discoveries no less important. Rita's "sadism," in fact, was not yet recognized as such; rather, it was described in terms of aggression. It was not until the analysis of Trude in 1924 that anal and urethral sadism were recognized, and not until analyses of Ruth and Peter in 1924–1925 that the notion of oral sadism appeared—after the beginning of Melanie Klein's analysis with Karl Abraham, who certainly exerted a decisive influence on this point. Erna, analyzed from 1924 to 1926, provided even richer material than Rita, if we can judge from the length of the passages devoted to them. However, Rita's case remains a very important one. With the publication of *The Psycho-Analysis of Children* in 1932, Melanie Klein's work had exhausted the knowledge accumulated in the treatment of Ruth, Peter, Trude, and Erna, and they are not discussed again except in retrospective or historical texts. Rita, however, remains at the center of Melanie Klein's conceptualization. This privilege is almost certainly due to the fact that her analysis, besides bringing out what is *important* (but which can sometimes be found more clearly in other analyses), helps more than any other to bring out what is *essential*—that is to say, the central and exclusive character of the oedipus complex both in neurosis and in normal development.

We know that twenty years later those who tried to expel Melanie Klein from the British Society of Psycho-Analysis reproached her with having given rise to dissidence by removing the oedipus complex from its role as the nucleus of mental life and by attributing this primary organizational role to the depressive character. But between 1923 and 1933, the first Kleinian system would rather have attracted the opposite reproach, for the predominant orientation of this period was the attachment of all manifestations of instinct and all forms of defense mechanism to an oedipus complex that was complete, "total," or "enriched," and described in much greater detail and in forms infinitely more varied than in the Freudian conception. During these years Kleinian psychoanalysis appeared not as dissident but quite the opposite; if we allow that the essence of Freudian psychoanalysis is defined by the interpretation of the oedipus complex in and by the transference, the first Kleinian system may be considered an extension of Freudian theories, and perhaps even as "ultra-Freudism" (in the sense in which, at the time of the Restoration, people spoke of ultraroyalists, who were, in the famous saying, "more royalist than the King"). Melanie Klein was in this sense more Freudian than Freud himself in the period we are now studying.[6] It is Rita's analysis that was the source of this ultra-Freudism, and that is why Rita was brought up again in 1945, when the oedipus complex had to be linked with the "psychotic character." Now, while following the development, from 1923 to 1925, of the important elements of the first Kleinian system, we must not lose sight of the fact that each of them does not take on its complete sense until it is related to the oedipus complex, and that this omnipresence of the oedipus complex showed itself first, in the most obvious way, in the case of Rita.

10. The Discovery of Pregenital Sadistic Fantasies

Trude and the Discovery of Anal and Urethral Sadism

Expressed as a fantasy of stealing the unborn baby, Rita's oedipal hostility to her mother was described exclusively in terms of rivalry for the father's love and was thus related, as

---

[6] Maurice Merleau-Ponty—who was, together with Daniel Lagache (Melanie Klein's first French translator), the first in France to understand the importance of her work—had made a similar comparison in his lecture "Relationships with Others in the Young Child" (Merleau-Ponty, 1953, p. 23). Preoccupied with political questions, he had used the classical Marxist distinction between an ultrarevolutionary "left," a "center" (Leninist in Stalin's period), and an opportunist and revisionist "right" to describe Melanie Klein's position in the psychoanalytic movement. He classed her as the extreme left in comparison with the center (Freud) and the right (Anna Freud). His essential basis was the concept of the early oedipus complex.

a secondary yet important effect, to heterosexual genital impulses. In the development of the theory over the ensuing four years, this aggression, though never dissociated from the oedipus complex, was described with greater specificity, and was related more and more clearly to sadistic impulses; these were interwoven with the genital libido, without ever being confused with it, and so found their integration in the impulses and fantasies of the oedipus complex.

The first stage of this development is marked, in 1924, by the analysis of Trude (three years, three months old), a treatment which led to the discovery of anal and urethral sadism. Melanie Klein tells us about it herself:

> One of the cases through which the anal- and urethral-sadistic nature of these destructive impulses became clear to me was that of 'Trude'. . . . When she came to me for treatment, she suffered from various symptoms, such as night terrors and incontinence of urine and faeces. Early on in her analysis she asked me to pretend that I was in bed and asleep. She would then say that she was going to attack me and look into my buttocks for faeces (which I found also represented children) and that she was going to take them out. Such attacks were followed by her crouching in a corner, playing that she was in bed, covering herself with cushions (which were to protect her body and which also stood for children); at the same time she actually wetted herself and showed clearly that she was very much afraid of being attacked by me. [Klein, 1955, p. 134]

The revelation of the anal and urethral elements is based on the association of aggression and the child's incontinence, and on the obvious appearance, in the game she suggested, of the early sexual theory of the anal child. This association of aggression and early sexual theories, seen here on a purely clinical plane, rapidly became one of the important points of the Kleinian theory of early sadism.

More specifically, the bond between the anal stage and aggression was at that time already recognized in classical psychoanalysis. Freud (1905b) had linked the element of anal erotism with the anal mucosa, and the active element with an "instinct to master," the source of which is muscular and goes

back first to the ego instincts; it is initially independent of sexuality even though it "may become united with it at an early
stage owing to an anastomosis near their points of origin" (p.
193; quoted by Laplanche and Pontalis, 1967, p. 217). This
instinct to master the object in an active way forms the sadistic
component of the anal-sadistic stage: "Activity is supplied by
the common instinct of mastery, which we call sadism when we
find it in the service of the sexual function" (Freud, 1913, p.
322; quoted by Laplanche and Pontalis, 1967, p. 217). We know
that while Melanie Klein was analyzing Trude, Karl Abraham
(1924) distinguished two phases in the anal-sadistic stage, characterized by the two dimensions—erotic and sadistic—of this
stage: "1. That anal erotism contains two opposite pleasurable
tendencies. 2. That similarly two opposite tendencies exist in
the field of sadistic impulses" (p. 425). In anal erotism the ple-
sure is first in the expulsion of the feces, then in their retention.
In sadism, the opposition is between destroying, and preserving
in order to dominate: "The component instinct of sadism, as
it exists in the infantile libido, also shows us two opposite pleasurable tendencies at work. One of these tendencies is to *destroy*
the object (or the external world); the other is to *control* it" (p.
428). These two oppositions form a unified whole: "The analysis
of neurotic patients has taught us that the second, *conserving* set
of tendencies that spring from anal and sadistic sources— tendencies to retain and to control the object—combine in many
ways and reinforce one another. And in the same way there is
a close alliance between the *destructive* tendencies coming from
these two sources—to expel and to destroy the object" (p. 429).
Between these two anal-sadistic configurations, Abraham establishes a genetic and a dynamic order. The impulse to reject
and expel precedes the impulse to hold and keep, and the latter
arises from the repression of the destructive tendency. The
distinction between the first and second phases of the anal-
sadistic stage has an essential place in psychoanalytic psychopathology, because the passage from one to the other also marks
the beginning of object-love: "at the dividing line between those
two phases there takes place a decisive change in the attitude
of the individual to the external world. Indeed, we may say that
the dividing line is where 'object-love' in the narrower sense

begins, for it is at this point that the tendency to preserve the object begins to predominate" (p. 432).

Melanie Klein gradually integrated this conception into her theory. In 1924 she adapted it thus: the anal-sadistic impulse aims not only at the control of the object or its appropriation; it also, in its earliest phase, aims at the destruction of the object. From that point there ensues a period of several months during which it links the sadistic dimension of oedipal hostility and death wishes toward the rival with anal and urethral sadism, following which this dimension is linked with sadism in general (including oral sadism). In the child's rivalry with the parent of the same sex, the motive of the death wishes is provided by the oedipus complex and thus by the genital instincts, but the content of the fantasies in which they are expressed is inspired by the anal-sadistic and urethral-sadistic instincts discovered in Trude's analysis.

This juncture between the early oedipus complex and anal sadism has already been described as a phenomenon operating in early sexual theories. Trude, exactly like Rita, was jealous of her mother, then pregnant with a little sister born when Trude was two years old; she wanted to be the mother of this child of the father, and to take her mother's place with him. But this early oedipus complex is contemporary with the anal-sadistic stage: it begins after weaning under the influence of the conversion of oral libido from the mother's breast to the father's penis, and is accompanied in succession by the anal stage of sadistic destruction and rejection of the object, and by the later phase of conservation and dominance of the object. It is the interweaving of nascent genital impulses with anal-sadistic impulses that gives rise to the sadistic and anal theories of the conception and birth of children. In the case of Trude, the theory of birth was that of the anal child: the unborn baby was identified with the feces. In the ensuing years, Melanie Klein developed an idea she does not seem to have immediately applied in Trude's case: anal aggression is aimed not so much at the feces as objects to be expelled as at objects—in the first instance the mother's body—which are attacked in these fantasies by means of the feces, identified with dangerous substances. We may, however, wonder whether this idea is not anticipated in "A Contribution to the Psychogenesis of Tics" (Klein, 1925), a text we placed in the proto-Kleinian period because of its predominantly clinical and theoretical content, but which was written after Rita's analysis and contemporary that of Trude. In it Melanie Klein wrote about Felix: "It became clear that he had also experienced the repressed wish to insult the [head]master with coprophilic language and to smear him with faeces. This again took us back to the primal scene when the same wish had arisen with regard to his father and had been expressed by passing a motion and screaming" (p. 114). She was thus taking up again, from a new point of view inspired by Abraham, a fact already noted by Freud (1918), who had stressed the sexual character of defecation as a reaction to the primal scene, in which sexual excitation is expressed: this reaction "is a sign of a state of excitement of the anal zone (in the widest sense) [of the word]. In other similar cases an observation like this of sexual intercourse has ended with an emission of urine; an adult man in the same circumstances would have an erection (p. 81). From Melanie Klein's new standpoint, this reaction has an aggressive value: the feces are in fantasy the instruments of anal-sadistic impulses aimed at the destruction of the object.

Ruth, Peter, and Oral Sadism

In the case of Trude urethral-sadistic impulses were combined with anal impulses, and Melanie Klein discovered them at the same time. In this case too the source is Freudian, and the closest influence is that of Abraham, who had published in 1920 an article entitled "The Narcissistic Evaluation of Excretory Processes in Dreams and Neurosis." There, repeating Freud's views, he stressed the beneficent *or destructive* omnipotence attributed to urine and feces. This idea first appears in Melanie Klein's work in the postscript, written in 1925, to the paper on tics: speaking of a child, Walter, whose analysis had just begun, she notes the repeated occurrence, in the course of the sessions, of "an outburst of rage, accompanied by aggressive motor discharges, and a representation of anal and urethral dirtying attacks—all directed against the parents in sexual intercourse" (Klein, 1925, p. 126).

It is generally considered, quite rightly, that Melanie Klein's theories are characterized by her insistence on oral sadism. This was, however, the form of sadism she discovered last. All the oral elements of the material provided by Rita and Trude had at the time been connected with oral erotism. It was two other children, Ruth (four years, three months) and Peter (three years, nine months) who led her to this discovery, as she notes in "The Psycho-Analytic Play Technique" (Klein, 1955):

> But in other analyses, carried out in 1924 and 1925 (Ruth and Peter, both described in *The Psycho-Analysis of Children*), I also became aware of the fundamental part which oral-sadistic impulses play in destructive phantasies and corresponding anxieties, thus finding in the analysis of young children full confirmation of Abraham's discoveries. These analyses, which gave me further scope for observation, since they lasted longer than Rita's and Trude's, led me towards a fuller insight into the fundamental role of oral desires and anxieties in mental development, normal and abnormal. [pp. 134–135]

Melanie Klein goes into more detail in a note: "This growing conviction about the fundamental importance of Abraham's discoveries was also the result of my analysis with him, which began in 1924 and was cut short fourteen months later through his illness and death" (p. 135). The fragments published from Rita's analysis put the accent essentially on the oral frustration felt by the little girl, and include no detailed descriptions of oral-sadistic fantasies. Ruth, like Rita and Trude, had wanted to take from her pregnant mother the child she was carrying, to hurt her and to kill her. But whereas these attacks were attributed to genital jealousy in Rita's case, and anal sadism in Trude's, they are now linked with oral sadism, and the child's intense oral frustration is understood as the consequence, in fantasy, of the oral-sadistic murder of the mother by the little girl: "as a result of her desires to rob and kill her mother, she was afraid of being abandoned by her for ever or of never seeing her alive again, or of finding, in the place of the kind and tender mother who was saying good-night to her, a 'bad' mother who would attack her in the night" (Klein, 1932, p. 29). It seems that oral-sadistic fantasy in all its richness was discovered in Peter's analysis. We know that in May 1925 Melanie Klein had read a paper, never published, on the analogy between certain crimes and children's fantasies. She gave details on the material she used in a later text (Klein, 1927a). She had commented on two recent news items which had appeared in the Berlin papers: the arrest of two criminals, one of whom carried on homosexual affairs with young boys whom he then killed, decapitated, and cut into pieces which he burnt, the other of whom killed his victims and used their bodies to make sausages. She had compared these crimes with the fantasies of a child she identifies as Peter (1927a, p. 177). Peter had in fact constructed a fantasy in which, after practicing mutual masturbation with his father and his young brother; after representing this with dolls, he had cut off the head of one of them and sold the body to an imaginary butcher, keeping the head, which was the part he liked best. It seems that at a certain point in his analysis Peter represened in his play innumerable scenes of dismemberment and devouring, breaking a considerable number of dolls and figurines into pieces. As he was a clinically normal child whose analysis was purely prophylactic and whose serious infantile neurosis was revealed only by analysis (his parents, recognizing the excessive number of severe neuroses in their family and agreeing with Melanie Klein's views on psychoanalysis as "preeducation," had thought an early analysis might spare Peter this fate), Melanie Klein was all the more impressed. Moreover, the fourteen or fifteen months of this analysis corresponded almost exactly with the fourteen months of her own analysis with Abraham, who in these years (1924–1925) was writing his last works—those in which he goes most deeply into the analysis of oral sadism. All these experiences were to lead Melanie Klein to share absolutely the ideas of her psychoanalyst and to add her own discoveries to Abraham's picture of libidinal development. After a preambivalent oral stage, sadism accompanies the second oral stage, the two phases of the anal-sadistic stage, and the infantile genital stage, which all of are ambivalent stages in which the libido is combined with aggressive impulses. In the normal adolescent ambivalence is not superseded until the adult genital stage. From this point of view, sadism must be described at its three basic levels—oral, anal, and urethral—while a close bond is formed between the style of activity of the preambivalent oral impulses, objectless but free of sadism, and the postambivalent genital impulses, object-oriented but equally free of sadism. We shall see what influence this idea exerts on the conception of the early oedipus complex.

As far as sadism is concerned, it took Melanie Klein less than two years to discover all the variants of early sadism, which then took six or seven years to work out theoretically. In this field more than any other, the play technique, from the very moment of its invention, enabled her to reach material of extraordinary richness. The emergence of this material is all the more spectacular because its possibility could not be glimpsed in any of the proto-Kleinian theories.

11. Sadism and the Early Superego

In addition to providing data which enabled sadism to be completely described, the analyses of Ruth and Peter made it possible to go deeply into the related phenomenon of anxiety. Henceforth for Melanie Klein, anxiety, which Rita's analysis had already shown to be significant of guilt, appeared each time as the direct consequence of early sadism. We find here an essential element of Kleinian theory: the idea that anxiety is the product of fear of retaliation. This idea was not inspired by Ruth's and Peter's analyses; we saw it already in the analysis of Erich, whose fear of being killed by his father was linked with his own death wishes against him, and not, as classical theory would have it, with a real or fantasized threat of castration on a phylogenetic basis of primal fantasies. From this period on Melanie Klein was led to think that the unconscious is dominated by the talion principle: "an eye for an eye, a tooth for a tooth." If a child is afraid of castration, it is not because of death wishes but because he has wished to castrate his father. If he has conceived death wishes against his father he will be afraid of being killed by his father. According to this formula—which corresponds to the turning of impulses back upon the person, as described by Freud—there corresponds to every specific sadistic fantasy an anxiety fantasy, identical with it in even the slightest details, in which the subject undergoes what he has forced his objects to undergo in his sadistic fantasies. Thus, each discovery of a new source of sadistic aggression brings with it the discovery of a corresponding typical anxiety or, more precisely, a corresponding anxiogenic fantasy which represents, in the form of an anxiogenic situation, a turning against the subject of the corresponding sadistic fantasy. The evolution of the theory of anxiety situations thus runs exactly parallel to that of the theory of sadism. Erich was afraid of being killed by his father. Rita feared her mother might destroy the inside of her body, did not dare to play at being the mother of her doll, and insisted on being closely tucked up in her beclothes to avoid being attacked in her sleep by the bad introjected mother. Trude was afraid that her body might be emptied of feces (identified as babies) by her mother, and Ruth and Peter were terrified of starving and of being cut into pieces and devoured by their parents.

This notion of the fear of retaliation is closely bound up with the notion of the introjected object or, in later Kleinian language, of the internal object. The concept of the introjected object and that of the fear of retaliation are directly interdependent; the latter transforms the real objects that are attacked into vengeful objects, for the unconscious. Because of the child's belief in the omnipotence of thought—preceded, according to Abraham's theory (1920), by belief in the omnipotence of excrement used as destructive weapons in sadistic fantasies—the child lives on two levels; on one he is capable of experiencing reality and having relatively "realistic" relationships with his real parents, but on the other—which constantly infiltrates the first—he believes he has really destroyed and injured them, and so fears their vengeance. The object relations of the young child take place both in a relationship with real objects and in a relationship with imaginary objects. These imaginary objects, which Kleinian theories between 1923 and 1927 describe as exclusively sadistic and vengeful, are produced by introjection of the real parents, at whom the sadistic fantasies are first aimed. Between 1923 and 1927 the description of the introjection mechanism—which was later to be linked with the oral-sadistic fantasy of cannibalistic incorporation, wherein the subject incorporates, by swallowing, objects which, damaged by being devoured, become vengeful internal persecutors—had not yet been made. It was worked out from the analysis of Erna, conducted between 1924 and 1926, but only after that analysis had been completed. Melanie Klein noted the existence of introjected objects before she could understand introjection itself. The concept of the introjected object, in the actual genesis of Melanie Klein's ideas, which is different from the logically coherent order in which they were later to be presented, came not from the discovery of the process of introjection but from the idea of the fear of retaliation. In this sense it seems the concept of introjection had not yet acquired its Kleinian, or even its Freudian meaning. The use she then made of it was much closer to the very loose definition Ferenczi (1909) had given when he introduced the term; he connected the concept closely with that of transference and described under it processes we would now consider projective: "Whereas the paranoiac expels from his ego the impulses that have become unpleasant, the neurotic helps himself by taking into the ego as large as possible a part of the outer world, making it the object of unconscious phantasies" (p. 40). Introjection was defined then, by a vague reference to absorption into the body, as a way of extending interest to objects via their integration into the subject's fantasies. Around 1926 the word did not seem to have a much more precise meaning for Melanie Klein, who described the introjected object as an object whose essential characteristic is that it does not correspond to the perception of it, because of the distortion that follows its integration into the world of fantasies, which the child has difficulty in distinguishing from reality.

These menacing introjected objects constitute the nucleus of the superego. Between 1923 and 1927, Melanie Klein's description of the superego, in accordance with her preoccupations, began with its close links with sadism and the oedipus complex. The definitive theory, which involves a split between a "good" and a "bad" superego, did not appear until 1927, when the evolving concept of introjection led to an extension of the role accorded this mechanism.

Like the introjected objects which are its nucleus, the young child's superego is at first of an extreme strictness and cruelty, with no direct connection with any actual demands made by the parents on the child. Melanie Klein (1927b) instances the case of four-year-old Gerald, one of her first patients in London,

> whose parents have not only never punished or threatened him but who are really unusually kind and loving. . . . On account of the well-known formula which prevails in the Ucs this child anticipates, by reason of his own cannibalistic and sadistic impulses, such punishments as castration, being cut to pieces, eaten up, etc., and lives in perpetual dread of them. The contrast between his tender and loving mother and the punishment threatened by the child's super-ego is actually grotesque and is an illustration of the fact that we must on no account identify the real objects with those which children introject. [p. 155]

This cruelty of the superego is the direct consequence of the predominance of sadism in the initial phases of its formation, and its conceptualization follows the same stages as that of sadism: first conceived as the product of fear of retaliation arising from Rita's oedipally inspired attacks against her mother, it is after Trude's analysis conceived as having anal-sadistic and ure-thral-sadistic dimensions, and then, after the analyses of Ruth and Peter, a fundamental oral dimension. The young child's superego is thus conceived as stricter than that of the adult, and as all the more cruel because it corresponds to a more archaic phase of development.

On this point Melanie Klein stood in complete contradiction to the psychoanalytic theories then generally accepted. We know in fact that Freud considered the superego to be heir to the oedipus complex, and thus a process taking place during its period of decline. The Kleinian theory, on the contrary, holds that the superego is constituted at the very beginning of the oedipus complex, which is itself described as occurring much earlier than in the Freudian view. For this reason Melanie

Klein completely recasts the views expressed by Ferenczi and Abraham, her initial inspiration. These two authors had already sought to define superego precursors and the feeling of guilt. Ferenczi had described a "sphincter morality" linked with toilet training, which he considered to be a "physiological precursor of the superego" at the anal stage. Abraham had suggested the cannibalistic stage as an origin of anxiety; he thought guilt feelings appeared at the first anal-sadistic stage. For both men, these were but embryonic forms of the working out of a process which took place only in the course of the oedipus complex, whose late occurrence they maintained in accordance with Freudian chronology. Melanie Klein was influenced by them, but she did not work out her wider conception of the superego as an extension of her precursors' research. Such a procedure would have presupposed that she took as her deliberate aim the reconstitution of the origin of this process. But we know that she proceeded in exactly the opposite way: having no intention at the outset of going deeply into this question, she found herself faced with material from the analyses of Ruth and Peter (the first she conducted using the play technique), in which guilt played a predominant part. From a strictly Freudian point of view, which this material confirms in all particulars, she linked the superego with the oedipus complex, whose onset she then had to move to a position earlier in the child's life. She stressed the fact that her modifications were limited to that: "To sum up my conclusions: I wish first of all to point out that they do not, in my opinion, contradict the statements of Professor Freud. I think that the essential point in the additional considerations which I have advanced is that I date these processes earlier and that the different phases (especially in the initial stages) merge more freely into one another than was hitherto supposed" (Klein, 1928, p. 197).

Thus, the Kleinian theory of the early appearance of the superego was first imposed by clinical practice, and was at the beginning entirely independent of the problem of the origins or precursors of the superego. The interpretations given to Rita show that at that time the archaic superego was still conceived as fear of revenge for an aggression connected with oedipal hostility. It was only at a second stage that a deeper examination of sadism led to a recasting of the hypotheses of Ferenczi and Abraham, an alteration whereby sphincter morality, oral-sadistic anxiety, and anal-sadistic guilt were quite naturally ascribed to the operation of a superego already in place. This superego, linked from the outset with oedipal conflict, is introjected under the influence of the first genital impulses, which in the final analysis account for its formation, even if the anxiogenic content has to be ascribed to oral-sadistic and anal-sadistic impulses infiltrating them in the initial stages of the oedipus complex. From this "ultra-Freudian" or "ultraoedipal" point of view the oral-sadistic and anal-sadistic elements of the superego could not be the precursors of the genital superego. Even if present initially, they are not primary but secondary, not organizers but organized; they provide not the intention but only the style of the archaic superego. Melanie Klein developed this point and later accepted the existence of oral precursors of the superego, and eventually an oral superego, but this was not the position she took between 1923 and 1927.

This theory of the superego had its effects on the technical conceptions to which it gave an added justification. It was during the 1927 controversy with Anna Freud that Melanie Klein insisted most firmly on the early appearance and the severity of the superego, which were the basis of the arguments she used in replying to the criticisms leveled at her. Anna Freud (1926–1927), interpreting the Freudian views in a very restrictive sense—far more restrictive than Freud's own comments on the analysis of little Hans—believed that children are much more dependent on real objects than are adults, and much less dependent on the superego, which is still embryonic or weak. Thus the fear of sanctions and the wish for the parents' approval, and in some cases that of the psychoanalyst, carry much more weight than guilt feelings properly speaking. The frequency of tantrums in young children is cited as an argument in support of this thesis and is interpreted as a sign of a weak superego. This conception provides the theoretical justification of the technical precepts Anna Freud borrowed from Hermine von Hug-Hellmuth: the inadequacy of a purely psychoanalytic and interpretive attitude, caution in the analysis of the oedipus complex, the necessity of an educative attitude, and the inculcation of moral standards and values during the "educative and curative treatment." Melanie Klein's exactly opposite theory of the superego allowed her to argue in defense of her technique. The child's superego, according to her, is no weaker than that of the adult; tantrums are the product not of a weak superego but of an excessive and overbearing superego that brooks no compromise.

The child's superego, menacing and sadistic, is essentially identical with that of the adult. The only notable difference is one of style: the adult superego appears less cruel and more highly developed. Even so, it is only a superficial difference: in both the adult and the young child the deep layers of the superego threaten castration, dismemberment, and devouring; these threats are simply covered over in the adult by superficial formations from a later period. Behind these appearances the reality is the same: "in contrast to Anna Freud, I am led to believe from the analysis of children that their super-ego is a highly resistant product, at heart unalterable, and is not essentially different from that of adults" (Klein, 1927b, p. 155). Children's apparent absence of guilt is accounted for by the immaturity of their ego, which is incapable of defending itself adequately against the excessive demands and terrifying threats of the superego: "The difference is only that the *maturer ego* of adults is better able to come to terms with their super-ego" (p. 155). The material provided by the analysis of children must be interpreted as proving an inadequate defensive strategy of the ego against the demands of the id but also against those of the superego. For this reason Anna Freud's technique is completely wrong: coming to the aid of the ego in its struggle against the id, she reinforces an oppressive superego whose existence she ignores, but which is at the very root of the child's difficulties. She thus increases the child's anxiety instead of reducing it, and exerts an "unnecessary harshness" (p. 144) by activating the child's anxiety and guilt without allaying them through interpretation.

From Melanie Klein's point of view, the main enemy of the child's ego, and of the analyst, is not the id but the superego, the source of anxiety, guilt, and tantrums. The violent actions and sadistic fantasies of children are not the direct emanation

of impulses but are responses of the ego to the threats of introjected objects forming the nucleus of the superego. The
child's sadism is certainly primary: it causes the distortion of
introjected images. But once the introjected objects make their
threats from within, the child transfers onto real objects the
threats coming from the superego. He thus enters into a vicious
circle (Klein, 1927a, p. 179) in which actual sadism reinforces
the sadism of introjected objects and vice versa. When primary
sadism is constitutionally excessive, or when the ego is very
immature, the only possible defense against these terrifying
affects is repression of the sadistic fantasies, which is inadequate
because it prevents the abreaction of sadistic impulses by symbolic means in fantasies and play, thus leaving them intact so
that massive episodes of the return of repressed material are
inevitable. But there is also repression of the guilt feeling itself,
which returns in the form of the need to be punished. This
vicious circle continues in the unconscious and inspires tantrums which thus have the triple significance of satisfaction of
sadism, an inadequate defense of the ego against a cruel superego, and (insofar as they lead to repressive measures) the
satisfaction of a need for punishment which originates in the
superego. The child's "bad" and antisocial behavior (but also
that of the adult, as Freud had seen) thus indicates a defeat of
the ego by the id, but more particularly by the superego. This
defeat was seen in 1927 as the exclusive result of the weakness
of the ego, which was incapable, in economically unfavorable
conditions, of using an effective defensive strategy based on
sublimation. This theory was later followed up in greater detail,
but the failure of the defensive process was always, in the later
development of Kleinian ideas, related to this vicious or "bad"
circle, which was to become an important concept in the Kleinian system; later, in 1937, it was to be opposed by a healing
"good circle," as "good" and encouraging aspects of the superego were discovered. Their strength or weakness were to become important factors in the entry into the "good" or "bad"
circle. But this phase was preceded by a period during which,
as we have just seen, the theory of the superego concentrated
essentially on the following elements: oedipal origin; early appearance; extreme cruelty due to the fear of retaliation for

sadistic fantasies; and the crushing power of the superego in relation to the ego.

12. The Early Oedipus Complex in Girls

Parallel with this first theory of the superego, Rita's analysis confirmed, following an analogous train of thought, the fact—already anticipated in the proto-Kleinian system—of the early appearance of the oedipus complex, whose link with sadism, anxiety, and the superego was to be made clearer by the analyses of Trude, Ruth, Peter, and Erna. Starting from Rita's analysis, the general direction of the evolution of the oedipus complex was clearly shown: starting point through the oral frustration of weaning; first phase of the positive complex in the first half of the second year; phase of repression and negative complex from the middle of this second year; final phase of the positive complex with a quantitative increase in genital impulses at the time of the "classical" oedipus complex described by Freud, which thus coincides with the third and final stage of a long evolution. The analyses of Trude, Ruth, and Erna made clear the impact of oral and anal sadism on the initial forms of the oedipal conflict, while that of Peter made it possible to fix the Kleinian conception of the development of the oedipus complex in boys. One of the peculiarities of Melanie Klein's description of the oedipus complex was the reversal of the usual point of view, which considered the female oedipus complex a modified and incomplete form of the male complex. The difference was that she discovered the early oedipus complex in the analyses of little girls before meeting it in the analysis of boys, Peter in particular. This was partly a matter of chance, as the play technique was first applied to three little girls before being applied to Peter. Nevertheless, we may speculate that this chance, which played an undeniable part, coincided with a necessity inherent in the nature of the archaic oedipus complex, the initial phases of which are easier to demonstrate in girls than in boys. Melanie Klein's description of the archaic oedipus complex involves, besides the recognition of its early appearance, the complete revision of the Freudian theory of female sexuality, the reinterpretation of the manifestations of penis envy, and the recognition of a feminine complex in the boy, balancing the masculine complex of the girl. These factors meet to make Melanie Klein's description of the male oedipus complex an application to the case of the boy a genetic scheme that first took shape in the analysis of the feminine form of the archaic oedipus complex.

Weaning and the First Feminine Phase

The first stage of the female oedipus complex begins with weaning. This idea, imposed by Rita's analysis, was affirmed by Melanie Klein as early as 1924 at Salzburg, and remained one of the permanent points of her doctrine: "I regard the deprivation of the breast as the most fundamental cause of the turning to the father" (Klein, 1928, p. 193). Oral frustration causes the abandonment of the mother as the privileged object of the little girl's libido. Between 1923 and 1927, the following elements were added to this basic fact.

1. Anal frustrations undergone during toilet training add to hatred of the mother and precipitate the conversion to the father.

2. Under the influence of Helene Deutsch, Melanie Klein (1928) noted that "the genital development of the woman finds its completion in the successful displacement of oral libido on to the genital" (p. 192). But unlike the Viennese psychoanalyst, she thinks that this displacement occurs extremely early, that it is active from the emergence of the first genital impulses, and that it provides a quantity of libidinal energy indispensable to the conversion to the father and the beginning of the oedipus complex. It thus follows immediately after weaning.

3. Genital impulses appear from the second half of the first year. Their reinforcement by oral libido after weaning is facilitated by their feminine and receptive character: the little girl's libido is not at first male or phallic as Freud thought; from the very beginning it has a specifically feminine and receptive aim: this proximity of the aim of the libido and that of genital libido facilitates the transfer of libidinal energy from one aim to another.

4. From the beginning, the female genital impulses are accompanied by an "unconscious awareness of the vagina" and of its "oral" and receptive function (Klein, 1928, p. 192). This awareness is accompanied by sensations in that organ which give rise to typically female forms of masturbation (p. 192). This receptive libido, enlarged by the addition of oral impulses, will therefore turn toward an object it can incorporate.

5. The father's penis is the object which succeeds the mother's breast. This conclusion, proceeding directly from Rita's analysis, had already been suggested by Melanie Klein at the Salzburg Congress in 1924. Children first conceive and desire coitus as an oral act, and the receptive aim common to the vagina and the mouth favors the "displacement of oral libido on to the genital" and gives the first oedipal instincts a character that is both oral and vaginal.

6. This mixed instinctual character—oral and genital—gives its special coloration to the first position of oedipal rivalry with the mother: "envy and hatred of the mother who possesses the father's penis seem, at the period when these first Oedipus impulses are stirring, to be a further motive for the little girl's turning to the father" (Klein, 1928, p. 192). This idea is one of the contributions of Ruth's analysis, and has two aspects, logically distinct but discovered simultaneously by Melanie Klein. The first is the part played by infantile sexual theories as organizers of the oedipal wish, a role already glimpsed in the paper read at Salzburg. It is from the theory of coitus as an oral act that envy and jealousy of the mother arise, because in the child's fantasy she incorporates the object, the father's penis, to which the little girl's desires are now turning. This first point appears to have been acquired at the end of Rita's treatment, in accordance with the idea of rivalry; the child's hostility against her mother appeared as a consequence of the incestuous desire for the father. In a second phase, Melanie Klein shows, this hostility is expressed in pregenital sadistic fantasies organized by the sexual theories in which the beginnings of the oedipal tendencies are expressed, while they lend them in return their anal-sadistic and oral-sadistic coloration. We know that this demonstration of anal and then oral sadism was the product of analyses carried out in 1924 and 1925.

7. In a context very near to this, the same relationship exists between the oedipal identification with the mother and pregenital sadism: "In the girl, identification with the mother results directly from the Oedipus impulses" (Klein, 1928, p. 193). This identification is accompanied by feelings of rivalry and hostility which combine with oral-sadistic and anal-sadistic impulses: "this identification coincides with the anal-sadistic tendencies to rob and destroy the mother" (p. 193). The first position of rivalry with the mother is thus marked by sadistic fantasies of extraordinary violence, the intensity of which may end by masking the oedipal genital tendencies, even though the sadistic impulses are placed at their service: "The early stages of the Oedipus conflict are so largely dominated by pregenital phases of development that the genital phase, when it begins to be active, is at first heavily shrouded and only later, between the third and fifth years of life, becomes clearly recognizable" (p. 197). The Kleinian theory, then, includes both an affirmation of the primacy of genital impulses in the initial phase of the oedipus complex and an explanation of the fact that this supremacy is difficult to trace.

The second phase of the female oedipus complex, marked by abandonment of the father and a return to the mother, is also caused by the convergence of several factors. They all have the same characteristic: they arise at least partially from the first oedipal position, and, although their development depends on it, they nonetheless lead to its reversal.

The first of these factors is linked with the progressive overlapping of the genital tendencies by sadistic impulses. The emergence of oedipal impulses was contemporary with the appearance of sadistic impulses, which reach their peak, according to the descriptions of Abraham, to which Melanie Klein adhered more and more in the course of 1924 and 1925, at the time of the oral-sadistic stage. At this moment the balance of power is favorable to the oral-sadistic and anal-sadistic impulses, which submerge the genital libido. The excessive sadism causes the introjection of objects fantastically distorted by omnipotence, which gives an appearance of reality to the imaginary attacks of which they are victims, bringing with it the fear of retribution. The little girl who wants to destroy her mother, cut her into pieces, devour her, take from her the father's penis and the children—real or imaginary—she is carrying is introjecting an injured mother whose vengeful attack she fears more and more, and against whom she defends herself by fantasy counterattacks which become more and more sadistic. She thus enters the "vicious circle" under the influence of a cruel and tyrannical oral-sadistic and anal-sadistic superego which threatens to devour her, cut her in pieces, etc. The terror of the introjected mother, which prevented Rita from playing at being the mother of her doll, identified with the baby she wanted to steal from her real mother, is the specific anxiety situation of the girl. It is at the root of her oedipal guilt: "Because of the destructive tendencies once directed by her against the mother's body (or certain organs in it) and against the children in the womb, the girl anticipates retribution in the form of destruction of her own capacity for motherhood or of the organs connected with this function and of her own children" (Klein, 1928, p. 194). This anxiety, which causes the abandonment of the girl's first position at about fifteen or eighteen months, is comparable with the boy's castration anxiety: "The girl's very intense anxiety about her womanhood can be shown to be analogous to the boy's dread of castration, for it certainly contributes to the checking of her Oedipus impulses" (p. 195).

The second group of factors bringing on the abandonment of the first oedipal position comes from the relationship with the father. The precipitating factor is the frustration, in this relationship, of oral and genital desires. While the father's caresses "have now the effect of a seduction and are felt as 'the attraction of the opposite sex' " (p. 192), the absence of direct oral and genital satisfaction in the heterosexual relationship leads to a disappointment more or less easy for the little girl to bear. The ability to tolerate this new frustration depends in fact on the way the oral frustration of weaning was born. From this point of view the first preoedipal reaction to the mother rests entirely on the archaic oedipal relationship with the father. After a time varying in length—depending on the girl's ability to tolerate the frustration, and thus on the quality of her earlier relationship with her mother—the disappointment of her incestuous wishes will cause them to be abandoned, just as a few

months earlier the frustration of weaning had caused the rejection of the mother as an object. The relationship with the
father is influenced in another way by the attitude toward the
mother. Genital impulses and hatred of the mother combine
in the first oedipal position to consolidate the attachment to the
father. If hatred for the mother predominates as a motive of
the incestuous choice of the father by the receptive genital tendencies, this heterosexual relationship will be all the weaker
and all the more vulnerable to the attacks of the maternal superego. Not only will the father be abandoned as an object of
love, in accordance with the threats and demands of the introjected mother, but he will be hated in his turn as a frustrator.
The hatred of men which is at the origin of female homosex-
uality in certain of its forms goes back to this stage.

The Phallic Phase

At the confluence of these two processes—growing terror
of the introjected mother and disappointment in the father—the
little girl reverses the initial position and enters the second
phase of her oedipal development. She turns away from her
father, comes closer to her mother, and from then on considers
her father a rival. This is a phase which Freud observed and
described as the phallic phase; he viewed it as marking the entry
of the girl into the oedipal situation. In one sense Melanie Klein
confirmed Freud's conceptions: a masculine phase really does
exist in the little girl before her entry into the oedipus complex.
She also allows that this phase is characterized by penis envy,
the little girl's wish to possess the male genital organ, a theory
which at the time was opposed by most women psychoanalysts.
The essential elements of the Freudian characterization of the
phallic phase are well known; Laplanche and Pontalis (1967)
summarize them as follows: "the child at this stage, whether
boy or girl, knows but one genital organ—the male one—and
the opposition of the sexes is equivalent to that of *phallic* and
castrated. The phallic stage corresponds to the culmination and
dissolution of the Oedipus complex; the castration complex is
predominant" (p. 309). As far as the girl is concerned, they
describe the particular form taken by her castration complex:

"In the girl, the absence of a penis is experienced as a wrong suffered which she attempts to deny, to compensate for or to remedy" (p. 56). Penis envy they define as the "fundamental element in female sexuality and root of its dialectics":

> Penis envy originates in the discovery of the anatomical difference between the sexes: the little girl feels mutilated in comparison with the boy and wishes to possess a penis as he does (castration complex). Subsequently, in the course of the Oedipal phase, this penis envy takes on two secondary forms: first, the wish to acquire a penis within oneself (principally in the shape of the desire to have a child), and, secondly, the wish to enjoy the penis in coitus. [pp. 302–303]

From the beginning of the first truly Kleinian ideas the empirical data described by Freud were accepted; the difference was with regard to the interpretation of most of them. According to Melanie Klein, the child at the phallic stage is not ignorant of the difference between the sexes and the existence of the vagina, but only misunderstands them. The ignorance is purely conscious, while the knowledge of the vagina is unconscious and repressed during the phallic phase. In the girl the phallic stage does not correspond to the peak and decline of the oedipus complex, but to the decline of the first feminine position. Castration complex and penis envy may be prevalent, but they cannot be described as the "fundamental element in female sexuality and root of its dialectic." In fact, any dialectical point of view is excluded. The phallic phase is not a moment of negation indispensable to the evolution of the oedipal process, but a fact irreducible to any logical development or extension of the idea; the phallic phase can be deduced from the oedipus complex no more than can the oedipus complex be dialectically engendered by the phallic phase. The whole of the process of the phallic phase can be explained as the meeting of two lines of development which cross, though their sources are different. The oedipal development, properly speaking, comes from the genital impulses. The negative elements of the complex can be linked with different instinctual sources: the oral-sadistic and anal-sadistic impulses which the oedipus complex organizes before being submerged by them. Penis envy does not originate in the discovery of the anatomical difference between the sexes. According to Melanie Klein, the difference is unconsciously known from the first emergence of the genital impulses, and thus is part of the first oedipal phase. We may therefore summarize Melanie Klein's attitude in 1927 as follows: following the first feminine position, the girl's phallic phase is not the manifestation of early genital tendencies but on the contrary shows their first repression; the instinctual source of this negative oedipal phase can be found in the sadistic tendencies which form the early superego.

The girl's entry into the phallic phase presupposes a defeat of her infantile genital erotism. The intensity and duration of this phase depend on the seriousness of this defeat. The genital impulses of the first oedipal stage are weakened by the frustration they undergo: the father's penis cannot replace the mother's breast as a source of real satisfaction; the maternal tendencies cannot be satisfied. Genital erotism is thus disappointing, and its failure renews the original frustration of weaning. At the same time the oral-sadistic and anal-sadistic tendencies reach their maximum, and, by virtue of the fear of retribution, the fear of the introjected mother's vengeance becomes terrifying. It leads to abandonment of the first oedipal position by a process which owes nothing to a logical development of the situation, but which shows the influence of disturbing intrapsychic forces—the sadistic impulses. From then on, the little girl turns away from the father, who is refusing her coitus and maternity, and hates him as a frustrator, just as earlier she hated the mother who frustrated her by weaning and toilet training.

She now turns to the mother to placate her; or, more precisely, she turns to the real mother to placate the cruel introjected mother. From this point of view, entry into the phallic phase is accompanied not at all by contempt or devaluation of the mother, and the supremacy of the penis is only a derivative of this reconciliation with her. In this new situation, the little girl who hates her father because of the frustration she has suffered considers him a rival for her mother's love. The fantasy of having a penis has two sources. It betrays the permanence of the primal oedipal desire (to steal the contents of the mother's body: feces = children = penis) in a displaced form (to steal the father's penis), which causes less anxiety because, at this stage, the father who has been loved up to now is not introjected as a sadistic persecutor and does not seem very dangerous. It also expresses the wish to overcompensate for the guilty and anxiogenic hatred of the mother by fantasies in which the girl, thanks to the penis stolen from her father, has sexual intercourse with her mother and gives her children. This corresponds with the overcompensation of the initial wish to steal her offspring. In this overcompensation, first mentioned in the 1928 article, we can see the ancestor of the notion of reparation.[7] Penis envy thus appears as the accompaniment in fantasy of an offshoot of the initial oedipus complex, distorted by displacement and inversion. It is thus the product of a work of defense: "Identification with the father is less charged with anxiety than that with the mother; moreover, the sense of guilt towards her impels to over-compensation through a fresh love-relation with her" (Klein, 1928, p. 193).

The phallic phase at its peak is thus characterized by a negative or inverted oedipus complex: the girl in her imagination adopts a masculine position; she wants to be a boy and dreams of giving her mother children, of taking her father's penis, and of driving him away and excluding him. This purely defensive phallic phase has no power to give rise to the classical oedipus complex, except by its failure. As Freud saw, the little girl has to give up her masculine position in order to enter the oedipus complex. But this factor is not unique and determinant. In particular, the hatred of the mother, which provides a powerful motive for the abandonment of the masculine position, does not come from the castration complex: the imaginary injury of the absence of a penis can give rise to this hatred only by reactivating the primal hostility against the mother which the phallic phase had simply displaced onto the father. If the phallic phase disappears it is because "against this new love-relation with her there operates the castration complex which

[7] The words "wish to restore" were italicized there by Melanie Klein. The notion of reparation was explicitly stated in "Infantile Anxiety Situations Reflected in a Work of Art and in the Creative Impulse" (Klein, 1929).

makes a masculine attitude difficult, and also the hatred of her which sprang from the earlier positions. Hate and rivalry of the mother, however, again lead to abandoning the identification with the father and turning to him as the object to love and be loved by" (Klein, 1928, p. 193). But this new transformation is finally possible only because the decrease in sadistic impulses reverses the balance of forces in favor of the genital impulses. Then the fear of the introjected mother weakens because the fantasy attacks aimed at her are less infiltrated by oral and anal aggression, and are more exclusively attached to true oedipal rivalry based on genital impulses: "if there is a more positive relation to the mother, built up on the genital position, not only will the woman be freer from a sense of guilt in her relation to her children, but her love for her husband will be strongly reinforced . . ." (pp. 193–194). Although this idea is not explicitly stated, it seems that Melanie Klein was admitting in 1928 that late oedipal rivalry with the mother gave rise to the introjection not of a menacing superego but of an ideal to be imitated, one in which the destructive dimension faded into the background. From that point the superego has two successive levels corresponding with the three stages of the oedipus complex:

> From the early identification with the mother in which the anal-sadistic level so largely preponderates, the little girl derives jealousy and hatred and forms a cruel super-ego after the maternal imago. The super-ego which develops at this stage from a father-identification can also be menacing and cause anxiety, but it seems never to reach the same proportions as that derived from the mother-identification. But the more the identification with the mother becomes stabilized on the genital basis, the more will it be characterized by the devoted kindness of a bountiful mother-ideal. Thus this positive affective attitude depends on the extent to which the maternal mother-ideal bears the characteristics of the pregenital or of the genital stage. [p. 195]

We would most nearly approximate Melanie Klein's position by saying that in the rivalry with the mother in the first oedipal stage, the girl and the introjected mother vie with each other in sadistic attacks, while in the final oedipal position they view with each other in tenderness and love for the father. Here Melanie Klein was influenced by Abraham, but went further: the genital libido is itself free of ambivalence, and this can be observed from the early genital stage. From this point of view, Melanie Klein connected all the hostile elements of the late complex with survivals and attentuations of the sadistic elements inherited from the two earlier forms. Apart from this difference, she adheres essentially to Freud's description as regards the peak and decline of the girl's postphallic oedipus complex. The only difference we can see concerns the idea that the feminine complex, far from fading out progressively and incompletely, is repressed like that of the boy under the influence of a feminine anxiety similar to castration anxiety. But this is only an attentuated repetition—not going so far as the adoption of a masculine position, and limited to the abandonment of the choice of incestuous object—of the abandonment of the first incestuous love for the father under the effect of fear of the introjected mother's vengeance.

13. The Early Oedipus Complex in Boys

We have already seen that Melanie Klein did not describe the male oedipus complex until after she had described the female complex. Having viewed the oedipal manifestations of Rita, Trude, and Ruth without her observations being clouded by the need to fit them into a schema constructed for boys, she had been able to consider the feminine oedipus complex as an autonomous process rather than as a modification of the masculine one. She had observed a more complete parallel between the masculine and feminine forms of the complex than Freud had admitted; the same origin in both cases, in the genital impulses peculiar to each sex; the same cause for repression, in the anxiety characteristic of each sex (castration anxiety for the boy, fear of being internally devastated, robbed, and made sterile by the introjected mother for the girl). When Peter's analysis enabled her, in 1924–1925, to study the initial stages of the masculine complex, she reversed Freud's approach and conceived the boy's development on the model of that of the girl. This was not without difficulty: genetically, the order of the stages appears identical in both sexes, but their significance is different. Like the girl, the boy passes through a first *feminine* phase of oral-sadistic and anal-sadistic rivalry with the mother. Like the girl, he is led by the fear of the introjected mother to adopt a masculine position because of the repression of his feminine complex. But this position, conforming as it does to his genital orientation, is maintained at the time of the classical oedipus complex, of which it marks the beginning. From then on, the parallel is incomplete: the third phase is lacking in the boy. We have the following diagram.

	First phase	Second Phase	Third Phase
Girl	♀	♂	♀
Boy	♀	♂ ——————→	♂

It was probably in order to maintain a strict parallel that Melanie Klein was led to the hypothesis of a first positive oedipal phase in the boy, preceding the feminine position. But here the demands of symmetry and of chronology are difficult to reconcile, as the boy's feminine position is contemporary with that of the girl. So Melanie Klein has to admit a considerable overlap in the primary stages of the oedipus complex. The priority of the boy's masculine position is affirmed. Maintaining that "the Oedipus tendencies are released in consequence of the frustration which the child experiences at weaning" and "they receive reinforcement through the anal frustrations undergone during training in cleanliness," Melanie Klein (1928) explains in almost the next sentence: "The boy, when he finds himself impelled to abandon the oral and anal positions for the genital, passes on to the aim of *penetration* associated with possession of the penis. Thus he changes not only his libido-position, but its *aim*, and this enables him to retain his original love-object" (p. 186). This text appears to suggest that in 1928 she admitted the existence of an initial masculine position based directly on genital impulses and preceding the feminine phase common to both sexes. But it should be noted that no Kleinian text ever described this masculine phase, except for occasional mentions of its overlap with the boy's feminine phase, to which she assigns characteristics allowing it to be distinguished from the corresponding position of the girl. A certain ambiguity, already present in the 1926 article, remained to the end: describing Melanie Klein's views, a commentator as intelligent and well qualified as Hanna Segal (1964) wrote:

> To both the boy and the girl infant the first object of desire is the mother's breast, and the father is perceived to begin with as a rival. . . . The father's penis quickly becomes both to the little girl and the little boy an alternative object of oral desire to be turned to away from the breast. . . .
>
> For the little boy this turning to the penis of his father as an alternative to his mother's breast is primarily a move towards passive homosexuality, but at the same time this incorporation of his father's penis helps in his identification with him and in that way strengthens his heterosexuality [p. 110]

In the final version of Melanie Klein's ideas, the boy's initial position appears to be a feminine one, and the model worked out in 1924 for the girl is applicable to the boy. In this sense our diagram certainly reflects Melanie Klein's final opinion. But this does not make it possible to integrate the initial heterosexual position postulated in the 1928 text for both the boy and the girl. If we wish to account exactly for these ideas, we have to admit a disjunction between the genetic (or, more precisely, the dynamico-genetic) order, and the chronological order. Thus, the feminine phases of both sexes would be contemporaneous, but the boy's would be, if not chronologically later, at least causally secondary to a primary, but not earlier, positive oedipal position: this emerges from Melanie Klein's insistence on the overlap and confusion of the initial stages of the oedipus complex, however clear the order of succession is in the case of the girl. So we have to accept the following diagram, in which the stages on the same horizontal line are contemporary but not homologous, as their dynamic and genetic homology (defined with respect to the primal or inverted char-

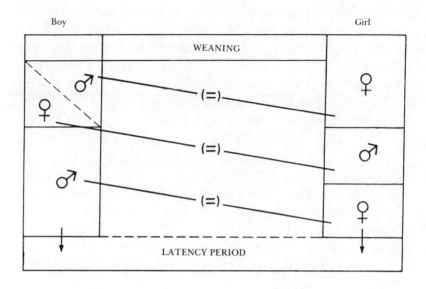

acter of the oedipal position) shifts in relation to their chronological correspondence; this is indicated by the slanting lines.

But whatever the theoretical difficulties raised by the question of the symmetry of the masculine and feminine forms, the
formulation of the boy's feminine phase is still the essential
contribution of the period 1923–1927 to the Kleinian conception of the masculine oedipus complex. It consists of a position
of rivalry with the mother, exactly identical in content with that
of the girl, and infiltrated by the same oral-sadistic and anal-
sadistic fantasies. "The tendencies to steal and destroy are concerned with the organs of conception, pregnancy and partu-
rition, which the boy assumes to exist in the mother, and further
with the vagina and the breasts, the fountain of milk, which are
coveted as organs of receptivity and bounty from the time when
the libidinal position is purely oral" (Klein, 1928, p. 190). So
even if the feminine phase was not recognized in 1928 as absolutely the first, it was nonetheless assigned an essential place
in the development of the boy, whose first fully developed oedipal stage—the initial heterosexual stage was the subject of a
theoretical postulate rather than a clinical observation—was
thus marked by a very early identification with the mother,

during which the boy wishes to bear a child. In this feminine position the boy suffers an irremediable frustration of his feminine desire for maternity, and this frustration is at the origin of "the male "femininity complex" (p. 190). This complex is in a way the equivalent of female penis envy; both desires are doomed to be disappointed and are at the root of a suffering which is never truly alleviated by later symbolic substitute satisfactions. Thirty years later, Melanie Klein linked this suffering, common to both sexes, with the primal longing for the breast. It is significant that in the 1928 article the word "envy," on five of the six occasions of its use by Melanie Klein, is connected with the male envy of maternity or with penis envy (pp. 190, 193, 195).[8]

Just as the woman never gives up her penis envy in the unconscious, so the man never gives up his envy of maternity, and "The Early Stages of the Oedipus Conflict" (Klein, 1928) outlines a psychology of the male femininity complex which bears a certain analogy with the description given by Abraham (1920a) in "Manifestations of the Female Castration Complex." According to Abraham, the normal fate of penis envy is to be transformed into the desire to receive a child from the father, a desire which at puberty has to be "detached from the idea of her father": "her libido, thus freed, has to find a new object" (p. 344). But where this evolution does not occur, or occurs only incompletely, the primal desire for a penis survives. It takes two different forms. In "the homosexual type" it takes the form of realization of the wish, whereby "the unconscious phantasies of the woman make the assertion: 'I am the fortunate possessor of a penis and exercise the male function' " (p. 348). In the "revenge type," characterized by the denigration of everything male, "in the refusal to acknowledge the significance of the male organ there is implied, although in a very mitigated form, an emasculation of the man" (p. 355). This wish to castrate the man is expressed in behavior aimed at disappointing, depreciating, and humiliating him.

---

[8] It should be noted that the remaining use of the word in this article occurs in the phrase "envy and hatred of the mother who possesses the father's penis" (p. 192). This notion does not appear in any of Melanie Klein's earlier writings.

We find comparable male types in Melanie Klein as regards the outcome of the femininity complex. In normal cases, the envy of maternity finds sublimated expression in paternity and in amorous relationships: "on the one hand his relation to women will be positive in character, and on the other the desire for a child and the feminine component, which play so essential a part in men's work, will find more favourable opportunities for sublimation" (Klein, 1928, p. 191). The equivalent of Abraham's "revenge type" is found in men who display aggression and contempt toward women. In these men, side by side with the refusal of the feminine role due to castration anxiety, we find dread of the introjected mother and revenge against the maternal superego: "This excessive aggression unites with the pleasure in attack which proceeds from the direct, genital Oedipus situation, but it represents that part of the situation which is by far the more asocial factor in character-formation. This is why a man's rivalry with women will be far more asocial than his rivalry with his fellow-men, which is largely prompted through the genital position" (p. 191). Like their female counterparts, these men despise, denigrate, and devalue the opposite sex.

The wish-fulfillment type is not found as such in the male femininity complex. It takes a displaced form which is nearer to sublimation, and thus to normal development, than it is to a neurotic character trait. Melanie Klein describes two outcomes of the femininity complex which can be connected with this type. In one, the man's "sense of being at a disadvantage is then concealed and over-compensated by the superiority he deduces from his possession of a penis" (p. 191). The virile protest is exacerbated, and in extreme forms it approaches to the "revenge" type. There is, however, another outcome of the envy of maternity: thanks to a "displacement . . . on to the intellectual plane" of his rivalry with women, a man finds an overcompensation in the feeling of his intellectual superiority, and in the most favorable cases he finds a symbolic equivalent to maternal fertility in intellectual, scientific, or artistic creativity.

But in most cases, the envy of maternity is carried over to the desire for paternity, bringing with it an overvaluation of the virile role, based on overestimation of the penis, a normal

phenomenon but one which bears the mark of overcompensation of the feminine wish to have children. This attitude
originates in the phase of decline of the boy's anal-sadistic feminine position, accompanied by entry into the phallic stage. In
this phase the boy can overcome his desire to steal his mother's
children, thanks to a decrease in pregenital sadism and the
reinforcement of genital impulses. The narcissistic overestimation of the penis that is characteristic of the phallic stage
expresses, in addition to this reinforcement, both a displacement and a negation of the envy of maternity, which were due
to a fear of retaliation by the introjected mother. But unlike the
girl, the boy finds, during this phase, powerful autoerotic and
narcissistic libidinal satisfaction in the possession of a penis,
while the real and easily verifiable presence of that organ allays
first the fear of being destroyed by the introjected mother and
then, as the new masculine position gains strength, the fear of
castration by the introjected father. Consistent with the boy's
biological sex and the direction of his impulses—a source of
satisfaction and of reassurance against anxiety—the phallic
phase enables the boy to achieve a satisfactory equilibrium,
which is maintained until onset of the latency period. On this
point Melanie Klein's position is the same as Freud's.

Her conception of the oedipus complex, then, is characterized essentially by a considerable broadening of the field of
phenomena linked with this complex. Far from being reduced
to a contemporary manifestation of the phallic phase, a relatively brief and intense crisis, the oedipus complex becomes a
complicated but well-ordered process which lasts several years
and includes the whole of the child's development between
weaning and latency. Its richness and innumerable variants, as
well as its role as organizer of the pregenital impulses, now
make it possible to connect it with almost all the processes of
the young child's mental life. The evolution of the superego in
particular is closely bound up with that of the oedipus complex,
and the description of their interaction stands as Melanie Klein's
most important theoretical achievement of the period 1923–1927.
Apart from a few details, this description remained to the end
an essential element of the Kleinian system. This theoretical
contribution is closely connected with the invention of the psy-

choanalytic play technique, the true source of Kleinian psycho-
analysis, and with its reflection on the principles of the
psychoanalytic treatment of children.

As early as 1927, it may be said, the nucleus of the Kleinian
system had taken shape. There were later additions, but unlike
the proto-Kleinian system it underwent no major changes;
when the discovery of the depressive position limited the role
assigned the oedipus complex in development, there were no
basic changes in the description of its internal organization, any
more than the change from the geocentric to the heliocentric
model in astronomy brought any modification of the description of the moon's orbit around the earth. The Kleinian system
of 1923–1927 was integrated into a larger system of which it
was no longer the center, but it remained to the end a constant
element of Kleinian psychoanalysis.

4

From Sadism at Its Height to Reparation Mechanisms

1. Melanie Klein's First Years in London

Melanie Klein's first years in London were spent in the preparation and writing of the great synthesis entitled *The Psycho-Analysis of Children,* published in 1932. There also grew up around her during these years a current of interest, sympathy, and collaboration. This movement was general enough in the British Society Psycho-Analytical Society for people to speak at times, from this period onward, of a British school of psychoanalysis as distinct from the continental schools. A passage from Ernest Jones (1957) gives a good account of the atmosphere that surrounded the creator of the play technique upon her arrival in London:

> In September [1927] Freud sent me a long letter complaining strongly about a public campaign I was supposed to be conducting in England against his daughter Anna, and perhaps therefore against himself. The only basis for this outburst was my having published in the *Journal* a long report of a discussion on Child Analysis. It was a topic that had for years interested our Society, which contained so many women analysts, and it had been further stimulated by Melanie Klein's coming to England the year before. [p. 145]

Jones was particularly sympathetic; he had invited Melanie Klein to London to deliver, during the summer of 1925, the series of lectures on child analysis which were to be the starting point of the work of 1932; he had also asked her to settle in the British capital after Abraham's death, a request motivated by both scientific and personal reasons.[2] Joan Riviere, one of Freud's closest British disciples—she had been analyzed by him in 1922 (Jones, 1955, pp. 456–457) and was carrying on a lengthy correspondence with him (Jones, 1957, p. viii)—was one of the first to become interested in Melanie Klein's work; there were also Susan Isaacs, Ella Sharpe, Alix Strachey, future translator of *The Psycho-Analysis of Children*. Nina Searl, who had begun to analyze children before Melanie Klein settled in England, was at first somewhat hesitant about Melanie Klein's technique and ideas, but quickly came over to her side and was the second analyst to use the play technique. Between 1927 and 1932 Melanie Klein's influence extended to the entire British Society, encountering none of the reservations and declared opposition that were to appear later. At that time Melanie Klein was by no means the only "Kleinian" in England, but she did not become the head of a school, followed passively by disciples on whom she imposed the product of her personal speculations. Soon her English colleagues reacted to her ideas, and reflected and wrote on facts discovered or brought to the fore by the psychoanalysis of young children: the origin of guilt feelings, the formation of the superego, the early development of girls. Sometimes they brought to light facts which she acknowledged, but it was exceptional at this time for ideas that were generally Kleinian and likely to remain so to be advanced initially by anyone but Melanie Klein herself. Her friends were interested mainly in finding arguments to support their convictions, and sometimes to allay their reservations about the new ideas. They compared Melanie Klein's discoveries with Freudian metapsychology and attempted to reconcile the two. But while they were

[1] According to Winnicott (1965), Jones had asked Melanie Klein to analyze a member of his family, probably a child. "Strachey said: 'If you are applying psycho-analytic theory to children, you should meet Melanie Klein. She has been enticed over to England by Jones to do the analysis of someone special to Jones' " (p. 173).

studying the theories of 1927 and the problems they raised, Melanie Klein was diversifying her experience and deepening her thought, and soon made important new discoveries.

Three of these are of particular note: (1) the discovery and exploration, under the name "phase of sadism at its height," of the nucleus of what we might call, after Wilfred Bion, the "psychotic part of the personality"; (2) the description and interpretation of early psychosis in terms of disturbance in the formation of symbols; and (3) recognition of the mechanisms of reparation. All three seem to have emerged, together with other, less important innovations, from the application of the play technique to schizoid children and, later, to frankly psychotic ones. These three ideas appeared in 1929–1930 in three articles published one after another in the space of a few months: "Personification in the Play of Children" (Klein, 1929b), "Infantile Anxiety Situations Reflected in a Work of Art and in the Creative Impulse" (Klein, 1929a), and "The Importance of Symbol-Formation in the Development of the Ego" (Klein, 1930a). Two years later *The Psycho-Analysis of Children* synthesized these ideas with those formulated earlier. It is this development we are about to examine. First, though, a point of some importance must be clarified.

During this period Melanie Klein's vocabulary and style were rapidly taking shape, acquiring typical features that made it possible to identify her writing from the very first lines. In 1926 and 1927 she had presented discoveries that were factual, or technical, but always concrete. After that, however, she undertook the task of formulating theories. this means that we will have to examine carefully her vocabulary, as it reflects the formation of her concepts. But this will sometimes be difficult: during her first years in London she was still thinking and writing in German. It is true that at a very early stage she published articles written directly in English, and of which we sometimes have no German version; examples are "Criminal Tendencies in Normal Children" (Klein, 1927a) and her contribution to a symposium on child analysis (Klein, 1927c; see also 1927b, 1930b, 1931). It is important to note, however, that her most important and innovative texts were written in German. This is the case with the three articles mentioned in the paragraph above. It is especially true of *The Psycho-Analysis of Children*, translated by Alix Strachey from a manuscript to which the author later made a large number of additions, so that for a long time the English edition lacked passages that were accessible only in German.

2. The Theory of Development

The Phase of Sadism at Its Height

Between 1927 and 1932 the essential part of Melanie Klein's work in the field of instinct theory was concerned with her theory of a phase when sadism is at its height. This theory held particular interest for her, as it enabled her to account for the severity of the superego introjected in the early stages of the oedipus complex, and thus to give a stronger theoretical foundation to her earlier discoveries and to explain the nature of the psychotic mechanisms functioning in this peak phase to make possible a revival of early psychopathology. From this point of view it is no exaggeration to say that it was the theory of the culminating phase of sadistic impulses that linked the discoveries of 1927 to those of 1929–1931, and gave the Kleinian system of 1932 its unity.

The idea of an unleashing of sadism during the initial stages of the oedipus conflict was indeed present from 1926, in "The Psychological Principles of Early Analysis," but the explicit notion of a peak phase of sadism was not worked out until later, probably in 1928, during the analysis of a psychotic child, Egon. In any case it was in 1929 that Melanie Klein introduced this concept explicitly, in the paper on infantile anxiety situations (Klein, 1929a). She gives it its name a few months later in "The Importance of Symbol-Formation in the Development of the Ego" (Klein, 1930, p. 219): *Höchste Blüte des Sadismus*, soon agglutinated to become *Höchstblüte des Sadismus*. This unusual expression, which seems strangely archaic from the standpoint of modern German usage, is not easy to translate. In a figurative sense it means "the golden age of sadism"; literally it means "the highest flowering of sadism." The phase

denoted by this technical term is certainly the "highest" manifestation of sadism, one characterized by the conjunction and
accumulation of three factors leading to the escalation (*Steige-
rung*) of aggression. One concerns instinctual sadistic *aims*
which, because of the overlapping of pregenital stages, are
added together, perhaps even potentiating one another, very
shortly after the beginning of the cannibalistic stage. Many of
Melanie Klein's readers will have noticed the frequency in her
work of the expression "by means of every weapon which sadism
can command"; far from being, as one might think, simply a
turn of phrase, it denotes this phenomenon with great precision. The instinctual aims of the sadistic impulses (to bite, soil
with excrement, cut up, burn, etc.) become in fact the weapons
in fantasy of an object relationship aimed at the annihilation
of the object.

This intensification of sadism by the proliferation of its
weapons is only the most obvious aspect of sadism at its height.
It has been insufficiently noted that the intensification of sadism
concerns also the *motives* for aggression (especially its instinctual
bases) and its *object*. By this is meant that for Melanie Klein
sadism has not truly reached its height until *all* the impulses
combine with the sadistic impulses proper to produce attacks
in fantasy against the object—or, more exactly, the objects, as
in this phase all objects are attacked through the one that represents them all. As far as the description of these two aspects
is concerned, the originality and depth of Melanie Klein's
thought, as well as its clinical richness, are no less than in her
inventory of sadism's weapons.

The impulses that accumulate to produce the intensification of sadism, then, do not compromise only the sadistic impulses proper. The oral activity of sucking also contributes,
insofar as it is the frustration of weaning which in Melanie
Klein's opinion sets off the simultaneous beginnings of sadism
and the oedipus complex. Early genital impulses play their part
in aggression against the rival. But neither the sucking impulses
nor the genital impulses can really increase sadism. This function falls to the *epistemophilic impulse,* which has very early and
intimate bonds with the sadistic impulses. The object of sadism
at its height is a composite image of both parents, so that a bad

relationship with one of them cannot be compensated by a good relationship with the other. The fantasy of the *combined parents* constitutes the monstrous object which can bring about the third type of sadistic identification.

A definition of the height of sadism might then be suggested that corresponds exactly to the use Melanie Klein made of this notion between 1927 and 1934. Sadism is at its height when the child is compelled by oral-sadistic, anal-sadistic, and urethral-sadistic impulses, and by the epistemophilic impulse, to annihilate the combined parents with all the weapons of sadism. But if this definition is to be fully comprehensible, the Kleinian notions of the epistemophilic impulse and the combined parents must be elucidated.

The Epistemophilic Instinct and the Height of Sadism

The notion of the epistemophilic impulse appears in Melanie Klein's work from the first formulation of her theories in 1926–1927. Even before that, her approach was always characterized by an emphasis on the desire to know and on intellectual sublimation. Her first psychoanalytic project, after all, was to free her son from common learning inhibitions by explaining sexuality to him at the oedipal stage. The theory of sublimation and inhibition was the very center of the proto-Kleinian system. To designate this desire to know, based in the last analysis on the sexual curiosity of the oedipal age, Melanie Klein did not need to have recourse to a special concept, and when she used the term "instinct to know" (*Wissenstrieb*[2]) she assigned it no special status among the manifestations of sexual curiosity. However, as we have seen, certain ideas already present in the proto-Kleinian period were retained throughout the various changes in Kleinian theory. This was the case with her idea that all sublimations are based on a nucleus of masturbatory fantasies (that is to say, on fantasies of the primal scene); it was the case also with an idea acquired during the analysis of Erich,

___

[2] This German word belongs to everyday language; the shortened form *Wisstrieb*, used by Freud and later by Melanie Klein, does as well. In order to respect this level of language, they might both be translated "urge to know" or "need to know."

that of the complete symbolic equivalence between the mother's body and the external world. Melanie Klein did, however, abandon the term "scopophilia" (*Schaulust*, which means both pleasure in seeing and the wish to see), a term linked with the theme of the primal scene, of which she had made considerable use in a number of clinical passages written before 1926. The term disappeared at about that time, and the realities it designated were then transferred to the epistemophilic impulse. It may well be that this is nothing but a change in vocabulary, a relatively unimportant modification of a notion already present in Melanie Klein's thought.

It seems, too, that on this point Melanie Klein was influenced by the British psychoanalyst Mary Chadwick, who in 1925 had published an article entitled *"Uber die Würzel der Wissbegierde"* ("On the Origin of the Desire to Know").[3] In fact Melanie Klein quotes this article on several occasions. When in 1928 she described the notion of *Wisstrieb* (the epistemophilic instinct), she took up again the theory that the man's overestimation of the penis and male intellectual capacities goes back to "the frustration of his wish for a child and to the displacement of this desire on to the intellectual plane" (Klein, 1928, p. 191). She stressed the point again in 1932, again quoting Mary Chadwick; the epistemophilic impulse is partly linked with the rivalry and envy harbored by men toward women. And in fact this link appears in Mary Chadwick's text. She begins, rather oddly, with two questions then in the news in Great Britain—women's right to higher education, and the censoring of several works detailing methods of contraception—and postulates an unconscious link between the two themes.

Turning to the evolutionistic hypotheses then in vogue, she reminds us that primitive peoples forbid women knowledge of certain secrets specially reserved for men; in addition, their beliefs deny the possibility of a woman's knowing by whom she is pregnant.[4] The general problem of curiosity and the desire

---

[3] Oddly enough, this article published in German by a British analyst has never, as far as can be determined, been translated into English. An abstract appeared in the *International Journal of Psycho-Analysis*, Vol. 6 (1925).

[4] An allusion to the Aranda of Australia, who are supposedly ignorant of the link between the sexual act and pregnancy.

to know is then stated, and the article sets out to describe the ontogenesis of this desire in accordance with the ideas then generally accepted in psychoanalysis; oral, tactile, visual, and auditory investigation of one's own body and its erogenous zones, until the moment when "the investigative instinct (*Forschungstrieb*), in accordance with the law of development of sexual impulses, turns toward other people; thus its role of erotic satisfaction appears in the context of infantile sexuality—that is to say, sexuality independent of the primacy of the genital organs" (Chadwick, 1925, p. 58). Of course this instinctual development is counteracted by the prohibitions imposed on instinct by education, and when Mary Chadwick attempts to evaluate their impact she lays down two principles which seem destined to become part of the Kleinian theory of the epistemophilic instinct. (1) For the child, to know is to possess: "there is a close relationship between knowing a thing and taking possession of it. In children's conceptions the two are often identified in such a way that knowledge acquires the full psychological value of satisfaction" (p. 58). (2) By virtue of this equivalence, frustration of the quest for knowledge is the same as depriving someone of the real possession of something; frustrations suffered in the realm of curiosity are no less painful than other frustrations: "It is for that very reason that frustration in matters of knowledge is so serious. It is as if the object of satisfaction were taken from the child's hand or mouth" (p. 58).

Her thinking here is very Kleinian; sexual curiosity is, depending on its fate—maintenance, repression, sublimation—the origin of either neurotic symptoms or successful sublimations, among which the epistemophilic instinct is in the front rank. According to Mary Chadwick, this sexual curiosity is essentially concerned with the question of the origin of children, and its frustration is bitterly resented; "Children feel shocked and humiliated by being deprived of knowledge they have so ardently coveted; they suffer a narcissistic hurt. They feel their ignorance as worthlessness compared with adults, whose knowledge they admire—by reaction against repressed envy—as though it were omniscience"; this feeling of narcissistic diminution" is bound together with another [feeling] which is related to it in content, concerning the lack of something adults possess—that is to say, with the castration complex" (p. 59).

Mary Chadwick next sets out to study the particular forms taken by the epistemophilic instinct in the two sexes. She thinks that in boys the tendency is reinforced by the normal fate of the femininity complex, a theory she borrowed from Otto Rank. When the boy has had to relinquish his passive homosexual wish to have a child by his father, he transforms, by displacement, his desire to have into a desire to know, "in such a way that this impulse to know is the only sure trace of the original desire, and proves that the effort to know the object has replaced the effort to possess the object" (p. 60). Thus the foundations are laid for future sublimations; the epistemophilic instinct, "displaced onto other objects, turns toward sublimated substitute versions of the desire to have a child." But this initial frustration, even when overcompensated, leaves a trace; envy of the woman's ability to have a child leads the man to refuse her access to knowledge, through an envious hate directed first at the mother by every child. Its genesis is outlined thus: "I. Hatred of the mother because of her prohibitions and her refusal to satisfy the eagerness to know, through all the stages: early oral, autoerotic, anal-sadistic, narcissistic, and phallic. II. Hatred of the mother because of her greater knowledge and her unwillingness to communicate it. III. Final displacement onto the epistemophilic instinct of the original desire to have a child when this desire has been shown to be unrealizable. IV. An effort to deprive the woman of the substitute satisfaction because she is still the rival, victorious on the real battlefield" (p. 65).

Such analyses must of necessity have struck a chord in Melanie Klein. She had studied comparable phenomena in the analysis of Erna; in Berlin she had perhaps met Mary Chadwick, who appears to have lived there in 1922 (when she attended meetings of the German Society of Psycho-Analysis) and who, like her, embraced a type of interpretation influenced by Abraham. At any rate Melanie Klein affirmed in 1927, at the Innsbrück Congress, the existence of an epistemophilic instinct; she at once affirmed its links with envy and rivalry, its natural unhappy fate, and its essential role in development. But in line with her discovery of the early stages of the oedipus complex, she was concerned not with the later curiosity of the child approaching latency, but with an early form of the epistemophilic instinct which Mary Chadwick had not envisaged: "The curiosity which shows itself plainly later on, mostly in the fourth or fifth year of life, is not the beginning, but the climax and termination, of this phase of development, which I have also found to be true of the Oedipus conflict in general" (Klein, 1928, p. 188). This early form of the epistemophilic impulse is experienced in an atmosphere of extreme frustration and pain, and is defined by an unhappy relationship with language, whose value for communication is sensed by the preverbal child, but from which he feels excluded because he cannot yet understand it. The whole of Melanie Klein's description suggests the idea of an actual traumatic situation; an unprepared ego is assailed by tensions that are too many and too strong, and cannot defend itself effectively: "We find that important consequences ensue from the fact that the ego is still so little developed when it is assailed by the onset of the Oedipus tendencies and the incipient sexual curiosity associated with them. The infant, still undeveloped intellectually, is exposed to an onrush of problems and questions" (p. 188). The ego fails to deal in any way with this "lust to know" because it lacks language, the only thing which would enable it first to recognize these questions consciously, and then to put them into words and communicate them. For this reason early sexual curiosity is of necessity doomed to be unsatisfied: "One of the most bitter grievances which we come upon in the unconscious is that these many overwhelming questions, which are apparently only partly conscious and even when conscious cannot yet be expressed in words, remain unanswered" (p. 188).

Given the traumatic dimension of this situation, we are at the level of the primal distress, Freud's *Hilflosigkeit;* by the relational dimension introduced by the relationship with language, however, we are already fully involved in the relational dimension of frustration (*Versagung*, refusal of satisfaction) and bitterness; "Another reproach follows hard upon this, namely, that the child could not understand words and speech. Thus his first questions go back beyond the beginnings of his understanding of speech" (p. 188). The result is an oppressive, crushing feeling of not knowing, all the more unbearable because wellfounded, as the child has no precise knowledge of sexual processes. Later, in both sexes, this specific feeling of frustration adds a particularly bitter component to the castration complex. Although the word "envy" does not appear in this passage, conditions conspire to give vent to this disappointment of the desire to know: "these grievances give rise to an extraordinary amount of hate" (p. 188).

Taking into account the frequent and early appearance of this tendency, recognized by Melanie Klein, we should try to discover the true nature of this "instinct to know." Indeed the German word *Trieb* is less technical than the English "instinct," but its use by a psychoanalyst implies that the reality has a certain relation with what Freud had described in the 1915 edition of *Three Essays* under the term *Wissenstrieb*. In Freud's opinion this is not an authentic instinct but a composite product; but it satisfies a component instinct, the pleasure-desire to see (*Schaulust*): "the instinct for knowledge. . . . cannot be counted among the elementary instinctual components, nor can it be classed as exclusively belonging to sexuality. Its activity corresponds on the one hand to a sublimated manner of obtaining mastery, while on the other hand it makes use of the energy of scopophilia" (Freud, 1905, p. 189).

Mary Chadwick suggested a different conception. To her the epistemophilic instinct, appearing before the oedipal tendencies but not remaining autoerotic, is one of those component instincts defined by the founder of psychoanalysis in 1905 (pp. 186–188); their characteristic is that they find their way to the object early, when all the other instincts are centered autoerotically on the appropriate erogenous zones, and thus well before the beginning of the oedipus complex. Melanie Klein (1928) took the appearance of the oedipal conflict back to the second half of the first year; she could scarcely then use the concept of component instincts, and she clearly designates the epistemophilic instinct as an oedipal tendency; its appearance on the scene, she says, is "bound" to that of the oedipal impulses, and its beginning is earlier than is generally thought, "which I have also found to be true of the Oedipus conflict in general"

(p. 188). But the interesting thing about this instinct, the origin of which is oedipal, is that it is deflected from its aim at an early stage by sadism, and that it enters very early into the orbit of aggressive impulses. It thus acquires an ambiguous status as an intermediary between the oedipus complex and sadism. It retains from its oedipal origin both its "voyeuristic" aim and its object, the mother's body: "This instinct, activated by the rise of the Oedipus tendencies, at first mainly concerns itself with the mother's body, which is assumed to be the scene of all sexual processes and developments" (p. 188). But sadism, without imposing on it a change of object, imposes a change of aim in accordance with the demands of the anal stage: "The child is still dominated by the anal-sadistic libido-position which impels him to wish to *appropriate* the contents of the body" (p. 188). For this reason the epistemophilic instinct follows the common destiny of all instincts at the beginning of the oedipus conflict; infiltrated by sadism, directed toward an aim it did not have initially, it is controlled for a while by the aggressive impulses and follows their lead in calling together the strongest defenses of the ego. It is a narcissistic hurt due to the traumatic nature of the irruption of the first questions into an ego without language, and guilt feelings arise from the "early connection between the epistemophilic impulse and sadism" (p. 188). All these are as many motives for the repression of this impulse, and afford a glimpse of a possible new explanation of intellectual inhibition.

But as regards the stages of development of the object relationship, the epistemophilic instinct takes on an important, if not exclusive, role in the processes leading to the height of sadism. It contributes, in fact, to the impetus setting off the phase of identification with the mother postulated by Melanie Klein in 1928. However, the expressions that can be cited here lack a certain precision, and do not give in sufficient detail the respective weights of the various factors which together determine the onset of this phase. Causal effectiveness is imputed without distinction to the early and intimate connection between the epistemophilic instinct, the sadistic "desire to take possession," and "the sense of guilt aroused by the incipient Oedipus conflict" (Klein, 1928, p. 188). "This significant connection ushers in a phase of development in both sexes which is of vital importance, hitherto not sufficiently recognized. It consists of a very early identification with the mother" (p. 188–189). It seems we could attempt, at least hypothetically, to allocate the parts played by the three factors concerned. Recall that the feminine phase is preceded, at least in the boy, by an active oedipal phase contemporary with the anal-sadistic stage, the genital elements of which are disguised by the sadistic elements to such an extent that in fact the overall significance of this phase appears more sadistic than strictly libidinal. These sadistic fixations bring with them the introjection of a cruel and terrifying superego, which quite soon causes the activity to be abandoned: the more cruel the superego, the more the father is feared as a castrator. Retaliation anxiety thus brings about abandonment of the boy's initial masculine position (remember that this position, invoked in the texts of 1927, does not appear in later Kleinian thought). The part played by anal sadism is equally clear: the femininity phase "has its basis on the anal-sadistic level" but gives it a new aim, that of possessing the feces, which are identified with children. We may recognize here a variant of the second aim of the epistemophilic instinct, but at this point what is the contribution of the epistemophilic instinct as such? It is, I would argue, to keep the mother's body and its contents in the position of object. In this sense Melanie Klein remains very close to Mary Chadwick, who defined the epistemophilic instinct as a component instinct, as the characteristic of component instincts is that their connection with the object is stronger and earlier than that of the other instincts (Freud, 1905b, p. 194). Instead of turning to the father and wishing to receive a child from him, the youngster remains fixated to the interior of the mother's body, and wants to steal from it feces, children, the father's penis, etc. It seems that the maintenance of this object tie can be attributed neither to anal-sadistic impulses nor to feelings of guilt. Instead it seems logical to attribute it to an instinct whose primitive object remains the mother's body; only the instinct's aim has come under the influence of sadism.

The theory of the epistemophilic impulse is thus more suggestive than precise. The question of its instinctual nature

is still obscure. To begin with it is not sadistic; it soon unites
with the oedipal impulses, but it is not genital. It embraces
scopophilic pleasure-desire and, although the indications are
vague, seems to have a source independent of the libido properly speaking, as also of aggression, and to unite rapidly with
both. Its most obvious function in the Kleinian theory of this
period is to denote a frustration of a very particular kind, in
which the fantasy dimension shows a marked ascendancy over
the dimension of reality; for if the reality of events forms an
irreducible part of oral frustration, the frustration of the epistemophilic instinct is a purely internal phenomenon to which
the real object does not contribute at all, as the demand to know
is frustrated only because it has not the instrumental means to
express itself and thus become manifest. This purely internal
frustration provokes rage and aggression the instinctual dimension of which, though not explicitly thematized, appears
with particular clarity. It represents a purely internal factor,
very largely independent of the environment, in the intensification of sadism, which thus begins its "highest flowering." It
is certainly the first appearance in Melanie Klein's work of those
early object relationships, independent of the activity of the
erogenous zones, which Fairbairn, Guntrip, and Willy Baranger
saw as the essential part of her contribution.

The Resources of Sadism at Its Height

The high point of sadism is the cannibalistic stage.

The high point of sadism begins with the onset of the
cannibalistic phase and lasts until the end of the first anal stage.

The hesitation evinced in these two statements, advanced
in successive articles of this period in the year 1929, marks a
certain embarrassment on the part of Melanie Klein, which we
might be tempted to relate to some difficulty in adapting Abraham's schema to her uses. But in Abraham's orthodox views,
the propositions are compatible; each of the transitions involved—from total cannibalism to partial cannibalism, from
ejection to retention—expresses an increase in the tendency to
preserve the object. It seems more satisfactory then, to view this
hesitation over the moment when sadism reaches its height as

rooted in a more profound difficulty, that of holding together two clinical realities which, considered in isolation, would militate toward two very different conclusions. For in one sense maximal sadism is that of the cannibalistic stage, the most brutal and radically destructive form of sadism, while in another it is that of the first anal stage, when oral attacks, far from having disappeared, are redoubled by anal and urethral attacks that enrich the basic tone with sinister harmonics. Melanie Klein (1931) quickly settled this question of timing: "the phase of development in which sadism reaches its height begins, in my opinion, with the emergence of the oral-sadistic instincts and ends with the decline of the earlier anal stage" (p. 239). This conception is found also in *The Psycho-Analysis of Children* (Klein, 1932) and became increasingly bound up with an insistence on the developmental and psychopathological significance of the frontier between the two anal stages. But as regards the definition of sadism in terms of the intensity or of the variety of attacks, Melanie Klein's uncertainty lasted longer.

If maximal sadism is defined as that expressed in intense direct attacks, an instinctual source will be viewed as more sadistic the closer it is to the oral stage. But if maximal sadism is defined as that which deploys all the resources at hand, a given instinct will be considered more sadistic the more its manifestations are mingled with those of other forms of aggression. Even if she at times contradicted herself in details, overall Melanie Klein tended to hold simultaneously to these two not very compatible presuppositions.

The theory of urethral instincts provides the most obvious example of this relative indifference of the author of *The Psycho-Analysis of Children* to the demands of systematic coherence. She recognized the early action of these instincts as early as Trude's analysis in 1924, but the analyses of Peter and Ruth made her realize, only a few months later, the predominant role of oral sadism. It was not until 1929 that she resumed the description and interpretation of urethral instincts, still hard to distinguish from anal impulses: "in the phantasied attack on the mother's body a considerable part is played by the urethral and anal sadism which is very soon added to the oral and muscular sadism. In phantasy the excreta are transformed into dangerous weapons: wetting is regarded as cutting, stabbing, burning, drowning . . ." (Klein, 1930a, pp. 219–220). In *The Psycho-Analysis of Children* urethral sadism acquires a particular status: of all forms of sadism it is "most closely allied to oral sadism" (Klein, 1932, p. 128). In the same work Melanie Klein announces her intention of pointing out "the great importance, hitherto little recognized, of urethral sadism in the development of the child" (p. 129). The destructive fantasies in which urine is represented as a substance which burns, dissolves, corrodes, etc., are in fact guided by the symbolic equivalence of milk and urine. Such fantasies in children are a "sadistic reaction to their having been deprived of fluid by their mother and are ultimately directed against her breast (pp. 128–129) via a mechanism which is all the more interesting because it serves as a paradigm for the formation of sadistic fantasies generally. This mechanism consists in the transformation of the child's pleasure in nursing, which is withheld, into its opposite, the destruction of the breast: "As a revenge for not getting enough milk from their mother they will produce in imagination an excessive quantity of urine and so destroy her breast by flooding it or melting it away; and as a revenge for not getting 'good' milk from her they will produce a harmful fluid with which to burn up or poison her breast and the milk it contains" (p. 213).

.Apart from this directly sadistic aspect, the urethral instincts play another important role in development. They make a considerable contribution to the displacement of libidinal interest from the mother's breast onto the father's penis. Beginning with the oral desire for the penis, identified with the nipple, a more specifically urethral interest in the penis develops because it produces urine more obviously than does the female urinary organ. This interest, which according to Melanie Klein is expressed by urinary incontinence, rapidly gains the significance of a masculine position in both sexes. Thus, whether in the evolution of sadism or that of the libido, urethral cathexis immediately succeeds oral cathexis. But at the same time, and always with the same wish to bring out the importance of the manifestations of urethral sadism, Melanie Klein (1933) presents the short-lived notion of a urethral-sadistic stage between the oral-sadistic and anal-sadistic stages. Thus urethral sadism achieves a certain autonomy in relation to oral sadism, as part of an evident attempt to account for the intensification of sadism by the simultaneous activation of all its resources. But in these conditions the notion of a privileged relationship between the oral and the urethral is difficult to maintain, and the urethral again moves toward the anal, both adding their specific "powers" to the oral resources: "The data I have been able to collect from early analyses reveal that between the oral-sadistic and anal-sadistic stages there exists another stage in which urethral-sadistic tendencies make themselves felt, and that the anal and urethral tendencies are a direct continuation of the oral-sadistic one as regards the specific aim and object of attack" (Klein, 1933, p. 253). In fact it appears as if the notion of stages is here practically emptied of its content, and that the interposition of a urethral stage between the oral and anal stages has not so much a genetic sense as a sense which for lack of a more appropriate expression we may call structural; by this is meant that anal sadism is not as immediately derivable from oral frustration as is urethral sadism. Here the three "stages" straddle each other to such an extent that they tend to peak simultaneously. As we approach the turning point of 1934, then, we see the notion taking shape of a sort of pansadistic period whose organization is described no longer in terms of instinctual aims, but rather in terms deliberately emphasizing the object: "the child enters a phase in which it directs every instrument of its sadism to the one purpose of destroying its mother's body and what is contained in it" (p. 253). But it is clear that such a "phase," in which the aims of the sadistic impulses are but instruments put simultaneously at the service of destroying the object, directly anticipates the paranoid position. It is not at all easy to reconcile the existence of such a phase with the theory of a well-differentiated urethral-sadistic stage or with that of a sort of primacy of cannibalistic attacks.

Does this mean that in 1933 Melanie Klein persisted in speaking from the genetic point of view, even when it had already become a conceptual straitjacket for her? Such a thesis is perhaps tenable as far as the classical theory is concerned, but her care to maintain the idea of a fixed sequence seems to us to answer a very precise demand: side by side with the succession of zones and aims, and partly corresponding with it, she distinguishes, in "The Importance of Symbol-Formation in the Development of the Ego" (Klein, 1930a), two clearly contrasted moments within the peak phase of sadism. The first is that of brutal sadism, naked and undisguised; it appears that in Melanie Klein's opinion all fantasied cannibalistic attacks are of this type. The second moment is that of a sadism that is at once refined and insidious, even hypocritical; it is characterized by processes at a greater remove from the imaginary destruction of the object. But it would be wrong to think that this sadism, anal and urethral in essence, is less intense than that of cannibalism. Kleinian theory was at this point sufficiently liberated from any influence alien to its own demands that it could forget completely Abraham's theory that the oral-sadistic stage, centered on total cannibalistic incorporation, is more destructive than the following stage. "The Psycho-Analysis of Children" put forward the idea that sadistic attacks of the second type arose from sadism at a higher level than that of brutal attacks; this affirmation was explicitly supported by metapsychological considerations which left no doubt as to Melanie Klein's evaluation of the phenomena. "In addition to the quantitative increase which the child's sadism undergoes at every point of origin, qualitative changes take place in it and serve to heighten it still further" (Klein, 1932, p. 132). From this point of view, it may be said, sadism is not really at its height until it is in possession of all its resources, when the urethral and anal elements have furnished their contribution of fantasies "whose number, variety and richness are all but inexhaustible" (p. 132). It is therefore essential for the theory of sadism at its height that the system of 1932 maintain the idea of a fixed genetic sequence enabling the distinction between the two forms of sadism to be based on the chronological succession of their fixation points. And if the theory of insidious sadism is so important to Melanie Klein, it is because it is a discovery whose clinical importance, on which she was to insist for the next thirty years, seemed to her to be paramount.

Brutal sadism uses teeth and jaws above all for imaginary attacks that consist of devouring, tearing to pieces, cutting up. When feces or urine appear on the scene it is to dirty or burn the object. Insidious or refined sadism uses these substances as magical and mysterious agents of destruction: "In the first part of this phase, . . . where open violence reigns, excrements are regarded as instruments of direct assault; but later they acquire significance as substances of an explosive or poisonous kind" (Klein, 1933, p. 132). The release of these fantasies is essential for the understanding of paranoia and persecution mania; paranoiac distrust can be explained by the projection onto the object of the insidious sadism of the subject, who fears to receive from his persecutor that which he has inflicted on him in unconscious fantasy. Thanks to this discovery, it becomes possible to assign precise fixation points to the two groups of psychoses which show elements of persecution most clearly:

> The first part of the phase when sadism is at its height is that in which the attacks are conceived of as being made by violence. This I have come to recognize as the fixation-point in dementia praecox. In the second part of this phase the attacks are imagined as being made by poisoning, and the urethral and anal-sadistic impulses predominate. This I believe to be the fixation-point in paranoia. [Klein, 1930, p. 232]

The analyses of John and Dick made it possible to delve more deeply into the kind of facts which were taken up afresh in later Kleinian theory under the heading of projective identification. The fantasies of John, who had a severe intellectual inhibition, involved dangerous animals against which he had to struggle unceasingly for fear they might destroy the entire world. These animals represented the feces of the child himself, which in imagination he put into his mother's body in order to hurt and poison her and to destroy the contents of her body. Fearing revenge, the child was terrified at the prospective presence, within his own body, of poisoned excrements the object of his attack might introduce magically and secretly into his bodily orifices. He was afraid not only of his own excrement but of the attacks the introjected object might carry out within him. This fact makes it possible to verify and reinterpret the theory of paranoia as Abraham had taken it from Stärcke and van Ophuijsen. It was hard to understand, according to this conception, how the fecal lump could be seen by the paranoiac as the penis of his persecutor. The discovery of insidious sadism enabled this point to be cleared up: the presence of dangerous excrement in his intestines is feared by anyone who has fantasized about magically putting his own poisoned excrement into his mother's anus; anal introjection is felt as a destructive invasion by anyone who has fantasized the destruction of the object by a similar invasion. It is now easier to understand why the paranoiac can neither expel the internal persecutor nor retain it; every time he evacuates it violently he fears its insidious return, more dangerous the more violently he has forced it out.

The Fantasy of the Combined Parents and the Height of Sadism

The theory of the two modes of sadism has made us familiar with the idea that the height of sadism does not coincide exactly with the earliest of its phases. Examination of the nature of the object of sadistic impulses confirms this thesis. According to Melanie Klein's ideas between 1927 and 1932, maximum sadism is aimed neither at the mother's breast nor at the mother herself, but at the two parents joined in coitus. To be more precise, two themes that were at first independent were fused in 1929, giving rise to the discovery of the unified or combined image of the parents, now designated by a special term (*vereinigten Eltern* and later, in texts written directly in English, *the combined parents*). The first theme concerns the development of aggression against the mother, the description of oral-sadistic attacks against the breast, then against the mother or the interior of her body. The second consists of the enumeration, increasingly detailed as the material collected by the play technique accumulated, of the variants of the sadistic conception of coitus and in the increasingly firm interpretation of the cruel aspect of the fantasy image of the primal scene in terms of fulfillment of desire.

The idea that the child's aggression aims at the breast before aiming at the mother as a whole object is not typical of Melanie Klein's early ideas. We do indeed find, around 1927, the idea that the cannibalistic stage implies biting the breast (Klein, 1927a, p. 170), but this is more an allusion to Abraham's ideas than the spontaneous development of a personal theme. It was only in 1932 that the idea was clearly affirmed that the first object is not the mother but the breast.[5] But before this idea really emerged, the Kleinian concept of the first object relations had already developed considerably. This development has scarcely been noticed up to now, and the reason can easily be guessed: in the texts of this period, though Melanie Klein did not explicitly state this, there is an appreciable difference between the evolution of sadism and that of the libido. From 1924 onward, in accordance with a conception universally recognized in psychoanalysis, Melanie Klein considered the breast to be the first object of the libido; her originality is seen in the theory that the frustration of weaning turns the child away from the breast and toward the father's penis. This theory has as a corollary that the first oedipal position is female in both sexes[6] and is based on a direct transference of the sucking impulses to the incipient genital impulses. As far as the object is concerned, the libido passes from the breast to the penis before attaching itself to the *person* of the parent of the opposite sex. But the sequence of objects of aggression is very different: there is nothing to indicate that Melanie Klein thought before 1929 that the frustrating breast is the object of sadistic attacks by the baby at the time of weaning.[7] Aggression is explored only in the context of oedipal rivalry, and through the content of anxiogenic fantasies which mirror it. This aggression against the rival, male or female, of the first stages of the oedipus complex is first described in terms of castration by biting, of theft or destruction of the children contained in the mother's body, or of the violent extirpation of the feces contained in her intestine. In the first texts presenting the play technique, these attacks are still described in very realistic terms, as aimed at the

[5] Before 1934, in the early stages, objects are "represented by their organs," between which there are multiple symbolic equations, but no passage designates the breast as a primary object of sadism.

[6] It is only in "Early Stages of the Oedipus Complex" (Klein, 1928) that we find the short-lived theory of a first masculine stage in the boy's oedipal development (See Chapter 3).

[7] Even in 1929 it is the mother that is meant, not the breast: "The oral frustration which turns the indulgent 'good mother' into the 'bad mother' stimulates his sadism" (Klein, 1929a, p. 214).

body, exactly visualized, of the mother as a complete person and the rival of the daughter, who herself fears very definite attacks on her own body; Rita feared that a mouse or a *Bützen* (genital organ) might come through the window and bite off her own *Bützen*. During a session, Trude hit her analyst in the stomach, clearly declaring her intention of opening it in order to remove the excrement. The internal or introjected character of the object which is the victim of the attacks, and whose vengeance is feared, is almost considered a defensive illusion, a disguise which can be shed as the analysis progresses:

> children begin to distinguish between the 'pretence' mother and the real mother and between the wooden baby-doll and the live baby brother. They then firmly insist that they wanted to do this or that injury to the toy-baby only—the real baby, they say, of course they love. Only when very powerful and long-standing resistances have been overcome do children realize that their aggressive acts were directed against the *real* objects. [Klein, 1926, p. 137]

It is not until 1928 that the idea appears that the first object of sadism is (1) the mother as a libidinal object and (2) the inside of her body as represented in fantasy. Even then these two views of the object are not linked with each other. The first is introduced only in reply to the question of why the superego of four-year-olds coincides with "an unreal, phantastic image of parents who devour, cut and bite"; it is because the one-year-old child "desires to destroy the libidinal object by biting, devouring and cutting it" (Klein, 1928, p. 187). As for the important discovery of the fact that it is the inside of the mother's body that sadism attacks, it occurs only in the process of describing and defining the epistemophilic instinct (p. 188). These two views merge because the object attacked does not coincide with a real object of perception but with an unreal object whose internal character this time is clearly stated: it is the mother as a bag of skin enveloping and containing the partial objects, "the scene of all sexual processes and developments" (p. 188). Here we must distinguish clearly two notions which the later development of Kleinian thought was to confuse, but which were still differentiated before 1934: (1) the primary object of sadism, which is in a way suggested by the epistemophilic instinct, is the interior of the mother's body, and what is aimed at is the contents more than the container as such; (2) this "object" is obviously a fantastically distorted image, an object of imagination rather than of perception. But the words "internal" in the expression "internal object" and "interior" in "interior of the mother's body or belly," though similar, are not yet synonymous. The only relationship here is one of simple common sense: it is precisely because they are internal that the contents of the mother's body are not visible and so are represented by fantasies rather than perceptions.

As Melanie Klein became better acquainted with the world of early fantasies, she realized increasingly that this interior of the mother's belly, the primary object of the epistemophilic instinct, is a prototype of all external reality. To be more exact, the imaginary contents of the mother's belly are prototypes of all external objects, while the body containing them is the prototype of the world: "The sadistic phantasies directed against the inside of her body constitute the first and basic relation to the outside world and to reality" (Klein, 1930a, p. 221). A few months later, the first passage in which the breast reappears, this time in the position of primary object, makes it clear: "In the earliest reality of the child it is no exaggeration to say that the world is a breast and a belly which is filled with dangerous objects, dangerous because of the child's own impulse to attack them" (1930b, p. 233). There is then, if we stick to the development of the object relationship as guided by the epistemophilic instinct, an increase in sadism due to the evolution of the object itself: if sadism as presented in the 1929 texts is directed from the beginning against an object which is perceived to be the whole existing world, it is understandable that sadism, already defined as maximal as regards both its instinctual energies and the resources at its disposal, should be so also by reason of the characteristics of its primary object.

Parallel to the evolution just described, the theory of the primal scene was gradually being transformed. We know that it was already of primary importance in the proto-Kleinian system; there it was designated as the core of the masturbatory fantasies whose sublimated activity give rise to talents, interests, play, etc. But the question then was only to describe, along classical Freudian lines, the sadistic conception of coitus as the child's mistake in interpretation, and the aggression aroused in the boy by the sight as directed chiefly against the father as rival. The first change in this image—but again in an isolated case, and without the observed fact being taken generally—came when Melanie Klein discovered that in Erna's eyes the manifestations of tenderness exchanged by her parents were intended only to persecute her by making her envious; such an observation implies that the parents are seen by the child as allied against her, which, according to the logic of Kleinian ideas, presupposes that prior to this they have been attacked together in the child's fantasies—as all fear is the mirror image of an aggressive fantasy. But this is not stated explicitly. A modification easier to relate to the chronology of Melanie Klein's discoveries came in 1927; the primal scene was conceived as sadistic under the dominant sadism of the child. But the suggested relationship was still conceived in vague terms and was still situated within the Freudian conception of mistaken interpretation; the child whose libido is closely linked with aggression and who desires coitus in a cannibalistic or anal form imagines that his parents practice it in such forms, the only ones he can imagine:

> We know from Freud that there is some unconscious knowledge which the child obtains, apparently in a phylogenetic way. To this belongs the knowledge about parental intercourse, birth of children, etc.; but it is of a rather vague and confused nature. According to the oral- and anal-sadistic stage which he is going through himself, intercourse comes to mean to the child a performance in which eating, cooking, exchange of feces and sadistic acts of every kind (beating, cutting, and so on) play the principal part. [Klein, 1927a, pp. 175–176]

We might thus say that this is a question of projection, not in the psychoanalytical sense of the term, but in the sense in which in psychology we speak of projection to denote processes such as this: "The subject perceives his surroundings and responds according to his own interests, aptitudes, habits, long-standing or transient emotional states, expectations, wishes, etc. . . . a particular businessman sees all objects in terms of what can be bought and sold ('occupational distortion'); a good-humoured person is inclined to view things 'through rose-tinted spectacles'; and so on" (Laplanche and Pontalis, 1967, p. 350).

Schaulust, the wish to see and the pleasure in seeing, is directed to the primal scene. When the epistemophilic instinct follows upon this "voyeurism," it concerns events and sexual processes supposedly occurring within the mother's body. This probably includes the primal scene, but that is not explicitly stated. Not until 1928 are we presented the fantasy in which the child expects to find, within the mother's body, the father's penis, incorporated there during coitus (Klein, 1928, p. 190). Everything was then ready for the unified image of the parents to be thematized (1929a, p. 213). Sadism is aimed at the destruction or theft, within the mother's body, not only of the feces and the children but also of the father's penis. Thus, none of the objects cathected by the child in the course of its development is spared by its aggressive impulses. The part objects of oral libido, the breast and the penis, and the more or less whole objects ("represented by their organs") of the first oedipal stages, are attacked simultaneously by a sadism from which nothing escapes—even less so because the mother's body is equated with the world in its entirety. Sadism is thus at its highest point when the object relation becomes more antioedipal than oedipal properly speaking. In fact, whether in the direct complex or in its inverted form, the sadistic attacks on one parent are accompanied by love and tenderness for the object of incestuous impulses. The child thus maintains a positive, encouraging, and reassuring relationship with the parent whose love matters most to him at a given moment. He has a recourse and protection against the imaginary attacks of the rival. The attack of the combined parents, however, wipes out this recourse almost completely. Against them the child is alone; he can find support from neither of the real objects, but only from the internal image of the "good" protective parents whose presence, in this context dominated by sadism, remains at least doubtful. According to the logic of the fear of vengeance, the child who attacks all his objects simultaneously fears them, like the young hero of Ravel's opera *L'enfant et les Sortilèges* (Klein, 1929a), all at once. The most intense sadism corresponds with the most terrifying and paralyzing anxiogenic situation, that which fragments and distorts the ego of the psychotic child. Detailed study of the theory of instincts reveals its close relation to one of Melanie Klein's most important discoveries, that of the specific features of infantile psychoses.

The discovery of the height of sadism and its triple genesis in the register of its origins, resources, and objects is certainly Melanie Klein's most decisive contribution to the theory of instincts. This is shown even more clearly by contrast, when we consider her indifference and conciseness when she treats of the later stages, generally. It is thus obvious that there is no Kleinian theory of the second anal stage as a phase of libidinal and aggressive development. It is never described except as a period of decrease of sadism; it remains outside the paroxysmal peak of destructive impulses, and the only distinction accorded it is drawn from its opposition to earlier stages rather than from its nature and its libidinal activity proper. In this Melanie Klein remains a disciple of Abraham, and goes even further than her master in her insistence on the antagonism between the two anal stages. This attitude is taken to such lengths that in all Melanie Klein's work not a single primary instinctual element—erotic or aggressive—is attributed to this phase; nor is a single sentence devoted to the sexual aim of retention or to the acquisitive instinct. What all other authors consider late anal impulses she generally places under the heading of overcompensatory strategies or reaction-formations intended to check and overcome the brutal or insidious sadism of the first anal stage. The second oral stage, then, is merely a stage of reaction. It occurs under the pressure of anxiety which could not be dissipated in the previous stage by use of the ejection mechanism. It is characterized by a transformation of the anxiogenic objects whereby their terrifying nature is considerably reduced. It is marked by the development of reaction-formations—distaste, order, cleanliness, pity—and by the quest for love and approval from the real objects. Finally, as we know, it marks the entry of neurosis into the psychological world; the specific neurosis whose fixation point is found here is obsessional neurosis, later to be described precisely as a reaction to an underlying psychosis, its function being to bind and master it.

Of the late stages of the oedipus complex Melanie Klein says practically nothing; at most she speaks of them only to define her position on what other writers have said. Thus, Karen Horney (1924) had distinguished two sources of penis envy. One, of very early provenance, was said to correspond to voyeuristic and exhibitionistic cathexes—that is, in Freudian terms, to one of those component instincts which do not join the mainstream of sexuality until rather late. The other, coming at a later stage, was described as a reaction to the disappointment of the oedipus complex. According to Ernest Jones (1927), whose ideas were similar, "it is the privation resulting from the continued disappointment at never being able to share the penis in coitus with the father or thereby to obtain a baby, that reactivates the girl's early wish to have a penis of her own". The "deuterophallic" phase is thus a regression to a "protophallic" phase, and the actual oedipal phase comes between the two. Confronted with such speculations, Melanie Klein's attitude remains vague, at least as far as explicit pronouncements are concerned. The underlying intention, to oppose the Freudian theory of an oedipus complex set off in the little girl by penis envy, could not but gain her adherence. But the forms in which this theory is expressed scarcely coincide with the experience gained in the psychoanalysis of children, and suggest a genetic model difficult to reconcile with the one Melanie Klein devised for herself. It is hard to see how to place in the sequence described by Melanie Klein—early oedipus complex, penis envy, later oedipal stages—the sequence suggested by Horney and Jones—early phallic phase, direct oedipus complex, second phallic phase. That is probably why *The Psycho-Analysis of Children* merely quotes these authors, taking no definite position on their hypotheses and noting simply that they have common preoccupations. All this is very remote from what really mattered to Melanie Klein.

3. Infantile Psychosis

Abraham's genetic concept was not only a theory of the development of the normal child; it was also the basis of a psychopathological theory of the fixation points of the various neuroses and psychoses, whereby each isolated phase was seen as corresponding to the fixation point of a well-determined clinical entity. We can distinguish Abraham's global intention from the concrete modality of its detailed realization. The principal motive of his attempt at systematization was the wish to solve the problem of "choice of neurosis" by exclusively genetic considerations, assigning to each phase of normal development the fixation point of one disease and one disease alone. Detailed correspondences between one stage and one affliction were not accepted in their entirety by Melanie Klein; in particular, until 1934 she was completely uninterested in depression and melancholia, conditions almost never found clinically in children despite the initial suppositions of her master (see letter of 7/10/23 in Freud and Abraham, 1907–1926). By contrast, she takes care to indicate the fixation point of schizophrenia and on this point diverges from Abraham; instead of connecting it as he did with an oral sucking fixation (which Abraham had advanced to explain psychotic withdrawal in terms of autoerotism) she based it on a cannibalistic fixation, thus assigning it the place he had accorded to manic-depressive psychosis. Until 1932 she remained, with this single exception, Abraham's faithful disciple in matters of psychopathology.

She did not, however, immediately support his psychopathological theories; rather, she reached them by an idiosyncratic route passing through clinical discoveries made in the practice of child analysis, a route unforeseen in Abraham's work. It was her clinical experience which governed her attitude to the theories of her predecessors. She hardly ever discussed and rarely used Abraham's contributions to psychopathology, but that was because prior to 1929 she was treating neurotic children she regarded as such. The disturbances they suffered went back to the early stages of the oedipus conflict, which she considered until 1934 to be the core of neurosis. Abraham's ideas were ill suited to support this approach, as they linked neuroses to relatively later stages, while the play technique made it possible to reveal their roots in the oral stage. It was not until

Melanie Klein was confronted in her practice with the technical and theoretical problems of infantile psychosis that she was obliged to seek out concepts that would allow her to master them. Some she found in Abraham, whose discoveries she referred to increasingly, but a large number she had to invent herself. Melanie Klein's most original contributions to psychoanalytic theory between 1927 and 1932 all proceeded, directly or indirectly, from her encounter with infantile psychosis, which related above all to the peak phase of sadism. The facts which she then discovered, and which she was the first to describe (not only in the history of psychoanalysis but also in that of psychiatry), as well as the classification and explanatory theories she suggested, made possible and largely anticipated all of the progress made in child psychopathology over the last half century. The resistance of child psychiatrists to psychoanalysis and the reticence of many analysts in the face of what they considered an arbitrary and speculative system have masked this historical fact. The controversies of 1943 had the effect of isolating the Kleinians for a long period, and the attitude adopted toward their contributions has sometimes taken on the nature of a conspiracy of silence. For some years now, however, we have had a better understanding of the psychopathological scope of Melanie Klein's work (see Giovacchini, 1972). In what follows it will be established that she had clearly formulated in 1932 almost all of the ideas which have transformed child psychopathology since 1945, including those which have asserted themselves most recently.

It was in 1929 that the question of psychosis was mentioned for the first time in her writings. This fact can be related to her analyses of Egon and Dick, which helped her gradually to an understanding of the world of the psychotic. In the first stage, Egon's treatment showed her a case in which play and free association was so inhibited that there was not sufficient material to interpret, while contact remained cold and distant so that nothing, neither symbolic images nor manifestations of emotion, enabled the analyst to intervene. In a second stage, the case of Dick, a mute and backward four-year-old child, enabled her to apply to an extreme case solutions that had succeeded with Egon. A child of about ten, Egon was a brilliant scholar, whose disturbances had not been apparent before the age of five; he had thus been able to acquire knowledge that in all probability had made his treatment easier. Although he had a nucleus of schizophrenia, it appeared in a form and under conditions that were favorable to its elucidation. His analysis was slow and difficult, and at first took a course that disconcerted Melanie Klein; the analysis lasted about two years and consisted of about 425 sessions. It was conducted between 1927 and 1928, only a few months after the interruption of Erna's treatment, which between 1924 and 1926 had enabled Melanie Klein to explore the nucleus of paranoia underlying a symptomatology of an openly obsessional type. Recalling a quarter of a century later the period of her first discoveries, she traced back to Erna's analysis her initial discovery of infantile psychosis. This child was "undoubtedly paranoic" (Klein, 1955b, p. 137); as Melanie Klein tells us, her case

> much helped to prepare the ground for a number of conclusions which I presented to the Tenth International Psycho-Analytical Congress in 1927, in particular the view that the early superego, built up when oral-sadistic impulses and phantasies are at their height, underlies psychosis—a view which two years later I developed by stressing the importance of oral-sadism for schizophrenia. [p. 135]

It is clear that here Melanie Klein is under a retrospective illusion, for "Early Stages of the Oedipus Conflict" (Klein, 1928) makes no reference whatever to the problems of psychosis. We must note, however, the continuity established by this passage between the analysis of Erna and the discoveries of 1929. This gradual transition was doubtless facilitated by Egon's treatment, which enabled her to confirm what had been learned in Erna's analysis, and also to adapt the technique to the particular need for making contact with psychotics, which in 1927 was a new experience for Melanie Klein. This explains the fact that when Dick was referred to her she was capable of finding very quickly the proper technical attitude, and to work out in a few weeks the fundamental concepts of her theory of infantile psychosis.

It was enough to collect together the intuitions aroused by the experience of the last five years, and to organize them, for this discovery to take shape. It was probably the most important discovery to date regarding infantile psychosis—the existence in the young child of forms of psychosis irreducible to those observed in adults. These appear to be determined by the failure of the ego to master sadism at its height by effective defense mechanisms; they are very frequent, and can easily be taken for backwardness. Beginning in 1929, Melanie Klein set forth eight theses.

● *Thesis 1. "Schizophrenia . . . is a far more general phenomenon in childhood than is usually supposed" (Klein, 1932, p. 135).*

A number of converging factors explain why this is so little taken into account. The first, and probably the most important, is that the child and the adult are not judged in the same way. Social standards weigh differently—sometimes more, sometimes less heavily—on the child than they do on the adult. In child clinics, deep disturbances in adaptation are hard to differentiate from episodic disturbances with no pathological significance. Many psychotic symptoms are easily attributed to naughtiness or, in other instances, to docility on the child's part. In analysis with Melanie Klein, six-year-old George was absorbed during the sessions in an endlessly repeated game. The chief of a band of hunters and wild animals, he was in perpetual battle with enemies also helped by ferocious beasts. Victorious, he killed his enemies and ate their animals, but new enemies inevitably rose, and the battle had to continue and the game begin again ceaselessly. This child, his analyst tells us, suffered not only from a serious neurosis; he also had paranoid symptoms. Entrenched in his fantasies, he was completely cut off from reality; he thought himself constantly surrounded by magicians, witches, etc. In this sense he was certainly psychotic. But to those around him such behavior, even if regarded as somewhat bizarre, was not usually considered pathological; for that the parents would have had to have more information and intuition than is usual. We may add that George, like Erna and a large number of children, did nothing to assist in his diagnosis: conscious of the strange and almost unbelievable nature of his reasons for anxiety, he remained absolutely silent about them, and had never confessed them to his family. And in 1929, it should be remembered, there was even less of a tendency to consult a psychiatrist or psychologist than exists at present. Thus, we often find in adult patients evidence of genuine psychoses suffered by them as children without their families having thought for a minute of consulting a doctor, even among those without disadvantaged backgrounds. Everything conspires, then, to conceal the frequency of infantile psychoses: the family's tolerance of pathology for which they are often at least partly responsible; the lack of psychological knowledge found in most people; and the particular lack of insight found generally in the parents of psychotic children.

● *Thesis 2. The clinical picture of infantile psychosis is sui generis.*

Irreducible to that of adult psychoses, this picture is characterized by the blurred and multiform nature of its symptomatology. As Melanie Klein (1930b) noted, "the diagnostic features of psychosis in childhood are essentially different from those of the classical psychoses" (p. 234). This is due to the nature of the child, a developing being, and to the functioning of his psychical equipment, in which fantasy and play are predominant; diagnoses are therefore made with greatest certainty using criteria that are "developmental" and concerned with play: fixation in the themes of play and activity at a stage which would normally have been passed ("I would say that the most sinister feature in a child of four would be the undiminished activity of systems of phantasy characteristic of a child of one year" (Klein, 1930b, p. 234)); clinical signs of backwardness; complete absorption in play and fantasy; extreme and "unreal" fierceness or goodness of characters in symbolic play; the stereotyped and repetitive character of such play; or complete absence of play or activity. But usually adults fail to notice such signs, and only the child analyst using the play technique can really establish the diagnosis of psychosis; the most characteristic signs of infantile psychosis are of such a nature that they appear completely only in the playroom.

Although the general features of the psychotic structure are the same in adults and children, in the latter their external manifestations are much more difficult to identify. Ideas of persecution and hypochondriacal fears readily take on the appearance of simple expressions of distaste or minor indispositions. Intellectual or academic inhibition is taken for laziness: "an incapacity to concentrate on any occupation, silly behaviour and talking nonsense do not strike us as so remarkable in children" (Klein, 1930b, p. 234). Catatonic obedience or negativism pass unnoticed or are dealt with by inappropriate educational methods. Hyperkinesis, stereotypy, and mannerisms are hard to distinguish from exuberance, minor compulsions varying from the normal, and play attitudes. Insofar, then, as classical psychiatry describes psychoses in terms of loss of contact with reality, definitions must be revised to meet the needs of a clinical approach to children, whose relationship with reality is totally different from that of the adult: the child lives in a world much more infiltrated by fantasies, in a physical world lacking any necessary regularity, and in a human world deformed by projections. "The foundations of reality relations in early childhood are of an entirely different order" (Klein, 1930b, p. 233), as the normal child shows behavior which in the adult would indicate psychosis. It is impossible to diagnose child psychosis without examining the structure of the fantasies: the content of anxiogenic situations, the type of defense mobilized against them. "In the earliest reality of the child it is no exaggeration to say that the world is a breast and a belly which is filled with dangerous objects, dangerous because of the child's own impulse to attack them. . . . for the psychotic the world is still a belly peopled with dangerous objects" (p. 233).

● *Thesis 3. The classification of infantile psychoses must have as its criterion the nature of the defense mechanisms brought into play.*

Melanie Klein does not consider submerging all the different forms of infantile psychoses in a general picture, too imprecisely defined. While stressing the existence of features common to infantile psychoses, contrasting them with adult psychoses, she nevertheless makes a sharp distinction between the forms she calls paranoiac and those to which she assigns the names schizophrenia, dementia praecox, and paraphrenia. The relationship with reality has only a limited interest if we try to make it, from an "adultocentric" point of view, the criterion of differential diagnosis between infantile psychosis and neurosis or normality; but it can be used in another way. It can be evaluated on the basis of forms of activity proper to children. Between the schizophrenic or paraphrenic child incapable of playing in the proper sense of the word and the normal child capable of multiplying his play scenarios and changing identifications, while remaining relatively "close to reality" in the choice of themes, are many intermediate stages. Certain paranoiac children recognize reality only in the context of their imagined experience of persecution (others deny reality in favor of the exclusive representation of fulfilled desires), whereas the neurotic child can recognize only a reality that is opposed to his desires. From this point of view both the ability to recognize all or part of external reality and the emotional value of what is recognized (exclusively frustrating, exclusively persecuting, or more diversified) are signs revealing not some inexplicable anchorage in a solid, reassuring reality but the type of defensive strategy used by the child against feelings of anxiety. Melanie Klein in fact observes that the anxiogenic situation is about the same, apart from its intensity, in most children, whether neurotic or psychotic (and among the latter, whether schizophrenic or paraphrenic).[8] The only things that vary are the mechanisms used to face the fear caused by this common fantasy, and the degree of elaboration and disguise of the earliest contents. The problem of "choice of disease" is thus posed in such terms that in order to solve it we must be able to cite either quantitative factors or factors involving the specific defense mechanisms used.

[8] The term *paraphrenic* is ambiguous; it is impossible to determine whether for Melanie Klein it designates schizophrenia alone or the group comprising both schizophrenia and paranoia (see Laplanche and Pontalis, 1967, p. 299).

Without excluding economic considerations (the two solutions are not incompatible), Melanie Klein chose the second path in 1929. Reporting Dick's case, she affirmed a theory which from this point on became central to her ideas: the quality of the relationship of the subject with external reality depends on the quality of his relationship with the introjected objects. And as the more or less disturbing nature of these objects depends on the projections of the subject himself and their more or less sadistic character, the relationship of a subject with external reality expresses in the long run his relationship with his own sadistic impulses. At the beginning of his analysis, Dick could not play because "the ego's excessive and premature defense against sadism checks the establishing of a relation to reality and the development of phantasy-life" (Klein, 1930a, p. 232). Against the "dread of what would be done to him (particularly by the father's penis) after he had penetrated into the mother's body" (p. 224), his only recourse was an extreme defense consisting of blocking every aggressive act on his part, and stopping all symbolic elaboration of his sadism. He then could not interest himself in reality for fear of destroying and being destroyed in return—hence the autism of his play and his object relationships. Erna gave to reality an attention that was sustained but completely falsified by distrust because, in accordance with the types of sadistic attack seen in the first anal stage, she was afraid of being in her turn the victim of insidious anal and urethral attacks—corrosive urine, explosive feces, poisonous gases magically and secretly introduced into the bodily orifices—of the sort she had directed against her mother's body. She needed, then, to keep constant watch on a reality always imagined as menacing, and all the more disturbing because it appeared harmless. Thus, relatively late infantile psychosis can be assimilated to paranoia. It goes back, as Abraham had established, to a predominant fixation at the first anal stage, reinterpreted in terms of insidious sadistic attacks. Dick's "schizophrenia" went back to an earlier fixation at the cannibalistic stage—contrary to the conclusions of Abraham, who thought he discerned predominant fixations at the sucking stage and so situated melancholia, the study of which was the starting point of his genetic system, at the oral-sadistic level. But whereas Abraham was above all anxious to make a nosological entity correspond with the activity of a precise group of impulses, Melanie Klein was concerned mainly with making distinctions among defensive strategies. This insistence on defense mechanisms is related to her insistence on the overlapping of stages and the interweaving of "all the resources of sadism." If there is no basic difference between the sadistic attacks in Dick's fantasies and those of Erna or Rita, the principle of differentiation among psychopathological organizations must be sought in the ego and its defenses. So in this unexpected way Melanie Klein, who had chosen to explore, by means of the play technique, the deepest layers of the unconscious at a time when most psychoanalysts were turning to the psychology of the ego and its defense mechanisms, finally found a route to the study of these operations. Thus, by a paradox not at all mysterious, it was she who, after Freud, contributed most to the theory of defense mechanisms: projection, reparation, splitting, etc.

As far as the psychopathology of infantile psychoses is concerned, the application of this thesis makes it possible to distinguish the two main forms: in paranoiac psychoses a projective relationship with reality predominates, while schizophrenic psychoses are accompanied by a retreat into the world of fantasy and play, a flight from reality, and at times the suspension of all interest in the outside world. Extending this notion of schizophrenic psychosis she presented one of her most decisive discoveries, in the form of the following thesis, which she was the first, and for a long time, with her British disciples, the only one to support.

● *Thesis 4. Infantile psychosis often masquerades as backwardness.*

The relationship between psychosis and intellectual defect had indeed often been observed before Melanie Klein. But this was in the context of adult psychopathology, and the link was considered terminal and fatal: according to Kraepelin, dementia praecox inevitably ended in a state of mental deficiency. Here the relationship is reversed. The link is initial, and psychotic anxiety comes first, blocking from the outset the development of affective and cognitive relations with reality. In the field of infantile psychopathology, no one had realized until then that conditions of backwardness could have any etiology but an organic one. Melanie Klein thus made a radical innovation, anticipating by approximately twenty years a viewpoint which became familiar to many during discussions of the work of Kanner.

● *Thesis 5. Infantile psychoses involving mental defect arise from a disturbance of symbolic thought.*

On this point too the scope of Melanie Klein's contribution is decisive, and it is perhaps the point on which her innovation is most radical. Today we are so sated with lectures on "the symbolic order," symbolic function, symbolic logic, etc. that we find it hard to imagine that there was a time when such terms were not much used. And yet Littré's *Dictionary* gives only the religious, rhetorical, iconographic, and chemical meanings of "symbol." We should remember that the works which have made popular the use of these notions come from three main sources. The first is Ernst Cassirer's *The Philosophy of Symbolic Forms* (1923–1929), the three volumes of which are exactly contemporary with Melanie Klein's contributions. The first of them, on language, was published in 1923, the year of publication of the two proto-Kleinian articles setting out the very first conceptions of symbolism which made possible the discovery of the play technique; the third, on the phenomenology of knowledge, appeared in 1929, a scant year before Melanie Klein's "The Importance of Symbol-Formation in the Development of the Ego." It is in this third volume, which she could not have known while writing her article, that we find the well-known pages devoted to the "pathology of symbolic consciousness." But we should remember that these developments concern only the pathology of mental defect, and that Cassirer is interested in the loss of the power of evocation and relation to the symbol; we shall see that Melanie Klein's discovery has an exactly opposite meaning.

The second source is the linguistic theories arising indirectly from the teachings of Ferdinand de Saussure. But here again it must be made clear that Saussure's definition of the

linguistic sign (not the symbol) went completely unnoticed during that author's lifetime. In 1929 only his few disciples in
Geneva and the researchers of the Prague Linguistic Circle, still
completely unknown, knew and referred to the *Course in General
Linguistics* (Saussure, 1915). Their work reached only specialists
until Claude Lévi-Strauss brought it to the notice of the edu-
cated public, setting up their method as a model for the hu-
manities generally. Use of the notion of the symbol appears
more characteristic of authors inspired by linguistics than of
the linguists themselves.

The third source is the work of Jean Piaget on the function
of the symbol. But his *La Formation du Symbole chez L'enfant* dates
from 1945, and interest in symbolic activities in the fields of
genetic and comparative psychology appears largely inspired
by Cassirer. Piaget did indeed take an earlier interest in symbolism, but this was at the time when he belonged to the Swiss
Society of Psycho-Analysis and took part in psychoanalytic con-
gresses; the symbolism of which he spoke at the time was the
symbolism Freud discovered and wrote about (Piaget, 1923).
Thus, in the field of the anthropology of symbols as in various
fields of psychology, Freud was the first to draw attention to
an order of realities that before had been largely neglected.

When Melanie Klein related the peculiarities of infantile
psychosis linked with mental defect to disturbances in symbol
formation, then, she did more than make an important clinical
discovery; at the same time she introduced the modern notion
of the symbol by adding a cognitive connotation to the concept
Freud had developed. In fact she knew no definition of symbolism other than Freud's; the nomenclature of typical images,
constituting a code directly available to the unconscious, the
phylogenetic origin of which was fairly generally admitted. Ferenczi, Jones, and she herself six years earlier had tried to describe its ontogenesis. But the idea of a relation between
unconscious symbolism and spoken language remained vague,
marginal, and at times a bit outlandish—Sperber's speculations
(1915), Freud's "The Antithetical Meaning of Primal Words"
(1910a); in any case it was still purely speculative. Melanie
Klein's originality was to relate Dick's inability to produce symbolic play and his inability to retain and correctly manipulate

verbal symbols as disturbances based on a more fundamental distortion of a function of symbolic representation the nature of which had yet to be discovered. She was all the more willing to undertake this search as the question was not new to her.

Recall that in proto-Kleinian theory symbolism was understood as an essentially libidinal process constituting the cathexis of external reality and the subjective operations relating to it, whether effective or cognitive. When in 1929 Melanie Klein took up the question of symbol formation, she cited her earlier theories as a basis for her discoveries regarding anxiety and sadism. She conceived this as a cumulative process; there was no question of giving up any of her conceptions of 1923. She simply added new data; "I can now add to what I said then and state that, side by side with the libidinal interest, it is the anxiety arising in the phase that I have described [sadism at its height] which sets going the mechanism of identification" (Klein, 1930a, p. 220).[9] But this presentation of the changes she was making presupposes the logical compatibility of the 1923 theory with that of 1929, an idea it is difficult to concur in. In the conceptions of 1923, the libidinal theory of symbol formation made it possible to reply to the question, How does the baby's libido come to attach itself to objects? But apart from the theory of an initial preobject state, the libidinal theory of 1923 is now of little interest. The problem it was intended to solve is no longer significant. The change from a conception in which libido is the motive factor to one in which this part is played by anxiety implies giving up the theory of primal narcissism and of an initial preobject state. In fact, in Melanie Klein's thought—and even earlier in that of Abraham, according to whom this affect appears at the oral-sadistic stage—anxiety by definition implies an object relation (apart from an important exception to which we shall return) and, more precisely, a sadistic attack on the object. To make anxiety a factor in symbol formation is to make the process begin at a time when object relationships are already formed. At the same time the entire meaning of the Kleinian

[9] This is not the identification of a subject with the libidinal "object," but identification in the sense of the "equation" of two things by a subject who thinks them identical.

conception of symbol formation is modified. Its function is no longer to account for the instinctual cathexis of the non-ego in general, starting from a state in which only the ego is cathected (ego being taken here in the sense not of a special structure but of the total personality or self); rather, it has now to explain how instinctual cathexis is transferred from certain primal objects to other objects. We are no longer dealing with the very general and by nature largely speculative problem of the instinctual cathexis of external reality, but with the much more limited question of the cathexis of certain aspects of reality, which initially have no biological or affective value:

> Since the child desires to destroy the organs (penis, vagina, breasts) which stand for the objects, he conceives a dread of the latter. This anxiety contributes to make him equate the organs in question with other things; owing to this equation these in their turn become objects of anxiety, and so he is impelled constantly to make other and new equations, which form the basis of his interest in the new objects and of symbolism. [Klein, 1930a, p. 220]

Symbol-formation is thus indisputably later than the establishment of object relations. To maintain the libidinal theory in the face of this fact is little more than rhetoric.

But although it is easy to discern the nature of the problem which interested Melanie Klein in 1929, it is less easy to understand the proposed solution. The main source of obscurity is the permanent confusion of two different realities which, however, she tends to distinguish in her vocabulary; these are *equation (Gleichsetzung)* and *symbolism* proper. Hanna Segal (1957) clearly distinguished these two notions: the *symbolic equation* is an early form of link between two representations which are purely and simply confused, with no possibility of their separation; but in symbolism proper two representations are related in such a way that one can take the place of the other, while at the same time they are clearly separated and recognized as distinct. Thanks to the symbolic significance of objects they can assist sublimation; thus a normal subject can sublimate fantasies and masturbatory tendencies by playing the violin with virtuosity, finding great satisfaction in doing so. The psychotic cannot do this; for him, "it would be masturbating in public" (Segal, 1957). Incapable of manipulating symbols, he remains trapped in equivalences or symbolic equations. Although care must be taken to avoid anachronism—after all, Hanna Segal made this enlightening distinction in 1957—it can be shown that in 1929 Melanie Klein held a position very near that of her disciple. The text of "The Importance of Symbol-Formation in the Development of the Ego" is in fact incomprehensible without this imputation.

Let us examine the logical difficulties this text presents. Two points appear especially difficult: how and why does the fear of part objects contribute to their equation with other things? And if it is true that this equation is the "basis of symbolism" how do we pass from the first to the second? In *The Psycho-Analysis of Children,* Melanie Klein (1932) put forward the following suggestion: "According to my view, the child's fear of its introjected objects urges it to project that fear into the external world. In doing this it equates its organs, feces and all manner of things, as well as its internalized objects, with its external objects; and it also distributes its fear of its external object over a great number of objects by equating one with another" (p. 147). This text suggests, indirectly at least, three successive phases of symbolic identification, discussed here in the order of the latest to the earliest (most primitive).

Equation between physical objects. The text appears to suggest that equivalence is directly established between one physical object and another. It is nonetheless probable that Melanie Klein conceived equations of this type rather as secondary to a comparison of each of the physical objects in question with a libidinal or anxiogenic object; this ontogenesis of the symbol had been envisaged by Ferenczi and Jones, whose position she had supported in 1923. Thus, when the analytic process was established and Dick became capable of symbolic play, the cathexis of any particular thing rapidly led to attempts to destroy or damage it; it then became disturbing and was abandoned for other things, with which the same process was repeated. There was apparently no direct relation between these objects—cupboard, washstand, electric heater—but only a simultaneous relation of each with the mother's body, with which they were identified in turn. Such "horizontal" equations of one thing with another are closely dependent on their common equation with an internal object. This preliminary form of identification must therefore be considered.

Equation between libidinal or anxiogenic objects and physical objects. The only idea Melanie Klein puts forward on this point is the following: this equation, motivated by fear of the introjected object, is carried out through projection. This mechanism likely seemed to her too commonly described to need a special development in this context; it is found, for example, at the origin of early phobias (especially the zoophobias of the first anal stage). Its forerunner is anal ejection; its function is to lessen anxiety by substituting for "a much feared object from which, because internalized, there was no escape onto another, external one, and one less feared at that" (Klein, 1932, p. 158). Here Kleinian thought is merely radicalizing the Freudian theory of phobia: it is easier to avoid the phobogenic animal than the father, who "can appear whenever he chooses" (p. 158). Similarly, it is easier to avoid the real father than the introjected father; thus, according to Melanie Klein, the projection mechanism functions between internal and external objects in exactly the same way as, according to Freud, displacement functions between the father (real and external) and his phobogenic substitute.

Symbolic equation between part objects. Nothing is directly suggested which could account for the formation of equations between part objects: feces, penis, breast, etc. Described by Freud himself and universally noted in dreams, myth, and folklore, they are attested before any projection. All organs, all physical products, are equated from the beginning in the unconscious. Equation is primary and does not have to be explained, at least in Melanie Klein's view. Thus, the theory of 1929 is aimed at describing the stages of the extension of symbolic equations and indicating their psychological meaning—that is to say, the economic finality of this process: to master anxiety by fragmenting it into small quantities thanks to its distribution over several objects. But the theory does not claim to tell us anything about the constitution of the equations themselves.

The reason is simple. At bottom Melanie Klein considers equation not as a positive fact resulting from an activity of the ego or the psychical apparatus in general, but rather as a purely negative fact. If libidinal or anxiogenic objects are "represented by their organs"—if breast, penis, feces, and children are constantly changing their meanings and cathexes—we should see in this not a semiotic fact resulting from a mental act of synthesis, but the result of an inability to discriminate. Here we are not within the range of symbolism properly speaking, which presupposes a secondary process (at least if we take it in the sense favored by Hanna Segal, which, as will be shown, is implicitly that of Melanie Klein) but in that of confusion and, in the language of the time, "affective logic," which ignores the principle of identity and non-identity. The verb *gleichsetzen* (the noun form is *Gleichsetzung*), by which she designates what is translated as *equate,* means "to put on the same footing" "to make equal." We find them for example in the following passage: "In the cannibalistic phase children equate every kind of food with their objects, as represented by their organs, so that it takes on the significance of their father's penis and their mother's breast and is loved, hated and feared like these. Liquid foods are likened to milk, faeces, urine and semen, and solid foods to faeces and other substances of the body" (Klein, 1932, pp. 156–157). It seems clear that such a system of reciprocal references without differentiation is on this side of the process of symbolization. For the rest, Melanie Klein, always careful to distinguish, in every order of reality, simple forerunners from genuine early stages, is content to consider equation as the *basis* of symbolism and of an interest in external objects. But there is a divide between the basis of symbolism and symbolism itself, and this divide is nowhere more apparent than in the clinical picture of psychosis.

In fact Melanie Klein very clearly contrasts, in the 1930 article on symbol-formation, two forms of the semiotic link between two realities. This opposition, though it harks back to the practical distinction between semiotic links (whether equation or symbolism) which inhibit the creation of fantasies and those which facilitate it, does not entirely obscure the theoretical distinction between equation and symbolism proper. Although starting point and intention are different according to whether we are interested in one or the other of these distinctions, they seem largely to coincide.

This conclusion must be obvious to anyone who reads carefully the report of Dick's analysis. When Melanie Klein undertook the psychoanalysis of this child, she found herself facing "a fundamental obstacle" (Klein, 1930a, p. 225) which she describes in terms of lack. He had no symbolic relationship with things, they had no emotional value for him, and therefore, when he manipulated objects, this strictly meant nothing; we cannot consider his play or activity as a symbolic representation with underlying fantasies.

> After a feeble beginning, symbol-formation in this child had come to a standstill. The early attempts had left their mark in one interest, which, isolated and unrelated to reality, could not form the basis for further sublimations. The child was indifferent to most of the objects and playthings around him, and did not even grasp their purpose or meaning. But he was interested in trains and stations and also in door-handles, doors and the opening and shutting of them.
>
> The interest in these things and actions had a common source: it really had to do with the penetration of the penis into the mother's body. . . . Thus what had brought symbol-formation to a standstill was the dread of what would be done to him . . . after he had penetrated into the mother's body. [p. 224]

Recall that this interest, the libidinal and sadistic meaning of which remains unconscious, is also the only one to be maintained (assuming that there were others) and is considered by Melanie Klein to be a true symbol despite the fact that it did not serve as a "basis" for later sublimations.

While capable of taking an interest in door handles, Dick was incapable of holding a knife, scissors, or any tool. This conduct had been preceded, during early childhood, by a refusal to chew his food. Melanie Klein's interpretation brings out simultaneously the equation between the inhibited actions and an oral-sadistic attack, and the paralyzing nature of this equation: "Dick's further development had come to grief because he could not bring into fantasy the sadistic relation to the mother's body" (p. 224). But the obvious idea here is that Dick's incapacities arose not from a lack of meaning or of cathexis of reality but, on the contrary, from too much meaning. If fantasizing activity is suspended, it is not in default of a certain symbolic relationship between biting to pieces and cutting with a knife, a relationship which would normally allow the sublimated discharge of aggressive impulses; rather, it is because this relationship is too pregnant; to cut with a knife is, in the unconscious, so confused with "attacking the breast with the teeth" that Dick cannot let himself do it, any more than the patient in Hanna Segal's example could let himself play the violin in public. The "symbol" is so little differentiated from the thing symbolized that it cannot escape the inhibition affecting the latter. Thus the supposed lack of the capacity of symbol-formation is translated not by an absence of meaning in the objects or activities relating to it, but by the uncontrollable proliferation of their meanings. If Dick lacks emotional relations with things, it is not because, shut into a preobject state, he would not give them any meaning (in which case he would be like the aphasics described by Cassirer, who lack the capacity of symbol-formation); rather, it is because for him "the world is still a belly peopled with dangerous objects" which must be avoided at any price (Klein, 1930b, p. 233). What is lacking in psychosis, and the lack of which is normal in the very first stages of the oedipus complex, is not the relationship between equivalent terms; rather, it is the capacity to distinguish between the symbol and the thing symbolized.

Unless this fact is at least implicitly recognized we cannot understand Melanie Klein's attitude at the beginning of Dick's analysis. We know that with this child she had recourse to a procedure rather like that advocated by Hermine von Hug-Hellmuth in 1920. As the child showed no play or spontaneous activity, Melanie Klein availed herself of his stereotyped interest in trains, which had been communicated to her by his family, and placed in front of him two toy trains unequal in size, expressing verbally the meaning she assigned them (the little train was the "Dick-train," and the big one was the "Daddy-train"). As soon as the child made a gesture or spoke a word, she interpreted. Unlike what is often imagined, such "barbarous"

procedures were not her habit: "in Dick's case I have modified
my usual technique. In general I do not interpret the material
until it has found expression in various representations. In this
case, however, where the capacity to represent it was almost
entirely lacking, I found myself obliged to make my interpretations on the basis of my personal knowledge, the representations in Dick's behaviour being relatively vague" (Klein,
1930a, pp. 228–229). But if Dick really lacked the capacity for
symbolic representation, how was it that his psychoanalyst could
establish contact with him by basing her ideas on a general
knowledge of symbolism? Was the active attitude adopted
aimed at teaching the child symbolic meanings he would not
know? Or was it not rather an act presupposing that the "general knowledge" taken as its basis applied also to Dick—that is
to say, that he had the capacity to understand symbolic equations?

     In fact the effect of these repeated interpretations can be
seen in a new ability to form and use symbols. But this acquisition does not consist in the formation of new semiotic links;
it is the awareness of equations which have been felt unconsciously. When real things have been differentiated from internal objects they cease to arouse excessive anxiety. The child
can then take an active interest in them, compare them, recognize them, and learn their names. It is clear, however, that such
a process concerns not the formation of symbols but their use.
The process by which we pass from symbolic equation to symbolism proper is not described in this context. Here we must
confine ourselves to recalling something Melanie Klein (1923a,
p. 86) noted earlier—that symbolism exists when repression has
rejected the representation of the thing symbolized in the unconscious, leaving the symbolizing image still in the preconscious—and her thoughts (reported twenty-five years later) on
realizing the importance of symbolism in play:

Peter . . . pointed out to me, when I interpreted his damaging
a toy figure as representing attacks on his brother, that he would
not do this to his *real* brother, he would only do it to the *toy*
brother. My interpretation of course made it clear to him that
it was really his brother whom he wished to attack; but the in-

stance shows that only by symbolic means was he able to express
his destructive tendencies in the analysis. [1955, p. 138]

Here again, thirty years after the proto-Kleinian system, the
need for symbolic expression was related to something like
repression. We thus have grounds for supposing that that was
Melanie Klein's opinion in 1929; but we must emphasize the
uncertainty of the evidence on this point.

What must finally be brought to light is the paradoxical
fact that the direction taken by Melanie Klein in 1929–1932,
which affords us a conception of the symbolic link in which we
have the constant impression that Hanna Šegal's distinctions
are already at work without their being explicitly formulated,
still does not yield an articulate theory of the nature of this link.
The only point to rouse Melanie Klein's interest is the practical
aspect, the fact that the link is working. In this sense the description of the symbolic relation is much less important to her
than determining the mechanisms which allow the thawing out
of sublimations and the symbolic fulfillment of instinctual desires that is observed when the analysis of a psychotic child
progressess. Having localized at the level of symbolic activity
the major disturbance in deficiency psychoses in children, she
deliberately neglects to formulate a theory of normal function
and turns rather to the description of the mechanisms of cure:
the distribution of identifications and the division of anxiety
leading to the determination *of its quantity.* That is why, at the
time of *The Psycho-Analysis of Children,* there was no theory of
this symbolism to which all sublimations are related, but only
a detailed theory of projection, splitting, and reparation, which
enable the use of symbols as a step toward sublimation. But
before coming to examine Melanie Klein's conceptualization of
these mechanisms, we must complete our study of the theory
of infantile psychosis.

● *Thesis 6. Disturbance of symbolic activity in deficiency psychosis
comes in the last analysis from the defensive conflict.*

Although Melanie Klein describes Dick's disturbance of
symbolic activity in terms of deficiency, she comes nowhere near

considering it a defect which could be cited as a primary factor in psychotic disturbances, accounting, for example, for the weakness of the ego and its inability to work out less mutilating defensive strategies. On the contrary, she believes that Dick at least, if not the psychotic child in general, suffers from an over-development of the ego. What paralyzes him and impedes his development is not a sadism more excessive than that of other children, but the too early and too considerable occurrence, presented by Melanie Klein as mere chance (in any case, she does not try to account for it), of a process in itself positive, the instinctual basis of which is genital and thus free from sadism, namely, "identification with the object attacked." Because of this identification, he cannot bear his own aggression. The re-action is pity, which forbids any sadistic manifestations at a time when sadism is normally at its height, and must find a means of expression. In order to check sadism, all activity, whether practical or fantasy, must be inhibited. So it is in a way an excess of the power of the ego that is at the origin of this arrested development which is Dick's deficiency psychosis: "The early operation of the reactions originating on the genital level was a result of premature ego-development, but further ego-development was only inhibited by it" (Klein, 1930a, p. 227).

● *Thesis 7. Infantile psychosis involves anxiety that is hidden but crushing.*

On this point too Melanie Klein, from her first experience of psychosis, goes beyond the common opinion of psychiatrists and of most of the psychoanalysts of her time. She does not fail to note that psychotics appear unemotional. The clinical picture of Dick includes "almost complete absence of affect and anxiety, a very considerable degree of withdrawal from reality, and of inaccessibility, a lack of emotional *rapport,* . . . indifference to pain" (Klein, 1930a, p. 230). She does indeed admit the clinical value of these reasons for the diagnosis of "dementia praecox" made by the London psychiatrist and psychoanalyst Douglas Forsyth, and the first session with Dick proved that the medical decision was right. But we know that if Dick was finally analyzed, it was precisely because Melanie Klein could see this superficial lack of emotion as a mask covering inexpressible anxiety, and did not hesitate to use an approach aimed at the fomentation—even the provocation—of fantasies. As the sessions followed one another, the weight of anxiety became more evident, and interpretations brought it into the light of day, which made it possible to leave it behind, once having felt it. Melanie Klein thus succeeded "in causing the anxiety to become manifest by diminishing it in its latent state" (p. 229). This is as much as to say that the absence of anxiety in the psychotic—child or adult—covers a hidden but crushing anxiety. This fact now seemed established in Melanie Klein's view, to such an extent that in *The Psycho-Analysis of Children* she no longer felt the need to argue in favor of her theory, mentioning it almost incidentally: "We know that the psychotic has a far greater quantity of anxiety than the neurotic" (Klein, 1932, p. 142).

● *Thesis 8. Infantile neurosis is a system of defenses against an underlying core of psychosis.*

To this may be added two corollaries: (a) this theory is especially true of obsessional neurosis; (b) infantile neurosis often shows pronounced obsessional features.

The theory of infantile neurosis, the first field of application of the first discoveries of Melanie Klein, received from 1929 the impact of the discovery of the peak phase of sadism and the corresponding psychotic anxiety. The contribution of *The Psycho-Analysis of Children* on this point did not consist in the repetition of the description of a well-known disorder; it lay essentially in the discovery of the early occurrence of certain forms of true obsessional neurosis (at least at the symptomatic level) and in the interpretation put forward for this. Again we should note that the very early existence of these forms was not unknown to Melanie Klein, as Rita was a typical example. But what from now onward characterized Melanie Klein's approach to the neuroses was, besides the exclusive interest in obsessional neurosis (there seems not to be a single mention of hysteria in her work between 1927 and 1934, except in a quotation from Freud), an original and neat theory, the clinical fruitfulness of which has often been noted, which makes it possible to account for both the oedipal nucleus of this disorder and its close relation to paranoia. The essential point of this concept is this: obsessional mechanisms, aroused by the demands of the struggle against the early anxieties typical of the first stages of the oedipus complex, attempt to reduce them by bringing into play procedures that are more advanced, less sadistic, and less violent than the defenses that are natural to the first stages of development. If they fail, they become fixed and consolidated into a structured neurosis, the formation of which expresses the extreme intensity of the early anxieties and thus of primary sadism. If they succeed, they are progressively abandoned or transformed into adaptive mechanisms corresponding to the genital level, and thus to the final binding of sadism by the libidinal tendencies.

Thus the conception put forward in *The Psycho-Analysis of Children* enables us to understand three facts of current experience:

1. The extreme frequency of obsessional mechanisms in infantile neurosis and even, it may be added, in the day-to-day life of the normal child, including life outside crisis periods. This only shows the activity of a group of instinctual and defensive processes the intervention in which is indispensable for overcoming cannibalistic and anal-sadistic tendencies: negation, overcompensation, reparation.

2. The disturbing prognosis of very early obsessional neurosis. The classical Freudian conception makes it difficult to understand why fixation should be more harmful than regression. The Kleinian conception of 1932 helps us to understand the early formation of neurosis by relating it to the blockage of the process of normal development under the influence of underlying psychotic anxiety. Obsessional neurosis is thus a compromise between what Bion was much later to call the "psychotic part of the personality" and the nonpsychotic part. In this sense the structured obsessional neurosis of the young child would be, rather than a genuinely neurotic state corresponding to adult obsessional neuroses, a borderline state in the sense in which Jean Bergeret understands the term, with no possibility of entering openly upon, and completely forming, a classical oedipus complex. This conception has the advantage of accounting better for the rigor of the superego in the neurosis of the older child or adult: "the severe super-ego in the obsessional neurosis is no other than the unmodified, terrifying super-ego belonging to early stages of the child's development" (Klein, 1932, p. 164). The main aspects of obsessional and compulsive symptomatology can easily be reinterpreted from this point of view: the frequent difficulties of obsessionals with their possessions, the compulsion to accumulate objects and then part with them, the compulsion to take and give back, all go back to the imago of the terrifying mother of toilet training, who demands back from the child "the faeces and the children it has stolen from her" (p. 164). Disgust at dirt, and the love of cleanliness go back to the subject's fear of his own excrement, which since the phase of insidious sadism has been identified in the unconscious with toxic substances. The need to control his surroundings corresponds to the need to control dangerous internal objects: id and superego projected onto real objects are easier to master than internal objects.

3. *The closeness of psychosis to obsessional neurosis, such that in the most serious cases the two disorders may purely and simply follow each other.* This is what happens in the development of certain very disturbed children who, during the first anal stage, pass through "rudimentary paranoid states" (Klein, 1932, p. 167) which are overcome in the next stage by the establishment of an obsessional neurosis. This early link between paranoid and obsessional states forms, as it were, a stepping stone to a possible regression. Thus the most serious cases of obsessional neurosis—precisely those in which this disorder follows a paranoid state—always carry the risk of developing into psychosis: "If his obsessional mechanisms cannot adequately overcome those disturbances his underlying paranoid traits will often come to the surface, or he may succumb to a regular paranoia" (p. 167).

4. Projection, Splitting, Introjection

Projection

The notion of projection, although it was to play a central part in Melanie Klein's theories, did not appear until very late.

She began to use the word and the idea in 1929. She needed a full six years of the practice of analysis by means of the play technique before her interest turned to projection. The surprising nature of this fact is redoubled if we remember that from 1926 onward she made abundant use of the concepts of introjection and the introjected object. She may have made no use whatsoever of the concept of projection, but that was certainly not through ignorance: it is a completely classical notion in psychoanalysis, and occurs in Freud's writings from the very beginning. What is more, Melanie Klein herself used the word at least twice, as early as 1921, and it is noteworthy that the use she then made of it directly anticipated that which became obligatory after 1929. Describing and commenting on a fit of terror on the part of Erich, she makes this remark: "the fear showed itself as the projection of his unconscious aggressive wishes" (Klein, 1921, p. 38). A few pages further on she writes: "he projects upon his father his own aggressiveness against the latter" (p. 44).

We find, then, in these early texts, not only a perfectly assured use of a classical Freudian notion, but already a personal touch in the emphasis laid on the fear of vengeance, which is exactly what the notion of projection indicates in Melanie Klein's final ideas. How, then, can we understand that she could, for such a long time, do without a notion that fitted in so well with her needs? The answer is simple: for several years she concerned herself with what was most urgent, that is, the exposition of the clinical facts upon which one of the 1926 theories was based: that "early" anxieties are fear of vengeance; that their content is the fear of suffering what one has oneself inflicted on the object in imaginary attacks; and that they must be considered as guilt feelings released by the first repression of the oedipus complex, due to the appearance of the early superego. Studying the theories of 1927, we have shown that it was probably the discovery of the meaning of night terrors that was at the origin of the simultaneous recognition of the early oedipus complex and the superego accompanying it. The notion of the superego was in 1926 a very recent discovery, made by Freud in 1923, the very time Melanie Klein was discovering the play technique. The way in which the Freudian texts of this time present the formation of the ideal of the ego, then the superego, accords an important place to identification, which is on several occasions considered in terms of introjection (Freud, 1921, 1923). Thus, when she had to describe the formation of an internal prohibition, Melanie Klein, following Freud's example, would quite naturally speak the language of introjection.

But the use of such a concept presupposes the incorporative, or more exactly centripetal, nature of the formation of the internal prohibition, starting from an external model; a position perfectly compatible with the Freudian conception, but which was to become more and more difficult to reconcile with the clinical results of child psychoanalysis, which very soon drew attention to the considerable difference between the prohibiting internal figures and the real parents upon whom they were supposed to be modeled. However this may be, Melanie Klein adhered for a long time to the idea that the superego, the product of an identification, was an introjected object. And insofar as this introjected object was fantastically distorted under the influence of the fear of vengeance, she tried for a long time to relate this distortion to the process of introjection. While doing this, she used a concept much nearer that delineated in 1909 by Ferenczi than the one her own writings after 1934 were clearly to define. And since, following him, she considered certain processes which resulted in fact from projection (especially, if we consult her final system, the fear of vengeance), to be the result of introjection (understood in a rather vague sense as inclusion in the ego by a sort of assimilation), it was inevitable that she should give up this notion. It is not, therefore, going too far to say that the spontaneous development of the theory of projection, begun in 1921 in the context of the problem of the fear of vengeance, was disturbed by the intervention of a theory of introjection suggested by Freud, but really coming from Ferenczi. It should be emphasized that this first Kleinian theory of introjection has the peculiarity, surprising to anyone familiar with Melanie Klein's later writings, of having no "interplay" with projection. On its reappearance, projection was associated with a mechanism which it seems legitimate to consider a form, the first to be discovered and described, of what was later to be called splitting; and from 1929 to *The Psycho-Analysis of Children* there was a growing relation between these two notions, at first largely independent; on the one hand the supposed forerunner of splitting and projection, and, on the other, that of introjection, incorporation, and internalization.

The Two Mechanisms of Personification in Play

If we can credit the index drawn up in 1945 by Melanie Klein's secretary and friend Lola Brook for the first edition of *Contributions to Psycho-Analysis* (Klein, 1948), "splitting" appeared in Melanie Klein's "Personification in the Play of Children" (1929b). Actually, in the English text of this article, it is a question of "splitting up." But it is important to emphasize that at this period Melanie Klein was thinking and writing in German. Here we notice a surprising fact: whereas the term "splitting up" occurs in two different passages of the English translation, its equivalent (*Spaltung*) does not appear in the German originals. When she quotes an article by Rado (1927), who had described a particular form of splitting of the mother's imago, she speaks of separation (*Trennung*, which is even more curious, as Rado had used the word *Spaltung*). When she speaks for herself about the mechanism to which she wishes to draw attention she uses the word *Zerlegung* (Klein, 1929c, p. 176). Is this term equivalent to splitting? The question seems difficult to answer. *Zerlegen* is an extremely common word which means, in logic or in chemistry, to break down or analyze, or, in mechanics, to dismantle. It implies a disarticulation which is not at all destructive, carried out along the natural separation lines of the parts, making it possible to put it together again by recomposition, synthesis, or reassembly. We can now observe that this term has part of its semantic field in common with, and another complementary to, the term *Wiederherstellung*, which was used shortly afterward to designate the process of restoration. It is nonetheless true that the function of this casual use of *Zerlegung* is to designate one of the processes later to be thought of in terms of splitting. It is one of the elementary constituents of the mechanism of personification (*Rollenbildung*), which itself makes only a fleeting appearance in the article in whose title it appears (Klein, 1929c). Personification, which is observed in the play of the child who makes up the characters, plays them himself alternately, or makes his friends (or the analyst) play them, is described as a mechanism of release, in the sense used by Daniel Lagache, rather than a defense mechanism. Although Melanie Klein does not use the term "sublimation" in this context, personification has all its characteristics, especially that of producing pleasure. The function of this play mechanism is to fight against the early superego in a way that is at once radical, economical, and elegant. The young child's superego is excessive, heterogeneous, and unstable. It is difficult for the ego, starting from such a chaotic conglomeration of very varied identifications, to achieve the synthesis of a single identity. The effectiveness of personification comes from its mode of operation; far from exhausting itself trying to maintain this nearly impossible synthesis, the ego gives up the effort and splits up (*verlegt*) the contradictory identifications, or lets them split themselves up. These identifications are *projected* onto the characters of the game. Thus distributed or divided (by a mechanism called *Teilung* or *Verteilung*), they can be faced one by one by an ego which is all the stronger because it no longer wastes its energy in maintaining the synthesis. Moreover, as a sort of bonus, the ego is reinforced by new possibilities of facing anxiety offered by the distribution of imagos projected onto the characters in the game; thanks to this mechanism, it is not the terrible superego which has to be faced all at once, but one or another of the identifications that make it up; these are easier to fight, so that the ego has successes which encourage it, increase its confidence in its capacities, and thus reinforce it. Thanks to the use of "splitting up" and projection

> the synthesis of the super ego, which can be maintained only with more or less effort, can be given up for the time being and, further, the tension of maintaining the truce between the superego as a whole and the id is diminished. The intrapsychic conflict thus becomes less violent and can be displaced into the external world. The pleasure gained thereby is increased when the ego discovers that this displacement into the external world affords it various real proofs that the psychic processes, with their cath-

exis of anxiety and guilt, may have a favourable issue and anxiety
be greatly reduced. [Klein, 1929b, p. 205]

"Splitting up" is thus at the starting point of a sequence of
psychical processes ending with the distribution of anxiety. It
is this last result which matters, and later texts, returning to this
phenomenon, no longer use the expression "splitting up."

The intrinsic interest of projection very soon shows itself
to be greater than that of personification, to which it contributes. We would be right to think that the short-lived thematization of this personification mechanism was merely the sign
of a still fumbling attempt to reintroduce projection within
Melanie Klein's theoretical system. In fact the personification
mechanism was assuming a function which later was assigned
to projection, that of producing transference. This point appears all the more significant because the Kleinian conception
of transference, as it took shape in the argument with Anna
Freud beginning in 1927, is closely linked with the notion of
the introjected object. What the child transfers onto the analyst
is not his relationship with the real parents, but his relationship
with the *introjected* parents. Melanie Klein placed special emphasis on personification in 1929 because it afforded her an
opportunity, unavailable to her up to then because of her prej-
udice in favor of introjection, to consider the element of projection in transference: "I have now to point out the significance
of this mechanism in the mental life of adults also. I have come
to the conclusion that it is the basis of a phenomenon of great
and universal significance, one which is also essential to analytic
work in both children and adults, namely, of the transference"
(Klein, 1929b, p. 207).

We should remember that Melanie Klein always insisted
on the essentially mobile nature of transference, the rapid wav-
ering between positive and negative transference, and between
paternal and maternal transference, which may occur several
times in a single session. The notion of personification had the
advantage of bringing out this fact, insofar as the child, in an
analysis using the play technique, made the analyst play very
different parts in rapid succession: "If a child's phantasy is free
enough, he will assign to the analyst, during a play-analysis, the

most varied and contradictory roles. He will make me, for example, assume the part of the id, because in this projected form his phantasies can be given outlet without inspiring so much anxiety" (pp. 207–208). Thus, this mechanism works not only for the superego, but also for the id, its antagonist: thanks to this procedure the ego can vary its identifications and attitudes in the context of strategies of alliance with the superego against the id or, conversely, with the id against the superego. Insofar as an internal aspect of the subject is personified in play, the latter brings about by its very nature an intersubjective relationship on the model of an intrasubjective one, or, which is the same phenomenon considered from another angle, a dissociation and redistribution of two aspects of the personality between the two partners in play—the self and the other. The adaptive aspect of this process is obvious in the context of the psychoanalytic play technique: "a weakening of the conflict or its displacement into the external world by means of the mechanisms of splitting up and projection, is one of the principal incentives to transference and a driving force in analytic work" (p. 208). What is important to emphasize in the description of this play behavior is that the return to the notion of projection is not the result of a theoretical step, of some realization of the ambiguities of the notion of the introjected object or of the difficulty of understanding the fear of vengeance in purely introjective terms; rather, it is governed by the need to determine the scope of therapeutic efficacy inherent in the play itself, independent of the concerted use of play activities as the vehicle of psychoanalytic communications, and with the aim of learning to derive the best advantage from this spontaneous behavior.

At the beginning, the theory of projection had nothing whatsoever to do with the notion of introjection. It was, however, closely linked with a mechanism that appears to represent the first form of splitting discovered by Melanie Klein—"splitting up"—and though the following quotation may evince rather a clumsiness of expression than a meticulous weighing of the terms in which she expresses herself, it makes clear, from the first use of these concepts, the common source and the identical orientation of the two processes: "I have come to the conclusion that this splitting of the super-ego into the primal identifications introjected at different stages of development is a mechanism analogous to and closely connected with projection" (p. 205). But now, without projection ever losing this fundamental property of acting on split aspects of the real person or his internal imagos, the accent was to be placed on the movement of projection rather than on the splitting of the superego, the thematization of which was not taken up again until later, and under different names.

Projection, Deflection, Ejection

Once reintroduced, the notion of projection remained rather vague for a time. It designates, essentially, a movement of externalization to which Melanie Klein had not given a technical name when she glimpsed for the first time, three years before describing it more completely, the play procedure just mentioned. Projection is "expelling the father and mother whom, in the elaboration of the Oedipus complex, it has absorbed into itself . . .," an expulsion which "contributes in great measure to the pleasure derived from the game" (Klein, 1926, p. 133). The fact of physically throwing an object away seems to be the most pregnant concrete model of the mechanism of projection; thus, when Dick threw out a little cart damaged in a previous session, "he was indicating an expulsion, both of the damaged object and of his own sadism (or the means employed by it), which was in this manner projected into the external world" (Klein, 1930a, p. 226). In 1931 the joining of introjection and projection took place, but in a passage in which it is only alluded to, and the emphasis on the element of throwing away appears in the temptation to revise the terminology and call it *extrajection* (Klein, 1931, p. 244). It is not until 1932, in the *Psycho-Analysis of Children*, that we find a clearly expressed theory of projection, its functions, and its precursors.

From then on the name of projection is no longer applied to every "extrajecting" process. Its use is limited by the clear determination of the meaning of connected terms: deflection (*Abdrängung*), displacement (*Verschiebung* or *Verlegung*), ejection (*Ausstossung*). In short, deflection is the ontogenetic precursor of projection. Projection has as its instinctual basis and physical prototype the ejection of the feces, the dominant process in the first anal stage. The result of projection is the displacement of the aim, or the object, or both, as well as the source of danger. Although deflection is the forerunner of projection, it remains distinct from it, and is not one of its early forms. We know that this distinction between mere precursors and early stages (*Frühstadien*) was very important to Melanie Klein. The theory of deflection is the first example in Melanie Klein's work—and one of very few—of the affirmation of a psychological phenomenon the direct or indirect observation of which is not possible in analysis through play. It is in fact an absolutely primal process the notion of which is borrowed from Freud, and which is part of the theory of the death instinct. One of the great theoretical innovations of 1932 was in fact Melanie Klein's support of this concept, enunciated in "Beyond the Pleasure Principle" (Freud, 1920), support which has sometimes been considered superficial or based on error. It has been said in particular that under the name of death instincts Melanie Klein in fact deals with aggressive impulses, thus mistaking the deepest nature of the Freudian death instinct: the repetition compulsion and the tendency to self-destruction. However, while referring directly to Freud's theory, she enriches it considerably by adding the critical dimension it lacked, yet without subtracting what is in fact essential to the Freudian speculation: the indefinite return of the same thing, primal masochism. Extending Freud's reasoning on the work of the death instinct against the organism itself, and extending her own clinical discoveries according to which anxiety arises particularly from aggression, she arrives, at the convergence of these two lines of inquiry, at the following thesis: "the destructive instinct is directed against the organism itself and must therefore be regarded by the ego as a danger. I believe it is this danger which is felt by the individual as anxiety. Therefore anxiety would originate from aggression" (Klein, 1932, p. 126).

Thus, what in Freud remained a hypothetical and disembodied process was filled with concrete reality and could therefore be placed in the general context of the psychoanalytic theory of defensive processes. When in fact Freud places the conflict between Eros and Thanatos at the outset of psychical life, when he supposes a struggle between the death instinct and narcissistic libido, it is very difficult to consider this primal confrontation a defensive conflict arising from the law common to this order of processes: increase in intrapsychic tension; automatic anxiety; defense against the impulse. In fact, at no point did Freud consider relating these discernible stages through an analysis of the abstract process he describes and of the observable concrete manifestations. The struggle between death instinct and narcissistic libido is resolved by a compromise: part of the death instinct is turned away, diverted or *deflected* to the exterior, which provides an object other than the self and a possibility of discharge compatible with the demands of the narcissistic libido. The death instincts deflected outward become the aggressive instincts properly speaking, and the death instincts remaining "inside" retain their masochistic orientation. Although Freud did not mention this explicitly in 1919, it is probable that this deflection of the death instinct is part of the behavior of expulsion of what is bad or unpleasant, characteristic of the "purified pleasure-ego" of the beginning of life (Freud, 1915a, p. 136), and also of the behavior of rejection and expulsion through the mouth which is at the basis of negation. (Freud, 1925, p. 237).

Melanie Klein takes over the Freudian theory as a whole, stressing two points that seem to her to constitute its essence.

1. The deflection of the death instinct is the origin of sadism and not only of aggression. Melanie Klein has sometimes been accused of using the term *sadism* in a diluted or even erroneous sense, forgetting that sadism is not only aggression, even extreme aggression, but the combination of aggression and sexuality. The accusation is certainly not groundless, but we should note that the deflection of the death instinct brings about the first interaction between Eros and Thanatos; if the impulse and the instinctual aim of sadism represent the contribution of the death instinct to this mixture of instincts, its object is assigned it by the life instincts. Besides, when Freud deals with the parallel process, the fate of the death instincts which have maintained the self as their object and are neither more nor less bound by the life instincts than those which have been deflected, he does not hesitate to consider them the initial forms of ma-

sochism. No valid objection against Melanie Klein could leave Freud unscathed, and if we admit the Freudian notion of primal masochism we must admit also the perfect legitimacy of Melanie Klein's explanation of the origin of sadism.

2. This deflected death instinct begins the first object relationship. In the original conflict between life instinct and death instinct, the libido is narcissistic to exactly the same extent as the death instinct is masochistic. The initial state of the instincts, for Melanie Klein in 1932 as well as for Freud, is an objectless one. Object interest is prepared by sadism—which since 1929 has given us a foretaste of the text devoted to Ravel's *L'enfant et les Sortilèges* (Klein, 1929a) and the clinical discoveries resulting from the analyses of Egon and Dick. This priority of the sadistic cathexis of externals is the result of the action of the narcissistic libido mobilized by the anxiety aroused by the danger of self-destruction. The result is a tendency, permanent in Melanie Klein's work from 1932 on, to consider that in the formation of object relations and, more generally, relations with external reality, the motive element is provided by sadism, as libidinal cathexis only follows and counterbalances the death instinct.

On this basis she makes four additional points.

3. The process of deflection establishes the basis of projection. It remains separate from it. It is a process, whereas projection is often defined as a mechanism. On this point, Melanie Klein (1932) refers to Freud: "He considers this process fundamental to the individual's relations to his objects and to the mechanism of projection" (p. 126).

4. The ego is present from the beginning of life. We are told nothing about the nature and the degree of organization of this first ego except that, fed by the energy of the narcissistic libido and thus by the life instinct, it serves to deflect part of the death instinct.

5. From the beginning this ego has a second line of defense against the destructive instincts: it mobilizes part of them against the others. The first operation of the ego is the institution, by deflection, of the forerunners of object relations and projection; its second action consists in organizing the internal field of

instincts by introducing a break which is the initial form (not the forerunner) of its topical organization into separate parts:

> It seems to me that the ego has yet another means of mastering those destructive impulses which still remain in the organism. It can mobilise one part of them as a defence against the other part. In this way the id will undergo a split which is, I think, the first step in the formation of instinctual inhibitions and of the super-ego and which may be the same thing as primal repression. [Klein, 1932, p. 127]

6. The split in the id is made possible by the incorporation of the object. Melanie Klein (1932) believes that the presence of the incorporated object (*einverleibt*, not introjected or internalized), in a way she does not outline in detail, facilitates the introduction of discord into the id. The incorporated object is considered "the vehicle of defense against the destructive impulses within the organism" (p. 127), an idea which leads to an admission of the simultaneous occurrence of the process of incorporation of the object and that of the splitting of the id: "We may suppose that a split of this sort is rendered possible by the fact that, as soon as the process of incorporation has begun, the incorporated object becomes the vehicle of defense against the destructive impulses within the organism" (p. 127). This passage gives rise to two questions. First, there is ambiguity where the chronological sequence is concerned, and even more on the causal order of the operations she is describing: the incorporation of the object and its action as a defensive element are simultaneous, as they are also, it appears, with the split in the id. But what is the position relative to deflection? Should we admit strict contemporaneity between incorporation, precursor of introjection, and deflection, precursor of projection, or does projection, as it appears, come first? Moreover, in this passage the inncorporated object is the agent of defense. But the same text imputes the initiative of this same defense to the ego. Does this mean that the ego and the incorporated object are purely and simply confused, and that the ego as a distinct entity is formed only by, and in its identification with, the incorporated object? Should we, on the contrary, consider the

ego to be the instigator of a process of which the incorporated object is only the executive agent, and thus postulate an ego in existence before any object relationship which would be responsible for the deflection, while the incorporation of the object and the active defense of this object came only in a second stage, producing a process—the splitting in the id—which would be essentially second? It seems that these two questions, purely speculative in any event, remain unanswered in the Kleinian system of 1932.

Whatever the answer to this thorny question, it is important to state firmly that deflection gives rise to sadism, projection, and object relations, which establishes a fundamental relationship and a common nature between these three types of phenomenon, of which the clinical texts of this period of Melanie Klein's work give us continuous illustrations from 1929 onward—and even, though only implicitly, from 1926. We can thus explain the tone, surprising when compared with that of Melanie Klein's earlier texts, of this purely theoretical passage based entirely on reasoning and on comments on Freud's work. By moving in this direction she found a means, not of protecting herself against critics who accused her both of heterodoxy and of carrying allegiance to Freud far further than was necessary, but of placing on a metapsychological footing a relationship clinical experience had forced her to recognize among hating, fearing, the projection of hostile impulses, and an interest in persons and things that allows the early discoverey of any hostile impulses and the creation of a defense against them. This point should be emphasized, as Melanie Klein's speculations on the death instinct were not well regarded in the international psychoanalytic community. We need not linger over the curt dismissal such ideas met in most quarters, but should note that Jones, who was close to Melanie Klein for such a long time, never followed her on this point. Stating very strong personal reservations on the theory of "Beyond the Pleasure Principle," he noted in 1957 that only three psychoanalysts still supported the concept: Karl Menninger, Hermann Nunberg, and Melanie Klein (Jones, 1957, p. 299). Even a commentator as benevolent as Willy Baranger, an Argentine psychoanalyst who translated *Developments in Psycho-Analysis* (Klein, Heimann, Isaacs, and

Riviere, 1952) into French and wrote a study on the ideas of Melanie Klein (Baranger, 1971), considered the 1932 theory of instinct to be an extraneous element which masked and distorted the essence of Melanie Klein's discovery. The "instinctivist speculation" he mentions may represent either a survival, the remnants of an uncritical support of Freudian theories (but then it must be explained why this part of the theory was maintained to the end), or an artificial attempt to hide the extent of her divergences from Freud under the appearance of a stubbornly proclaimed allegiance (but then it would have to be explained why on this point Melanie Klein chose to remain faithful to the letter of Freudian doctrine, when even the most authoritative supporters of orthodoxy had long given it up). But it is more illuminating to admit that such tenacity in the defense of an unpopular idea must surely be due to the great impact on her of certain clinical facts met with in child analysis, and of the conceptualizations by which she was trying to account for them. It may have been essential, as a result of Dick's analysis, for her to find a means of conceptualizing the regular conjunction of sadism, projection, and an interest in external reality; no other motive can explain the persistence, in the successive versions of Melanie Klein's conceptions, of a theory of deflection of the death instinct.

We must, then, bring out the links uniting deflection and projection in the thought of Melanie Klein. The change from one of these phenomena to the other presupposes two intermediate processes: (1) internalization of the object and (2) its anal-sadistic ejection. The first result of the deflection of the destructive instinct is the constitution of the object as such, and also as a dangerous object. If it is true that the libido follows only paths mapped out by the death instinct, and that, as Freud (1915a) says, hate is older than love (p. 139; cited in Klein, 1932, p. 135), then it is inevitable that the first object incorporated should be an object that is attacked, and thus a dangerous object. At this point the beneficent effect of deflection is partly canceled, because the source of danger is again located "on the inside." The process of expulsion must therefore be renewed, in different conditions, on the basis of an earlier history (deflection, constitution of an external source of danger, and its internalization), by a more developed ego, with more differentiated impulses and more elaborate motivic, perceptual, fantasy, and verbal schemas. Melanie Klein places this moment, when the internalization of dangerous objects becomes truly anxiogenic, during the phase of sadism at its height, when the cannibalistic manifestations of the second oral stage and the rejecting manifestations of the first anal stage overlap. Under the influence of the anal impulses, which at this stage have an essentially externalizing and centrifugal aim, the process of externalization will take the form of anal-sadistic ejection (*Ausstossung*) the prototype of which—at least in Abraham's theory—is defecation. The application of this anal process to the incorporated object is all the more understandable because it is a part object. As such, it comes within the sphere of symbolic equations described by Freud. According to the salient idea of all Melanie Klein's writings on this point, this part object is either a breast or a penis, or—more probably—an ambiguous and composite imago which is neither one nor the other and yet both at the same time, in accordance with the typical indifferentiation of terms symbolically equated but not yet symbolized in the proper sense of the word. However that may be, there is an "equation of the introjected object with faeces" (Klein, 1932, p. 145). This application, typical of the first anal stage, of the ejection process to a "bad" introjected part object constitutes the first form of projection. The first mechanism to deserve the name is thus based on the first anal stage, and comes before the divide between the fixation points of psychoses and those of neuroses. It is the normal prototype of frenzied projection. In order to appear, it needs an internal source of danger and the localization of this source of danger in a part object, the corporeal prototype of the evacuation of the feces.

Projection and the Mechanisms Producing Symbolization:
Division and Distribution of Anxiety

During the first anal stage these conditions are fulfilled simultaneously and to a high degree. It is thus not surprising that at this moment the child's fears "push the effectiveness of its mechanisms of projection to their furthest limits" (Klein, 1932, p. 146). In fact, due to the intensity of the sadism, the terrifying part objects must absolutely be ejected from within. But this process, by definition strictly defensive and determined by the urgency of the fear of the introjected objects, results in the differentiation and enrichment of object relations. In this sense it belongs not only to the psychology of the emotions, but also to that of cognitive development, because it is at the origin of the inspection and exploration of the external world: "the child's fear of its introjected objects urges it to project that fear into the external world. In doing this it equates its organs, feces and all manner of things, as well as its internalized objects, with its external objects; and it also distributes its fear of its external object over a great number of objects by equating one with another" (p. 147). It is therefore the external objects which are anxiogenic and which must be watched if the self is to be protected. The subject functioning in this way will perhaps have a perception of reality distorted by his projections; in any case he will have contact with it, having passed the stage of autism. Governed by the fear of the terrifying introjects of the phase of sadism at its height, projection is transformed into true adaptive behavior thanks to the meeting with an instinctual factor—the insidious nature of the anal attacks, which necessitates constant supervision of the sources of danger—and with the mechanism of division or distribution (*Verteilung*). By a strange turn of events, the child's fear of vengeance contributes to the attentive observation of reality: "The quality of secrecy and cunning which it attributes to those attacks leads it to observe the world about it with a watchful and suspicious eye and increases its relations to reality, though in a one-sided way"; for this reason, "its fear of the introjected object is a constant incentive to keep the mechanisms of projection in operation" (p. 146). As for distribution, this is the mechanism we have already seen at work in personification; it has an essentially economic significance; it causes anxiety to be split up into small quantities which the ego can face without too many risks, which enables it to obtain "proofs that the psychic processes, with their cathexis of anxiety and guilt, may have a favorable issue and anxiety be greatly reduced" (Klein, 1929b, p. 205). But we know that this quantitative aspect is of necessity accompanied by a qualitative aspect, highly positive as far as sublimations are concerned, because it helps us to understand in the last analysis why the child interests itself in external objects which are at first completely indifferent. For an external object or activity to acquire a certain interest, it must be dangerous. But it must not be too dangerous, or the child would turn away from the external world. So a certain optimal danger or anxiety is necessary to ensure the development of interests and activities on the basis of symbolism. The function of distribution is precisely to ensure this quantity (*Dosierung*) of anxiety. This goes beyond the theory of personification, but its essence remains and is merged in a more comprehensive conception. The process of the splitting up, projection, and distribution of the superego is not reduced to the formation of play-characters or even to the production of a transference; it has a much wider significance and in fact applies to the entire ensemble of relations with external reality. As its scope is recognized, its instinctual bases become more clearly defined.

As for the notion of splitting up, it disappeared along the way. We might, it is true, consider this disappearance only apparent: there is no need for an active mechanism intended to split up he superego when it is not yet really constructed and organized in a coherent way. Moreover, distribution appears to have inherited the main functions of splitting up. But the important question is to know whether the "splitting up" of 1929 is, in Melanie Klein's work, another name for the process which was later to be called splitting, or whether in fact it is a different mechanism. Whether these two mechanisms differ as do *Zerlegung* and *Spaltung* or whether they are simply two forms of "splitting," it is essential to note that the action variously described as splitting up, division or distribution (*Zerlegung, Verteilung, Dosierung*) implies above all what we might call the aspect of fragmentation, a distribution over a multiplicity of objects, which Melanie Klein considers inherent in projection. As such, it does not appear to constitute a mechanism truly distinct from projection. That is why the terminology that designates it remains unstable and inconsistent, and why it gives rise to affirmations which appear enigmatic but which, as we must admit if our hypothesis is to be correct, are perfectly well-founded: splitting up is a process "analogous to and closely connected with projection" (Klein, 1929b, p. 205).

Though we must not underestimate the many links between projection and splitting, they cannot be considered analogous. Splitting (*Spaltung*), which does not appear under this name in Melanie Klein's work until 1932, is an operation distinct from projection, following it and not appearing unless projection has in some way prepared the ground for it. But the most important difference between splitting up, a simple mode of functioning of projection, and splitting, is probably tied up with their instinctual nature and genetic level: the first is the chief means of working through sadism at its height; the second does not reach its full flowering until the first has fulfilled its functions and sadism is mastered.

Splitting in the Theory of 1932

The splitting of the imagos is presented in *The Psycho-Analysis of Children* as a mechanism characteristic of the second anal stage. It is therefore relatively late; in particular, it is contemporary with repression. So from the very beginning we must take care not to confuse it with the early *splitting in the id* which we have met under the heading of the first defensive operations connected with incorporation of the object "and which may be the same thing as primal repression" (Klein, 1932, p. 127). The splitting of the id is a hypothetical process described in the context of a speculative reconstruction of the earliest stages of the defensive process; by contrast, the splitting of imagos is a clinically observable process. The use of the same word—a very common one in German—to denote these two realities simply indicates that Melanie Klein, who was then working out the concept of the splitting of imagos, had not yet decided to reserve for its exclusive designation a convenient and common word of everyday language. Correlatively, she also speaks, in some passages, of the division (*Teilung*) or separation (*Trennung*) of imagos when she obviously means splitting in the proper sense of the word (Klein, 1932, p. 222). But even if her vocabulary

is still uncertain, the concept has already acquired such consistency that it can be identified without risk of error.

Splitting, a typical mechanism of the stage when sadism is
no longer at its height, is soon accompanied by an awareness
of the fear of vengeance. This apparent paradox is easily explained: at the stage of sadism at its height, the fear of suffering
the retaliation of the object attacked was too crushing to reach
consciousness; it was denied, especially by ejection and projection. When these processes have enabled sadism and anxiety
to be worked through, and especially when libidinal impulses
are beginning to prevail over sadistic impulses, the ego can
become aware of its fear of retaliation by the object. From then
on, taking into account the development of instincts in which
the urge to save the object prevails over the urge to destroy it,
the ego submits to "the severe super-ego and . . . the prohibitions imposed by the super-ego" (Klein, 1932, p. 153) instead
of trying to eject or annihilate it as in the first anal stage. As
we know that intersubjective relations are modeled on intrasubjective ones, we should expect this modification of the attitude toward the superego and internalized objects to be
accompanied by a corresponding transformation in object relations; to the ego's submission to the power of the superego
is added "an acknowledgement of the power of the object" (p.
153). Thus, at the second anal stage the ego "tries to master
anxiety by attempting to satisfy the demands both of the external and internalized objects" (p. 153). We know that this
method enables the ego to find in the love and approval of its
external objects the denial of its fears about the dangers threatening it from the introjected objects. In this way object relations
and relations with reality enable the ego progressively to gather
strength against the superego. This establishment of "good"
object relations is possible only through the splitting mechanism, which allows a relationship with a "good" object not dominated by sadism;

> This process of relating to objects is brought about by a splitting
> up of the mother-imago into a good and a bad one. The existence
> of this type of ambivalence towards the object indicates a further
> step in the development of object-relations, and also helps to

modify the child's fear of the super-ego. This fear is displaced
onto the external object and then spread over several objects by
means of displacement. As a result certain persons take on the
significance of the attacked and therefore threatening object,
others—particularly the mother—take on the significance of the
kindly and protecting object. [p. 153]

We can see the part played by splitting in Melanie Klein's
ideas in 1932. It is exactly correlative with reparation mechanisms and, like them, allows an escape from the "vicious circle."
Ambivalence, therefore, changes its sense completely. In Freud
and Abraham it has a negative character. For the latter it is
characteristic of the intermediate stage of the development of
object relations; it begins with the cannibalistic stage and does
not end until the adult genital stage. It extends for a long
distance between an oral sucking phase, preambivalent because
preobject, and a postambivalent object phase which enables it
to be superseded. For Melanie Klein, by contrast, it is positive
in that it allows love and hate to be sorted out and separated.
For her predecessors it corresponds to the combination of love
and hate in relations with the same object, and notions such as
sadism and the conflict of ambivalence are very closely associated with it; as Laplanche and Pontalis (1967) write, it "is exhibited above all in certain pathological conditions (psychoses,
obsessional neurosis) and in certain states of mind such as jealousy and mourning. It is characteristic of certain phases of
libidinal development in which love and destructive tendencies
toward the object are to be found alongside each other: namely,
the oral-sadistic and anal-sadistic stages" (p. 27). It therefore
has a distinctly pathological connotation. But to Melanie Klein
the very idea that an object relationship could fail to involve
ambivalence seemed hard to imagine, as any libidinal movement
toward the object is secondary to an aggressive movement
which, in the best of cases, it aims to requite. So what Freud
and Abraham call ambivalence is in her view part of a second
phase in which aggression is no longer dominant and so can be
faced by the ego. As it is seen from a general point of view very
different from that of Freud or Abraham, ambivalence has to

be redefined; Melanie Klein always applies the term—without taking the trouble to say so explicitly—to the ambivalence already formed by the splitting of the imagos. That is to say that when sadism is no longer at its height hate is mitigated (*mildern*) by love (1952) and ambivalence appears in the relationship with the introjected object. But as soon as ambivalence appears, the urge to save the introjected object also appears, and prevails over the urge to destroy it by ejection. There is also splitting, which allows the separation of love and hate and their distribution over different objects. In short, as soon as ambivalence toward the internal object appears, it disappears from the conscious mind because splitting also comes into play. In this sense, and despite the differences we have seen, splitting recovers, in the 1932 theory, one of the functions formerly attributed to splitting up—that of putting some order into object relations: classifying them, diversifying them, and thus ending up with the necessary quantity of anxiety.

Splitting thus immediately shows itself capable of molding the oedipus complex, whether classical or late, and stimulating the various reparations and sublimations which accompany it: "In dividing its mother into a 'good' mother and a 'bad' one and its father into a 'good' father and a 'bad' one, it attaches the hatred it feels for its object to the 'bad' one or turns away from it, while it directs its restorative trends to its 'good' mother and 'good' father and, in phantasy, makes good towards them the damage it has done its parent-imagos in its sadistic phantasies" (Klein, 1932, p. 222). The dissociation of the introjected objects into "good" and "bad" is both the immediate forerunner and the precipitating factor of the late oedipal opposition between the rival and the object of incestuous love, clearly differentiated. In this sense the most essential splitting in the 1932 theory is certainly not that of the maternal imago, as it was to become after 1934. In 1932 the real point of impact of splitting is the terrifying imago of the combined parents, on which, at the stage of sadism at its height, all the resources of sadism, and thus all the fears, are concentrated. The decisive moment of the decline of sadism is when this paralyzing imago can be defeated. Then

his imago of the combined parents is still more completely separated . . .; and his mother will become pre-eminently the object
of his libidinal impulses, while his hatred and anxiety will in the
main go to his real father (or father's penis) or, by displacement,
to some other object, as in the case of animal phobias. The
separate imagos of his mother and father will then stand out
more distinctly and the importance of his real objects will be
increased; and he will now enter upon a phase in which his
Oedipus trends and his fear of being castrated by his real father
come into prominence. [Klein, 1932, p. 246]

Thus, each time splitting is alluded to in *The Psycho-Analysis
of Children,* it appears as the typical mechanism of the later
phases of the oedipus complex as described by Freud. It is
splitting that makes possible children's sexual play with each
other, to which Melanie Klein generally attributes a positive
and highly adaptive value; these activities

not only gratify their libido but enable them to search for manifold confirmations and refutations of their various fears in connection with the sexual act. I have repeatedly found that if such
sexual objects have acted in addition as 'helping' figures, early
sexual relations of this kind exert a favourable influence upon
the girl's relations with her objects and upon her later sexual
development. . . .

In serving as a proof grounded upon reality of the existence
of the 'good' penis, the girl's relations with her brother fortify
her belief in the 'good' introjected penis and moderate her fear
of 'bad' introjected objects. [pp. 223–224]

It is splitting that makes possible the formation of the ambivalence complex toward the rival—that is to say, in Melanie
Klein's sense, in causing the apparent manifestations of ambivalence to disappear. In adolescence,

The erection of new principles and new idealized father-
imagos and the heightened demands on himself are used by the
child for the purpose of moving away from his original objects.
By doing so he is able to call upon his original positive attachment
to his father and increase it with less risk of coming into collision

with him. This event corresponds to a splitting [*Spaltung*] of his father imago. The exalted and admired father can now be loved and adored while the 'bad' father—often represented by his real father or by a substitute such as a schoolmaster—summons very strong feelings of hatred which are common at this period of development. [p. 189]

Thus, it is through ambivalence (in the Kleinian sense of the coexistence of two split object relations) that the ambivalent conflict (in Abraham's sense of a conflict between love and hate) can be overcome:

In splitting his father-imago, he diverts his aggressive traits to other objects. If, therefore, we bring together his over-compensatory admiration for some objects and his excessive hatred and scorn for others, such as schoolmasters, relations, etc., which we uncover during analysis, we can also find our way in the case of the older boy to a complete analysis of his Oedipus complex and his affects. [p. 82]

Splitting is a mechanism able to make love and hate compatible by dividing and distributing them (*teilen, verteilen*). It is therefore one of the mechanisms which can determine the possibility of a strong object relationship. It allows definitive genital cathexis of the oedipal object and identification with the idealized rival. It enables the subject to approach to reality and to project, from a certain stage of development, benevolent and helpful internal figures upon real objects. We should, then, stress the bonds uniting, in particular, splitting and reparation mechanisms. "As a result," writes Melanie Klein, "certain persons take on the significance of the attacked and therefore threatening object, others—particularly the mother—take on the significance of the kindly and protecting object" (p. 153). So the child finds in reality "good" objects which he can introject and with which he can identify: "The individual becomes increasingly successful in overcoming anxiety thanks to the progressive development of the infant towards the genital stage during which it introjects more friendly imagos. . . . It can now employ restitutive mechanisms and reaction-formations of pity towards its objects so as to placate the super-ego" (p. 153). We are thus led to describe in these terms the process leading to the setting up of the mechanisms of reparation and pity: splitting, projection, introjection. But what is the nature of this introjection?

The Concept of the Internal Object and Difficulties in the Notion of Introjection

We know in fact that all of Melanie Klein's texts prior to *The Psycho-Analysis of Children* relate introjection to the presence "inside" of bad objects attacked primarily by sadism, and whose vengeance is dreaded. The fact that "good" internal imagos exist, forming the counterpart of "bad" imagos, was recognized in 1929 (see Klein, 1929b, p. 203) without being fully integrated into the theory. It is not until 1932 that we find passages describing internal imagos in terms of sadism or violence and giving a disturbing picture of the "internal world." These facts can be correctly appreciated only in the light of the following ideas: (1) in spite of appearances, there is no theory of introjection in Melanie Klein's work before 1932, and in any case not even an apparent one before 1931; (2) the theory put forward in 1932, relatively incoherent, was not fully worked out until 1934.

Let us examine the first of these affirmations. It is true that in the texts published by Melanie Klein from 1926 onward the words "introjected object" and "introjection" appear with some frequency. For this reason and because, moreover, everyone knows that after 1934 her work contains a fully developed theory of introjection and its relations with projection, splitting, etc., it is quite natural to assume a perfect continuity in her successive uses of the word. But this continuity does not exist, and there seems to be very little connection between true introjection and what was meant by the word around 1927. We have already seen that the notion of introjection is used to denote the phenomenon of fear of vengeance in one of its most remarkable effects, the "fantastic distortion" of the imagos of real objects, starting from their exact perception. When the term "introjection" appeared in 1926, the accent was placed not on the mechanism but on its result, the presence of an "introjected object." As far as the meaning of this term is concerned, it clearly appears as the antonym of the term "real object." It designates the imaginary prohibiting figures discovered on analyzing the early guilt feelings of young children; the prototype is the introjected mother whose threats prevented Rita from playing with her doll: "the prohibition of the childish wish no longer emanated from the *real* mother, but from an introjected mother, whose role she enacted for me in many ways and who exercised a harsher and more cruel influence upon her than her real mother had ever done" (Klein, 1926, p. 132).

The first meaning of the notion of the introjected object was what Melanie Klein was soon to call an imago—that is to say, an unreal image of objects, the parents above all. But there is no mystery about the distortion of the imagos of three objects; it simply corresponds to the fear of vengeance. In this respect the child's confusion between prohibitions coming from the real parents and those coming from the introjected parents may be related to the distinction which, according to this same 1926 text, children in analysis make temporarily between the "pretend" mother of the game, and the real mother. This distinction appears in the course of working out interpretations that concern the wish for sadistic attacks and the resulting fear of vengeance, thus may be said to have a defensive meaning. It appears in a context of denial: "children begin to distinguish between the 'pretence' mother and the real mother and between the wooden baby-doll and the live baby brother. They then firmly insist that they wanted to do this or that injury to the toy-baby only—the real baby, they say, of course they love" (p. 137). But this is only an initial stage of the working out of interpretations; when resistances are finally overcome, the children realize "that their aggressive acts were directed against the *real* objects" (p. 137). Later still, toward the end of an analysis, children sometimes become capable of joking about the incredible fact that they really wanted to eat their mother or cut her up into bits (p. 138). Such texts suggest that the borderline between real objects and introjected or "pretend" objects is extremely tenuous, and depends largely on the weight of the defense mechanisms. Very "repressed" aggression can be expressed only against toys or those imaginary play people who seem to be the

first form under which introjected objects appear. Better integrated aggression can do without these disguises.

So what Melanie Klein was trying to express in terms of
opposition between the real and the introjected object is not
simply the unreal nature of the internal figures—again, this is
nothing but the imagos the child makes of his objects—but the
child's tendency to deny or fail to recognize the identity between
the play mother and the real mother. But Melanie Klein was
already aware of this mechanism in 1921, and she had called
it splitting (*Abspaltung*) at least once, linking it with ambivalence
(p. 1ff). From 1926 onward she never tires of describing the
immeasurable distance between the terrifying internal figures
and the real parents, the coexistence of two object relations
going on in parallel on two different levels with little interference. These descriptions put the accent on a state of isolation
of two simultaneous levels of experience which may at least
partially be imputed to the action of a defensive operation; but
they do not suggest a special term with which to designate this
lack of relations between the imago and the real object (usually
described as good). The clinical reality in question may well
coincide with the one which from 1946 onward was covered by
the concept of *schizoid splitting*, which should not be confused
with the splitting we have seen in the Kleinian theory of 1932
and which in 1934 became part of the depressive position. Thus,
whatever its central significance, the Kleinian notion of the
introjected object meant in 1927—and, it would seem, up to
1932—a mistaken apprehension of the complete identity of the
"unreal" imago and its real prototype, in which later Kleinian
theory was to see a form of splitting. This connotation is all the
more pregnant because Melanie Klein's descriptions of this period tend on the whole to oppose the introjected bad objects
to the good objects; in any event, the introjective significance
of the concept of the introjected object remained blurred for
a very long time.

In the definitive Kleinian theory, the fear of vengeance is
explained in terms of projection; we know that projection of
necessity implies a dissociation of elements which are then confused, an idea expressed in 1929 by the notion of "splitting up."
As early as 1926 certain clinical passages, especially the one just

quoted, seem to imply this interpretation: it is because they do not want to recognize that their aggression is directed against real objects that children come to distinguish between a "play" mother and a real mother; Rita feared the threats of the introjected mother because she wanted to steal the baby from her real mother, who was pregnant. But it was precisely in terms of introjection that Melanie Klein described this phenomenon between 1926 and 1932, and we know that it is probably because it represents in her view the beginning of the formation of the superego, which is considered essentially an introjective process. As a result, the notion of introjection loses all substance; in the following passage its appearance adds nothing to the sense, but rather tends to obscure it: "The child himself desires to destroy the libidinal object by biting, devouring and cutting it, which leads to anxiety, since awakening of the Oedipus tendencies is followed by introjection of the object, which then becomes one from which punishment is to be expected. The child then dreads a punishment corresponding to the offence" (Klein, 1928, p. 187).

Does this mean that an object which is attacked but not introjected would not be dreaded or punishing? Such a theory would suppose that introjection itself has the power to distort. Thus, the introjected object would punish not because it has been attacked in fantasy, because its vengeance is dreaded, and because it has been introjected, but by virtue of the very fact of introjection. One of the most striking consequences of this distortion of the concept of introjection is that it no longer fits the exact description of the facts revealed by means of the play technique. For several years, because she equated the introjected object and the object distorted by the fear of vengeance, Melanie Klein was to have great difficulty accounting for the existence of benevolent and helpful introjected objects. This difficulty was in a way secondary, resulting from the difficulty she had in exactly defining the extent of one of the facts she discovered in the course of her first analyses using the play technique: the severe superego of the early stages is not an exact image of the parents and of their demands, but a caricature. From a perspective that is always central to Melanie Klein, that of the analysis of anxiety and guilt feelings, the opposition between introjected and real parents reduces to the opposition between the unreal, cruel parents of fantasy and the real parents, who are good or almost so. The severity of the internal imagos and the primal superego does not derive—except in serious pathological cases (see Klein, 1927a)—from the severity of the real parents, which is always a great deal less than that of their "copies." This shows a certain tendency often noted in Melanie Klein's work, and often criticized (see, e.g., Devereux, 1970), to declare the parents "not guilty" and to lay the entire blame for sadism on the child.

But it is easy to understand that Melanie Klein's attitude is not based on some obscure tendentious motive, but rather answers the need to bring out the fantasy dimension in the formation of the superego, the unreal nature of the first imagos. It was important to her to oppose conceptions like that of Anna Freud which made the superego the late internalization of real parental demands. Such conceptions cannot account for the severity of these pressures—a severity which to a great extent they do not recognize. Thus, everything goes to add significance to this simple fact: the introjected object is ferocious; the real object is good and reassuring. We can understand, then, why it was an embarrassment to Melanie Klein when two of her patients—Gerald and George—produced for her benevolent imagos as unreal as their vengeful imagos. Gerald brought out, side by side with nasty and dangerous characters, a "fairy mamma," ideally good, whom Melanie Klein (1927c) considered nearer reality than the cruel imagos: "I discovered in him identifications which corresponded more closely to his real parents, though not by any means identical with them" (p. 157). This more realistic imago was nonetheless willing to help the child kill his father, castrate him, and eat his penis.

We note a certain perplexity two years later concerning the subject of George, whose personifications are compared with those of Erna, whose scenarios contained only two roles—persecutor and persecuted. Although we might expect that his case would be judged more favorable, Melanie Klein (1929b) reasons differently: "His ego identified itself more thoroughly with the id and was less ready to make terms with the super-ego. Anxiety was warded off by a noticeable exclusion of reality. Wish-fulfillment clearly predominated over recognition of reality—a tendency which is one of Freud's criteria of psychosis" (p. 201). We may note that such an affirmation is almost a contradiction in terms. In good Kleinian logic, an evaluation of George's sadism, less intense than that of Erna, should lead us to expect a less pessimistic diagnosis. Everything seems to indicate that in 1929 Melanie Klein considered these entirely good imagos to be merely the reversed doubles of the terrible imagos, lacking real consistency and stability. She notes in the same article "the excessively strong influence exerted by these extreme types of imagos, the intensity of the need for the kindly figures in opposition to the menacing, the rapidity with which allies will change into enemies. . ." (p. 204).

Such considerations are indeed enlightening, and directly anticipate the later ideas which make the "ideal" object of the schizoid position of 1946 a correlate of the "persecuting" object. But in 1929 the idea figured only in this passage, and was not taken up again for a long time. It seems to have had no function except to minimize the importance of the existence of helpful imagos. Though fertile and forward-looking, its difficulties seem very real. It led her to conceive another opposition, no longer between bad unreal objects and good real objects, but between unreal objects (both good and bad) and real objects: "I have come to realise that the operation of such imagos, with phantastically good and phantastically bad characteristics, is a general mechanism in adults as well as children. These figures represent intermediate stages between the terrible menacing super-ego, which is wholly divorced from reality and the identifications which approximate more closely to reality" (p. 203). Thus, the pregnant nature of the equation between real object and good object is such that this text, which begins by suggesting a neutral relationship to the criterion good/bad, continues as follows: "These intermediate figures, whose gradual evolution into the maternal and paternal helpers (who are nearer again to reality) may constantly be observed in play-analyses, and seem to me very instructive for our knowledge of the formation of the super-ego" (p. 203).

It was not until 1932 and the publication of *The Psycho-Analysis of Children* that Melanie Klein considered the possibility

of a process of introjection of good objects. Even here, we usually have to take into consideration a constant tendency to confuse good internal objects and real objects: "His belief in the
existence of kindly and helpful figures—a belief which is
founded on the efficacy of his libido—enables his reality-objects
to emerge ever more powerfully and his phantastic imagos to
recede into the background" (Klein, 1932, p. 148). Or, further,
"the . . . introjections of real objects, which are in fact well-dis-
posed to him . . . lessens the force of his fear of the terrifying
imagos" (p. 148). Thus, introjection can apply to good objects
insofar as they are real, but there is nothing to say that the
possibility is envisaged of an internal transformation or distortion (in the sense of wish-fulfillment) which could construct
unreal good objects from neutral or moderately "good" objects.
We can certainly envisage a mitigation of the terrible internal
objects by a process of this kind: so when the child approaches
the genital stage, "it introjects more friendly imagos" (p. 153).
But this is the fate only of the *bad* introjected object. Is it possible
to envisage in the Kleinian theory of 1932 the existence of *good*
introjected objects, distinct from good real objects, which would
be quite as real as the bad objects without being merely their
reversed doubles? Could we consider the possibility of a dis-
torting introjection producing good objects?

While the general direction taken by Melanie Klein up to
1932 seems to suggest a negative reply, there are two arguments
in favor of the possibility of such an introjection, as it were *in
extremis,* in the system of 1932. One comes from a description
of identification with the attacked object, first noted in the case
of Dick, in which it played a disturbing part scarcely in accord
with its evaluation in *The Psycho-Analysis of Children.* The other
is from a footnote containing a unique statement, the only one
of its sort in the whole book: "In Chapter VIII we saw how the
'good' breast becomes turned into a 'bad' one in consequence
of the child's imaginary attacks upon it . . . so that a primary
introjection of both a good and a bad mother-imago takes place
before any other imagos are formed" (Klein, 1932, p. 206, n.
4). This passage begins with an exactitude: nowhere else has
Melanie Klein affirmed the transformation of the "good" breast
into the "bad" one as the result of the attacks against it, or said

that relations with the "good" breast came before those with the "bad" breast. In an earlier article (Klein, 1929a) she had mentioned that oral frustration turns the indulgent "good mother" into a "bad mother." But this was the mother, not the breast, and the passage is ambiguous; it is the interpretation of a literary work, Collette's libretto of Ravel's opera *L'enfant et les Sortilèges.* The note is the only instance, in all the works published up to and including 1932, of such a statement; it shows, precisely in the field of the theory of introjection, that Melanie Klein's discovery of the depressive position in 1934 was already taking shape.

Introjection, Oral Incorporation, and Their Late Relationship

Attempting to account for the process of introjection, Melanie Klein assigned to it, as basis and instinctual prototype, oral incorporation; it appears that in this way the notion of introjection finally acquired a certain consistency. It should be made clear, however, that this development came relatively late and, particularly, after the reintroduction of the notion of projection in 1929. Thus, in 1932 introjection lost the apparent supremacy assigned it in earlier texts. It acquired in this way a clarity of outline which it previously lacked, but the condition of this clarification was a certain subordination of the theory of introjection to that of projection. The different moments of internalization now began to correspond to significant moments in the history of the development of projective processes. Despite this parallelism, the terms indicating the introjective processes are still more numerous and more precisely used than those corresponding to the semantic field of projection. It is relatively easy to separate out the term "identification," which is most often used in the material sense (to indicate not the process of identification but its products, what might be called "identificates" by analogy with the "introjects" of which certain authors speak). We can also distinguish incorporation, a libidinal process described by Abraham which is the oral conterpart of anal ejection, from introjection, of which it is the prototype. As for internalization, it corresponds to the vaguest terms—take into oneself, have within—which can apply equally well to the most primitive manifestations of cannibalism or to the most developed forms of introjection of the "good" object.

The first form of internalization to appear in the development of the child is, according to *The Psycho-Analysis of Children,* partial incorporation, coupled in theory with the deflection of the death instinct. The term appears to derive from Abraham, but Melanie Klein completely changed its sense. In Abraham, partial incorporation is the process of the first anal stage, and it is called partial because it does not aspire to the complete devouring of the object, which is the aim of total cannibalism. If the object is devoured only in part, it is to preserve it. This aspect disappears completely in Melanie Klein. To her, partial incorporation affects part objects (breast, penis, feces) scarcely distinguished from the (complete) objects they represent or whose place they take, and it seems clear that she sees it as a cannibalistic process: "As far as I can judge, the nucleus of the super-ego is to be found in the partial incorporation that takes place during the cannibalistic phase of development" (Klein, 1932, pp. 136–137); in this phase, "both real and introjected objects are mainly represented by their organs" (p. 136). This is used to account for the distortion suffered by the imagos: they "take the imprint of those pre-genital impulses" (p. 137).

There is a direct connection between this incorporation and the deflection of the death instinct. This first internalization would seem to follow that deflection and to involve an external object which has been made bad by this very first defense. "It would follow logically that the ego would regard the internalized object as so cruel an enemy of the id from the fact that the destructive instinct which the ego has turned outward has become directed against that object, and consequently nothing but hostility against the id can be expected" (p. 137). The genetic sequence is thus clear: deflection of the destructive instinct, followed by cannibalistic incorporation of the object, which in its turn governs projection properly speaking, based on ejection. Incorporation is a necessary stage between the first forerunner of projection—deflection—and projection proper:

> When, as a small child, he first begins to introject his objects—and these, it must be remembered, are yet only very vaguely de-

marcated by his various organs—his fear of those introjected objects sets in motion the mechanisms of ejection and projection, . . . and there now follows a reciprocal action between projection and introjection, which seems to be of fundamental importance not only for the formation of his super-ego but for the development of his object-relations and his adaptation to reality. [pp. 142–143]

As soon as internalization leads to projection, the 1932 text calls it introjection. It is only by being put into contact with projection that introjection can be described concretely, as a mechanism with a precise libidinal basis, incorporation, and as contributing to adaptation to reality.

It must be emphasized that the main body of *The Psycho-Analysis of Children* describes introjection almost entirely in its oral-sadistic aspects, as though it was difficult for Melanie Klein to separate this process from the "bad" connotation it had acquired by being used for six years to account for the anxiogenic distortion suffered by internal objects. If the idea of the introjection of a good object now appears, it is only in footnotes, as we have seen; in 1932 the Kleinian conception of introjection had not yet reached a point of equilibrium.

5. The Discovery of Reparation Mechanisms

The Circumstances of the Discovery

Neither the theory of projection nor that of splitting had reached its full development in 1932. That of introjection was still in the process of formation at that date, while that of symbolism was still very largely implicit. That of reparation mechanisms, by contrast, has in *The Psycho-Analysis of Children* the form it was to keep, in all its essentials, throughout the later theories. In this sense it is the most important discovery made by Melanie Klein between 1927 and 1932.

One of the terms belonging to the reparation series appears for the first time in "Early Stages of the Oedipus Conflict" (Klein, 1928). There it becomes part of a relational pattern typical of reparation mechanisms; equation of the child's and the mother's bodies, followed by real action on the more materially accessible of the two equivalents (the child's own body) in order to be reassured concerning the state of the fantasy body (the internal object). The girl, who in the course of her development has made imaginary attacks on her mother's body and its contents, fears the destruction of the interior of her own body. Hence the woman's preoccupation with her physical appearance: "At the bottom of the impulse to deck and beautify themselves there is always the motive of *restoring* damaged comeliness [*Selbstwiederherstellung*], and this has its origin in anxiety and sense of guilt" (p. 194). From the very beginning of 1927, Melanie Klein had described reparatory behavior on the part of the child but without using the word: discussing play involving the devouring of the father or mother, she notes that this play is invariably prolonged by reactive behavior: "the child now tries to make good and to atone for that which he has done" (1927a, p. 175). This is indeed reparation of the attacked object, but without the word and without the typical relational structure. In the oedipus text (Klein, 1928), both the word and the relational structure are present, but the point of application is not completely located. The question is not yet one of reparation of the damaged object, but of restoration of the self. It was not until 1929 that the word and all the aspects of the concept were finally associated.

"Infantile Anxiety Situations Reflected in a Work of Art and in the Creative Impulse" (Klein, 1929a) is an amazing article. Written in a few weeks on the occasion of two newspaper articles published in the *Berliner Tageblatt* March 11 and 23, 1929, it was read on May 15 at a meeting of the British Psycho-Analytical Society; it reproduces the two articles almost in their entirety. Although it is known as the text in which the notion of reparation is introduced, only five lines are devoted explicitly to this concept. The paper, Melanie Klein's first piece of writing on art, deals entirely with works of which she had no direct knowledge: (1) Maurice Ravel's opera *L'Enfant et les Sortilèges,* the libretto of which, written by Colette, she quotes from the review published by the Berlin paper of a performance at the Vienna Opera; and (2) the paintings of Ruth Kjär, to which

Karin Michaelis, a noted writer and journalist of the time, devoted her weekly column on March 23, but which do not seem ever to have been exhibited or to have become known in informed circles (it is therefore quite improbable that Melanie Klein had ever seen the canvases she discusses). Interestingly, the German version of this paper, published two years after the English version, shows considerable differences from it, an occurrence rather rare in Melanie Klein's work, another instance being the texts of *The Psycho-Analysis of Children*.

The general plan of the article is well-known: two pages, closely paraphrased from the review, describing the opera's action, followed by psychoanalytic comments on the text, and a discussion of the article by Karin Michaelis. In brief, Colette's libretto is as follows: a lazy child refuses to do his homework, is put on dry bread by his mother, and vandalizes the room. The objects and animals he has damaged or injured rebel and chase him into a garden, where the animals attack him. All ends happily, however, because he takes care of a wounded squirrel, an art which touches the hearts of all the animals. As for Karin Michaelis's article, it tells of a young woman impelled to paint because she cannot bear to see the empty space left on the wall of her home by a picture which has been removed. This empty space seems to coincide with an empty space she feels within herself, and she suceeds in filling it by painting half a dozen canvases which the author describes as masterpieces. In both cases Melanie Klein's interpretation links the spaces in question—the room, the garden, Ruth Kjär's home—with the mother's body, which is attacked in fantasy; "We see the incidents which took place inside the room now reproduced on a bigger scale in a wider space and in larger numbers. The world, transformed into the mother's body, is in hostile array against the child and persecutes him" (Klein, 1929a, p. 214). In Karin Michaelis's piece, the empty space where the picture had been coincides with the empty space within Ruth. This empty space corresponds with "the feeling that there was something lacking in her body" (p. 216), itself the expression of "anxiety lest the mother should in her turn rob the little girl herself of the contents of her body (especially of children) and lest her body should be destroyed or mutilated" (p. 217). When Ruth Rjär paints her mother's portrait, she *repairs* the damage caused her by her fantasy attacks: "the desire to make reparation, to make good the injury psychologically done to the mother and also to restore herself was at the bottom of the compelling urge to paint these portraits of her relatives" (p. 218). By symbolically restoring her mother and sister, she was restoring the maternal imago as an internal object, and so restoring herself. We can thus understand the narcissistic dimension implied in the 1928 text (the woman's concern with beauty as "self-restoration") and the tone, also very narcissistic, of Karin Michaelis's probably very idealized description of her friend Ruth Kjär. From the very first uses of the concept of reparation, then, we find the equation between, on the one hand, the world and the mother's body, which provides the model of container/contents (body/part objects and bodily contents: feces, children, father's penis, etc.) and, on the other, the child's own body. In the context of these symbolic equations the mechanism of reparation can be deployed.

But on the basis of this system of correspondences between the fantasized body of the mother and its equivalents, many defensive forms of behavior are possible: projection, splitting up, etc. We would be right to wonder how we can pass from the fear of vengeance on the part of the object to the reconciliation contained in the very notion of the mechanism of reparation. What is it that sets the child's feet on the road to reparation rather than on that of the indefinite repetition of sadistic attacks? This question remained open after the article on infantile anxiety situations. The beginning of a reply came some months later (Klein, 1930a), but it was rather different from the generally known theory. With reference to Dick's case—a case that is exemplary and at the same time extremely odd—Melanie Klein clearly links the mechanisms of restitution (*Zurückgebung*) with genital impulses and associates them with identification with the object, based on empathy (*Einfühlung*). Here she anticipates her later theory, but the peculiarities of Dick's case prevent her from extending her observations to all children. What was to appear in 1932 as the condition of a favorable development is here the origin of a pseudodebility of a psychic nature because of the prematurity of the simultaneous appearance in this child of reparation mechanisms and empathic identification with the object: "the genital phase had become active in Dick prematurely" (Klein, 1930a, p. 227). For this reason, his sadistic attacks against his mother "were followed not by anxiety only, but by remorse, pity and a feeling that he must make restitution" (p. 227). The child, capable too early of feelings of this kind, was still too involved in the sadistic phase to be able to give them the appropriate response—fantasies of active and constructive reparation, including some real action: "This early identification with the object could not as yet be brought into relation with reality" (p. 227). Dick, still incapable of directing his empathy, addressed it to material objects as well as to persons. The selectivity which would have allowed splitting up was still inaccessible to him. He could not enter upon true reparatory behavior, but could only forbid himself to approach his mother at all—whether at the level of sadism, libidinal impulses, or epistemophilia. This radical inhibition was at the root of Dick's psychotic withdrawal: "Side by side with his incapacity for tolerating anxiety, this premature empathy became a decisive factor in his warding-off of all destructive impulses. Dick cut himself off from reality and brought his phantasy-life to a standstill" (p. 227).

Another clinical example, that of John (Klein, 1931), brings forward a new idea by recalling the equation and the interplay between the mother's body, the child's own body, and the world which form the background for reparation fantasies. The reparation mechanism is connected, at least by virtue of being contemporary with it, with an ability to sort out good and bad objects; this idea anticipates the coming theory of the splitting of the object. Thanks to a reduction, resulting from the analysis, of his fear of the superego, John became capable of symbolically restoring his mother's body and his own by tidying his drawer (this was the drawer given to the child, of which he had the key, and in which he kept, between sessions, the toys used in them. By doing this "he was tidying his own body and separating his own possessions from the things he had stolen out of his mother's body, as well as separating 'bad' faeces from 'good' faeces, and 'bad' objects from 'good' ones" (p. 243). These two cases show the whole essence of the themes later developed in *The Psycho-Analysis of Children,* which we will now examine.

The Basis of Reparation Mechanisms in Genital Impulses

The theory that reparation mechanisms are based on genital impulses has as its corollary that the decrease of sadism is what releases these mechanisms. But as sadism begins to decrease from the borderline between the first and second anal stages, it is at this period that its influence diminishes, and so the reparation mechanisms, which reach their height at the genital stage, appear first in the second anal stage, of which they are in fact characteristic. These are the main points of the instinctual theory of reparation; although they are clear and logical, the details are sometimes complex, even confused. The main aspects of these details are as follows:

1. Despite appearances, reparation mechanisms have a single determining factor. The emergence of genital impulses and the decrease of sadism are not independent processes. On the contrary, they are closely bound, each being the correlate of the other. We know that Melanie Klein considers the genital impulses present from the sixth month of life, and that they set into motion the early oedipus complex. But during the whole period of sadism at its height, they are masked by the aggressive impulses which distort the manifestations of the oedipus complex, and make reparation impossible by giving it a catastrophic turn for the child when, as in the case of Dick, early genital impulses impose care for the object prematurely.

2. More difficult to accept is the fact that the reparation mechanisms are genital in essence, although characteristic of the second anal stage. On a logical plane things are indeed clear: since the genital impulses are present from the beginning of the early oedipus complex—and thus from weaning—and since according to Melanie Klein the libidinal stages overlap and interpenetrate to a great extent, it is quite natural that genital manifestations should be found from the age of weaning. It is equally comprehensible that reparatory manifestations should be impossible at the peak of sadism and that, because of this, manifestations whose instinctual basis is genital should

appear systematically and characteristically at the beginning of the second anal stage. But the problem remains of the relationship of reparation to the mechanisms proper to the second anal stage, particularly reaction-formation. This is a delicate point to which we must return at greater length.

The Trigger for Reparation Mechanisms: Not Anxiety but Guilt

The thesis that reparation mechanisms are triggered not by anxiety but by guilt becomes comprehensible only if we make it immediately clear that when forming her theory of reparation mechanisms Melanie Klein fundamentally altered her theory of anxiety. She now clearly distinguished guilt feelings from anxiety, of which they are a late development. The idea of guilt was henceforward limited to forms which appear to exclude the fear of vengeance but to imply identification with the object attacked by true sadism. Thus, oddly enough, the notions of guilt feeling and superego are separate in Kleinian theory and remain so. From 1923 on, Melanie Klein had considered the anxiety manifest in night terrors to be the result of oedipal guilt feelings. In 1926 she used the existence of very early guilt feelings as proof of the existence of an early oedipus complex. Now, limiting the scope of the concept of guilt, she described it as occurring later. But the initial superego remained at the stage of the early oedipus complex. Between 1932 and 1934, Melanie Klein was to allow that this superego causes an anxiety which is not yet a guilt feeling, but simply the fear of vengeance.

The most remote forerunner of this important distinction, destined to become and remain one of the most central elements of the Kleinian conceptions, appears in a text of 1927. There Melanie Klein distinguished two main types of manifestation of the feeling of guilt in clinical observation of children: it may be directly expressed either "as anxiety or in representations which imply over-compensation, which are the expression of reaction-formations" (Klein, 1927c, p. 147). In 1932, when she explicitly introduced this distinction between anxiety and guilt feelings, she referred back to her 1929 text (Klein, 1929a), where, however, the distinction occurs only implicitly. The first real statement of this thesis appears in *The Psycho-Analysis of*

Children: "The weak ego of the child cannot come to terms with such an unreasonably menacing super-ego, and it is not until a rather more advanced stage has been reached that its anxiety is also felt as a sense of guilt and sets the obsessional mechanisms in motion" (Klein, 1932, p. 170).

Of what does the distinction consist? Anxiety is purely egocentric—we might say narcissistic if that term were part of the Kleinian vocabulary—while the feeling of guilt is accompanied by concern for the object. We must admit, however, that the 1932 texts, though they leave no doubt that this idea was present in Kleinian theory at that time, do not give it any clear, complete, and detailed exposition. The idea of a link between the distinction between anxiety and guilt feeling on the one hand and the opposition of sadism and concern for the object on the other has indeed been considered since that period to be typically Kleinian. Edward Glover (1933) presents it as such in his recension of *The Psycho-Analysis of Children.* But Melanie Klein does not make the comparison explicitly; rather, she develops two parallel and relatively independent series of considerations.

In one she stresses the idea that anxiety shows two successive and distinct forms. The context and the underlying purpose of this idea, however, will surprise and even disappoint anyone who expects her to anticipate her future conception of depressive anxiety. Here she is entirely preoccupied with advancing her theory of a primitive superego. Fiercely unwavering in her purpose, she seeks to show the late, relatively superficial, or in any case very attenuated character of the anxiogenic situations recognized by classical psychoanalysis—in particular, anxiety for the loss of the object (Freud, 1926). The distinction between the two types of anxiety thus appears in an outburst of argumentation which limits its scope to an extraordinary degree. The central theme of the passage is as follows: the fear of losing the loved object does indeed exist in the young child, but it is preceded by the fear of suffering vengeance; there are anxiogenic situations earlier than those described by Freud. This text was written not to draw attention to the originality of the more developed later forms of anxiety but rather to determine their proper scope. In this context Melanie Klein

(1932) is led into an unsound argument in order to introduce such an idea: she defines concern for the object, if not as the characteristic manifestation of late anxiety, at least as one of its manifestations:

> Missing the loved or longed-for person, experiencing a loss of love or a loss of object as a danger, being frightened of being alone in the dark, or with an unknown person—all these things are, I have found, modified forms of early anxiety-situations, that is, of the small child's fear of dangerous internalized and external objects. At a somewhat later stage of development there is added to this fear a concern for the object itself. The child now fears that its mother will die in consequence of its phantasied attacks upon her and, in addition, is afraid that it will be left alone in its helpless state. [p. 179]

But if the child feels the need of its mother's presence, Melanie Klein thinks, it is in the context of the quest for reassurance against the earliest fears: it is to have proof that the real mother is kindly, and not to be confused with the terrible mother of fantasy. In short, this idea, preeminently Kleinian, of the existence of two forms of anxiety—one egocentric, the other altruistic—was of so little interest to Melanie Klein at this time that she introduced it seemingly by accident, in a passage in which the central question was not, "What are the most developed forms of anxiety?" but rather, "Is anxiety for the loss of the object not based on a deeper anxiety?" It must be noted also that in the whole of this passage there is not once any question of guilt feelings. The idea in fact occurs only once, in the initial pages of her chapter on early anxiety situations, and then in its broadest sense: "The presence and love of . . . real objects also has the purpose of lessening the small child's fear of its introjected objects and its sense of guilt" (p. 178). There is also no question of defense mechanisms in general, or of reparation in particular.

In the other series of considerations the explicit distinction between anxiety and feelings of guilt is connected directly with the study of restitutive tendencies. These two affects are all the more clearly differentiated when the child, in the course of its development, approaches the genital phase. "A pre-condition for the development of restitutive tendencies and of sublimation is that the pressure exerted by the super-ego should be mitigated and felt by the ego as a sense of guilt" (p. 154). For this transformation, then, two simultaneous modifications are needed. One, quantitative, corresponds to the rapid reduction of sadism during the second anal stage; the other, qualitative, receives no further specification. Melanie Klein simply studies the economic aspects of the phenomenon, perceptible especially in variations in the pressure exerted by the superego; these variations accompany the acquisition of guilt feelings properly speaking and may cause regressions: "The qualitative changes of the superego which are initiated by the accentuation of genital impulses and object relations influence the relation of the superego to the ego and precipitate a sense of guilt. Should such feelings of guilt become too overpowering their effect will once more be felt by the ego as anxiety" (p. 154). When a regression has taken place, the ego returns to earlier defense mechanisms, all of which consist of an attack on the object, and mainly to the ejection-projection of the superego. But what of the specifically qualitative aspect of the phenomenon?

When undertaking to distinguish anxiety from guilt feelings, Melanie Klein quotes Ernest Jones's "Fear, Guilt and Hate" (1929). There Jones distinguishes fear and guilt, and in addition differentiates two forms of each. He bases his general distinction between the two affects on phylogenetic and ontogenetic considerations, but it is psychoanalytic experience that enables the description to be improved. Nonetheless, though it is true that in the clinical experience of neuroses conscious anxiety usually masks an unconscious guilt feeling, we should be careful not to generalize the relationship: "The guilt itself proceeds from a yet earlier state of fear" (p. 445). It is this idea that Melanie Klein took up in 1932. It should be noted, however, that Jones himself refers to Kleinian conceptions, declaring his interest in the theory that "the genesis of the superego is to be found in the sadistic rather than in the phallic stage of development" (p. 449). From this point of view he undertakes to discover the first form of the feeling of guilt. It is associated, he thinks, with a primal anxiety arising from the lack of libidinal satisfaction before the establishment of object relations. Thus Jones places it in the context of the second Freudian theory of anxiety, which Melanie Klein never supported; she had discovered, before Freud (1926) published "Inhibitions, Symptoms and Anxiety," that anxiety is above all a fear of vengeance deriving from sadism itself. But Jones says himself that as far as this first form of instinctual inhibition is concerned, "It would not really be correct to speak of guilt in the full sense: one needs some such expression, as a 'prenefarious' stage of guilt. This must closely resemble the processes of inhibition and renunciation; the formula would appear to be the categorical: 'I mustn't, because it is intolerable'. It attempts thus to avoid the primary anxiety" (p. 449).

As for the second form of guilt feeling, it appears with object relations: "Here sadism combined with rage at frustration breaks through, love of the other person conflicts with dread of punishment at his hands (castration and withdrawal of the loved person), and the second stage, that of completely developed guilt, is constituted. Here we may describe the formula as: 'I shouldn't because it is wrong and dangerous' ". From this point of view, whatever the unacceptable aspect of the Kleinian notion (admittedly a bit strange) of a "guilt" both prenefarious and preobject, Jones's distinction has the merit of illuminating the subject of object relations and extensively elaborating the second form of the sense of guilt: "It seems to me highly unlikely that guilt ever appears in relation to an object who is simply hated: ambivalence is an essential condition of guilt" (p. 449). This idea is very likely the reason for Melanie Klein's interest in Jones's reflections, from which she borrowed two theories: (1) fear is older than guilt; and (2) guilt, properly speaking, presupposes love as well as hate.

The article setting out Dick's case (Klein, 1930a) gives us the first description in Melanie Klein's work of guilt as distinct from anxiety: "at this point there came into prominence the fact which I have already mentioned, and which was a determining factor in his development, namely, that the genital phase had become active in Dick prematurely. This was shown in the circumstance that such representations as I have just spoken of [i.e., sadistic attacks] were followed not by anxiety only, but by remorse, pity and a feeling that he must make restitution" (p. 227). It is clear that this passage anticipates Jones's second suggestion: there is no guilt without love. It is equally clear that the feeling of guilt described here is indissolubly linked with the need for restitutive action on the one hand and, on the other, with feelings implying a certain identification with the object; associated with these premature manifestations we find "early identification with the object" or "premature empathy" (p. 227). In this sense true guilt is closely connected with pity, which appears as a powerful impetus to reparation mechanisms. But such a connection has its problems, for in classical psychoanalytic theory pity is not usually located at the genital level, but at that of the reaction-formations of the second anal stage. This is precisely the point which Melanie Klein calls into question.

The Inclusion of Reparation Mechanisms in the Group of Reaction-Formations

The very nature of Kleinian theory necessitates a reevaluation of the mechanisms of reaction-formation. In the classical Freudian conception, in which sadism is never absolutely primal, it is possible to distinguish, from libidinal movements proper, movements which are essentially reactive, arising from the aim to defend against aggression, a defense which usually operates on the basis of the economic process of countercathexis. On this basis we can distinguish spontaneous love or good will, a direct expression of instinct, from the love often described as constraining (*zwanghaft,* often translated as "compulsive," a term overloaded with psychopathological connotations) and regarded as an overcompensation for repressed unconscious hate. But in the logic of the Kleinian conception, libido alone, uninfiltrated by sadism, is met with only in the preambivalent, preobject period of the oral sucking stage. Every object relation whatsoever is sadistic and anxiogenic before being libidinalized in a second phase.

But if it is true that Eros always precedes Thanatos, which cannot help but follow in its footsteps, any manifestation of libido and love will necessarily take a reactive form: there will be no need to distinguish in theory between instinctual libidinal manifestations and reaction-formations. So even if the reparation mechanisms occupy a privileged position in the sequence of reactive manifestations, they are indisputably part of it; there is a continuous series of intermediate stages between the most effective and "normal" restitutive attitudes and the most neurotic reaction-formations. Like the reparation mechanisms properly speaking, reaction-formations appear at the beginning of the second anal stage, "when the child's relations to the object have developed. . . . Moreover, . . . the contentment of its objects is also a guarantee of the child's own safety, and a safeguard against destruction from without and from within, and the restoration of its objects is a necessary condition for its body to remain intact" (Klein, 1932, p. 165). In short, just as the libido took the path trod by sadism when objects and the external world were to be cathected, it now follows the paths taken by the sadistic tendencies in their transformation into fear of revenge—paths traced by the system of symbolic equations between the mother's body, the external world, the internal world, and the child's own body. To ensure the safety of my body and my external world, I can restore the internal imago of the mother. And to do that I can, with the help of symbolism, offer drawings or cutouts to the real mother who corresponds to her in the external world.

In the details of reparation fantasies and reaction-formations, we find the libidinal countercathexis of what earlier was cathected sadistically. Just as the pregenital superego returns bite for bite, and as every detail of the punishment feared from the internal object is the rebound, onto the child's own person, of primal sadistic fantasies, so reaction-formations and restitutive fantasies repeat every detail of these fantasied attacks and try to *overcompensate* for them, to use a term which is not peculiar to Melanie Klein, but is used frequently by Freud himself. "Early analysis," she writes (Klein, 1932), "brings complete proof of the fact that the restitutive mechanisms are ultimately based on this law of similarity (or contrast) both in quantity, quality and in every detail" (p. 172).

It seems that in the group of reaction-formations, pity occupies a special place, and is particularly close to reparation mechanisms properly speaking. The decision in 1929 to comment on the plot of Ravel's opera was motivated by the link established by Colette between the helpful behavior of the young hero toward the wounded squirrel (a symbol, Melanie Klein tells us, of the penis in the mother's body) and the instant change in the attitude of the animals, threatening up to this point but now deeply moved; they withdraw, singing the child's praise. The German version of this article, published in 1931, gives details of the time of the occurrence and the significance of pity:

> In ontogenetic development sadism is overcome when the subject advances to the genital level. The more powerfully this phase sets in, the more able does the child become of object-love, and the more able is he to conquer his sadism by means of pity and sympathy [the more he expects friendship and love from real and introjected objects, the better he can value real objects for their effective capacity for love and their goodness]. . . . when the boy feels pity for the wounded squirrel and comes to its aid, the hostile world changes into a friendly one. The child has learnt to love and believes in love" (Klein, 1931b, p. 501).[10] Whereas the example of Ruth Kjär illustrates an impulsive form of reparation, in which the narcissistic element is present in an extreme form, in appearance at least, the example of *L'enfant et les Sortilèges* illustrates a spontaneous pity which at first does not correspond to any need in the child himself, but rests only on an empathic identification with the wounded animal.

The Psycho-Analysis of Children takes up this theme, reserving for pity a place very close to that of the reparation mechanisms, of which it very often appears to be the specific stimulus. We should note in particular that the 1932 text tends to consider the instinctual bases of pity to be genital and not simply late anal:

> The individual becomes increasingly successful in overcoming anxiety thanks to the progressive development of the infant

---

[10] The words in square brackets do not appear in the earlier English version (see Klein, 1929a, p. 214).

towards the genital stage during which it introjects more friendly imagos, resulting in a change in the character of the super-ego's methods.

When the hitherto overpowering threats of the superego become toned down into admonitions and reproaches the ego can find support against them in its positive relationships. It can now employ restitutive mechanisms and reaction-formations of pity towards its objects so as to placate the superego. [p. 153]

This passage appears to insist on the idea that the "reaction-formations of pity," far from being anal in character, become a way to "placate the superego" in exact proportion to the child's development "towards the genital stage." This text places pity in close relation to the attitude of support evinced by kindly real objects (incarnations of a tolerant superego), described elsewhere as a condition of successful entry into the latency period, and the intervention of which belongs of necessity to the infantile genital phase.

There are many indications of this relation: one need only mention the close links between, on the one hand, pity and identification (through the notion of empathy), and, on the other, identification and genital tendencies. It should be emphasized that Melanie Klein, who for the most part uses the term identification only in its material sense of a definite identification with some object, whole or part, scarcely uses it in its formal sense, except to affirm the connection of identification in general with the genital phase, as if this were in her view a different mechanism from the oral-sadistic mechanism of incorporation-introjection. Her article on symbol-formation (Klein, 1930a) makes it clear that this identification is in fact sympathy (*Einfühlung*), a term loaded with very positive connotations in the German cultural tradition, a fact sometimes glossed by the comparison with that movement toward another person known as sympathy, the etymological sense of which is the same as that of the German term for pity (*Mitleiden*, a suffering with). This movement is in the Kleinian sense projective rather than introjective. Identification with the attacked object is thus a mechanism unconnected with the introjection of that object; it has in fact the opposite meaning. Occurring early in development, introjection places a dangerous part object "inside," which then must be ejected into the outside world; watchfulness is necessary lest it return to the attack. It is from this watchfulness that the sense of reality arises in the first anal stage.

By contrast, identification with the attacked object occurs later and is linked with genital impulses. When this late mechanism is brought into action prematurely (as in Dick's case), it is because of the premature activity of the genital impulses; its effect is not comparable with that of the introjection of the "bad" attacked object, as it leads not to the destructive ejection of the object but to the breaking of the movement of projection, and thus of the link with reality, through a concern to protect the object. This, then, is a defense mechanism (distinct in 1932 from introjection) which may be projective, even if it is not always so, and whose instinctual basis is indisputably genital. Thus, the reaction-formation of pity is used more frequently as the genital stage is approached; the identification mechanism underlying it is that of identification with the damaged object, the precursor in the 1932 system of the notion of introjection of the "good" object as seen in the depressive position. There is nothing to distinguish pity from reparation mechanisms, either by the source of impulses or by the type of object relations.

Other reaction-formations—disgust, orderliness, cleanliness—are less commonly associated with pity and the reparation mechanisms. However, while one of the reaction formations, pity, tends to be closely linked with reparation, one of the mechanisms of this series tends to become separated from the others and to enter into closer relation with the reaction-formations. It thus appears to have more to do with the second anal stage than with the infantile genital stage. This is the mechanism of restitution, often considered the equivalent of reparation or restoration, to such a degree that translators render such terms almost indifferently. To be precise, however, *Wiedergutmachung* should be translated as reparation, *Wiederherstellung* as restoration, and *Wiedergebung* as restitution. Although it may indeed happen that the three terms are equivalent,[11] Melanie Klein

___

[11] When the girl thinks she has in reality despoiled her mother by her imaginary attacks, "This fear . . . goes to strengthen still further the ties that

shows a clear tendency to prefer the term restitution in the case of behavior inspired by fear of the threatening object, whether internal or external. In this sense the instinctual bases of restitution are usually anal rather than genital, and it corresponds to an object relation in which giving back is much nearer to taking than restoring is to destroying:

> In play analysis compulsive taking and giving back again finds very diverse expression. It occurs, together with anxiety and guilt, as a reaction to preceding representations of acts of robbery and destruction. . . .
> We then often see that in consequence of his rising anxiety, the child not only puts back what he has symbolically taken out of his mother's body, but also that by doing so, his compulsion to give, or rather to return [*wiedergeben*], is not being satisfied. He is incessantly compelled to supplement in all sorts of ways, what he gives back, and in doing so, his primary sadistic tendencies continually break through his reactive ones. [Klein, 1932, p. 167]

Restitution, more infiltrated with sadism and anxiety than reparation properly speaking, is thus in an intermediate position between pathological mechanisms, whether psychotic or neurotic, and normal ones. The ego making restitution is still struggling against an early type of anxiety, but uses for it more subtle means than projection by ejection—means which are used fully only at the genital level, in the struggle against guilt feelings: "Analyses of adults, too, have shown me that the wish to have a capital sum in hand for any contingency is really a desire for security, by being armed against an attack on the part of the mother they have robbed—a mother who was as often as not in point of fact, long since dead—and to be able to give back to her what they have stolen" (p. 168). As the strictly reactive aspect is much more important than the primary libidinal movement toward the object, restitution is much more exposed to the risk of failure than are the other reparation

---

bind her to her mother. It gives rise to an impulsion to make restitution and give her mother back all she has taken from her—an impulsion which finds expression in numerous sublimations of a specifically feminine kind" (Klein, 1932, p. 208).

mechanisms. In fact, the subject undertaking restitution is caught in an interminable sequence of obsessional actions in which the previous annulment is in its turn canceled by yet another counteraction: "we see the very neurotic child laboring under a constant compulsion to take in order to be able to give" (p. 170). It can suffer an even more serious failure when the patient, crushed by the impossibility of giving back everything, gives up the restitutive strategy and regresses to earlier defenses, as in the case of John:

> Whenever there was an increase in his fear of not being able to produce the right kind of thing or to give enough, or of not being able to repair what he had damaged, his primary destructive trends once more broke out in full force. He would tear, cut to pieces and burn the things he had made when moved by reactive tendencies—the box which he had stuck together and filled up and which represented his mother, or the piece of paper on which he had drawn (perhaps a plan of a town)—and his thirst for destruction would then be insatiable. [p. 169].

An obstacle to the success of restitution is that in it a residue of revenge survives. To pay off a debt—the German word *Schuld* means both financial debt and moral fault, and we know the use philosophers, especially Nietzsche (1887: 2nd dissertation, sections 19–20), have made of this double meaning—we must give back and count what we give back. This path is in itself a slippery one, and we shall see that of its very nature it constitutes an inescapable trap. It must first be emphasized, however, that the instinctual basis of restitution appears much more anal than genital. The problems of taking and giving back, and of behavior with regard to money in adults, are only its symbolic expression. The analysis of children often brings out more directly the anal nature of restitution: "Very often children will be interrupted in their representations of 'giving back' by having to go to the lavatory to defaecate" (Klein, 1932, p. 168). Thus, restitution is relatively distinct from reparation, just as pity is not a reaction-formation like the others. The field of reparation, like that of reaction-formation, is vast; it embraces the second anal stage and the infantile genital stage, and the two groups of mechanisms are in reality confused. But a frontier nonetheless divides this vast domain into two distinct regions, reparation and pity on one side, restitution and the other re-action-formations on the other, according to a simple criterion which comes down to distinguishing successful reactions and reparations from those which fail.

Successful Reparation vs. Omnipotent Reparation Doomed to Failure

We know that in Melanie Klein's definitive theories om-nipotent reparation is characteristic of manic defense. We may note that even before the theory of psychotic positions was elaborated she had made a clear distinction between two types of reparatory behavior, one based on the presence or absence of omnipotent thinking. In 1932 it was under the heading of obsessional mechanisms that she entered upon the study of disturbances in reparation caused by the illusion of omnipo-tence of thought. It is curious to observe, however, that it was in making this distinction that she introduced into her work for the first time a clear and detailed explanation of the fear of vengeance, attributing it to the child's belief in precisely this illusion. She was certainly aware of both the phrase and the idea; they are found on several occasions in the writings of the proto-Kleinian period, but they disappeared from her vocab-ulary after 1925. She now took up the idea again. Quoting Freud, Ferenczi, and Abraham, she resorted to the notion of narcissism, traditionally associated with the illusion of omnip-otence, but in scant agreement with the general direction of her thought; her later work does not mention it again. Thus, in 1932 she wrote that the phase of development "in which, according to my view, the onset of the Oedipus conflict and its accompanying sadistic masturbation phantasies arise is the phase of narcissism" (p. 171). Such a juxtaposition of terms may seem surprising. But that does not make it less coherent in the context of the reference to Abraham's conceptions, according to which the stage of narcissism and the total incorporation of the object corresponds with the libidinal phase of the second oral stage, or the cannibalistic stage. At this stage narcissism causes a general overestimation by the child of all the body's products "and a consequent belief in the omnipotence of its thoughts" (p. 171). By virtue of this overestimation, thought and action are equated, and the child makes no distinction between attacking in fantasy and attacking in reality: "As the result of this it feels guilty on account of the manifold assaults on its parents which it carries out in its phantasy" (pp. 171–172).

The obsessional's misfortune is that he tries to fight against the omnipotence of sadism with the omnipotence of reparation. He thus plays into the hands of a tortuous variant of the law of talion: "When their sense of guilt sets in motion obsessive actions as a defence, they will employ the feeling of omnipotence for the purpose of making restitution. But this feeling of omnipotence must now be sustained in a compulsive and ex-aggerated way, for the restitution, too, like the original destruc-tion, is based upon 'omnipotence' " (p. 172). In this game the dice are always loaded, by virtue of a genetic factor. The feeling of having destroyed is the heritage of a period of development in which the ego was incapable of submitting to the test of reality. The conviction of having destroyed the object is thus all the more rooted in the unconscious because from its origin it has escaped all doubt or critical examination. It represents a nucleus of absolute conviction, and its very entrenchment in the deepest layers protects it from any change. Reparation ten-dencies, on the other hand, appear at the beginning of the second anal stage; they belong to a more developed ego, which already knows, according to Nina Searl's profound observa-tion—quoted by Melanie Klein (p. 172)—that it is easier to break things than to put them together again. This ego already knows too much to give in to the illusion of its omnipotence for re-paration with the same blind faith with which, at the stage of sadism at its height, it believed in its omnipotence for destruc-tion. It is thus essential rather than accidental that reparation should suffer the same fate as the omnipotence of sadistic fan-tasies and be doomed to failure from the beginning: "reaction-formations set in at a stage of ego-development and object-relationship which presupposes a much more advanced rela-tionship to reality. Thus where an exaggerated sense of om-nipotence is a necessary condition for making restitution, his belief in the possibility of being able to do so will be handicapped from the outset" (p. 172). Because of this inevitable shift, obsessional reparation is an endless process that may take a variety of clinical forms, including doubts of one's ability to make reparation, forcing one to repeat, indefinitely, more or less magical efforts at reparation, as well as attempts to deny omnipotence of any kind since "every indication that he was using his omnipotence in a positive sense would be proof of his having used it in a negative sense" (p. 173). In the child, this latter attitude jeopardizes the possibilities of sublimation.

There is also a qualitative relationship between primal sadism, the illusion of omnipotence, and omnipotent reparation. In certain patients excessive primal sadism means that reparation, to be commensurate with the damage done, must take on megalomanic proportions. In such cases the impossibility of reparation dooms all constructive tendencies to radical failure.

But why do some subjects have to resort to omnipotent reparation, while others can avoid it? Melanie Klein indeed suggests what compels neurotics to retain their feeling of omnipotence or to regress to it; it is an excess of guilt arising from imaginary attacks against the parents. But what is the really effective differential factor? Why do some subjects whose sadism is "excessive" become obsessional, others manic, others pseudodebilitated psychotics, etc.? Melanie Klein did not tell us in 1932. At that time she indisputably recognized the existence of an omnipotent functioning of the reparation mechanisms, but she had not yet worked out a complete theory of omnipotent reparation, its causes, and its developmental effects. She was still quite a long way from her theory of the manic position.

The Discovery of Reparation Mechanisms Leads to the Final Formulation of the Kleinian Genetic Schema

At this stage of the development of Melanie Klein's thought, there could no longer be any question of "Abraham's scheme." This author's conceptions were by then integrated into a truly original theory, in which the phase of sadism at its height is opposed to a phase of reparation. This meant that the dividing line between the two anal stages was given a psychological and psychopathological significance which is sometimes very difficult to distinguish from that attached to the distinction between pregenital and genital impulses. The signs of this fluctuation were noted when we examined the fact that the reparation mechanisms, genetically characteristic of the second anal stage, have nonetheless a genital instinctual basis. It is true that Melanie Klein's position on this point is absolutely logical; but this is a global attitude going beyond the context of reparation mechanisms, extending out from them to the whole of Kleinian theory and combining with the results of her study of the theory of instinctual development. The end of sadism at its height and the onset of reparation mechanisms tend to coincide. Between partial love marked by a concern to preserve the object (the second anal stage) and object love excluding the genital organs (the infantile genital stage) the difference is less important than the resemblance. In addition, once Melanie Klein had recognized the frequency and original features of infantile psychosis, her interest became more and more centered on this question, and the dividing line between the two anal stages took on for her a value which was all the more fundamental because her discoveries had shown that the oedipus complex is not still to come for the child at the beginning of the second anal stage, but that it is already played out. In this way the dividing line takes on the significance of an ultimate trial, following which development is almost definitively determined and a second stage of development is begun marked by the establishment of a certain latency, through the elaboration of a mitigated and phallicized oedipus complex, the forms of which are determined by the experiences lived through—essentially on the level of fantasy—during the period of sadism at its height.

It is not surprising, then, that Melanie Klein, establishing the very close relationship between reparation mechanisms and reaction-formations, attached repression to the genital and the second anal stages indifferently. She could also write: "The relations of ego to the id, which in a somewhat earlier stage has been one of ejection, becomes in the later anal stage one of suppression of instincts—or rather, of repression in the true sense of the word" (Klein, 1932, p. 152). She saw no contradiction in justifying this statement by quoting a sentence from Freud (1926): "repression is a process which has a special relation to the *genital* organization of the libido and that the ego resorts to other methods of defence when it has to secure itself against the libido on other levels of organisation" (p. 125; quoted by Klein, 1932, p. 141). For her, the distinction she maintained verbally between the second anal stage and the infantile genital stage counted much less than that between the sadistic phase and the phase in which the primacy of love is beginning to assert itself. Though the opposition between pregenital and genital remained as important, its importance was no longer accorded a diachronic and genetic significance. That is, it is not the genital impulses which lend the development of the instincts its general tenor and rhythm; this part is played by the pregenital sadistic impulses, whose sudden irruption is followed by a considerable decrease. The genital impulses are present from the beginning, without any large or sudden variation in their intensity. Qualitatively, they are from the beginning the same as they are in the classical oedipal phase: directed toward the object and inspiring love and kindliness to such a degree that their premature appearance could cause in Dick a premature empathy catastrophic for his development. Thus, if we allow that between 1929 and 1932 the notion of reparation was Melanie Klein's deepest inspiration, we can understand that the general trend of her theoretical work was to pay increasing attention to the genetic dividing line between sadism and reparation, and to pinpoint as accurately as possible the processes occurring there which enable the former to be left behind.

Thus, Melanie Klein's two essential discoveries between 1927 and 1932 were those of a peak phase of sadism—the fixation point of psychosis—and of a mechanism, reparation, which enables it to be left behind. Everything thus conspires to make the moment when reparation enables sadism to be overcome the most central point in development; apart from a few rearrangements this idea, clearly stated in *The Psycho-Analysis of Children,* already contains the essence of Melanie Klein's most important discovery: that of the early depressive position, which she was to make two years later.

Conclusion

The description of the phase of sadism at its height is in-
dissociable from the discovery of the mechanisms of reparation.
Their conflictual sequence appears as the major event in the
development of the child.

By this is meant that the process through which Melanie
Klein discovered and thematized, following in the direct line
of Abraham, the existence of an extreme sadism, approximately
contemporary with that author's cannibalistic phase, is not, as
it might appear, independent of the process through which she
went on to make the discovery of reparation mechanisms. We
should note first of all, as an irrefutable fact, that the two discoveries were simultaneous and that both found their first important clinical illustration in the description of Dick's case. But
if we consider retrospectively the distance covered since the
oedipus complex was recognized in Rita's analysis in 1923, we
can see that as Melanie Klein went deeper into her concepts she
was led first of all to bring out earlier and earlier forms of
sadism, and then increasingly intense forms with regard to its
origins, resources, and objects. It was the same urge to explore
the deepest, earliest, and most extreme forms which showed
how interested she was in psychoses and which led her to recognize the dimensions of paranoia in Erna and autism—or, as
she put it, schizophrenia—in Dick. We can certainly attribute
this development of Kleinian theory to the accumulation of
clinical experience. Without a doubt it was her daily contact
with the earliest fantasies of young prepsychotic children that
concentrated her attention and forced her to interpolate into
her theories the description of this practical experience. Between 1929 and 1932 the impact of this clinical reality was such
that Melanie Klein was driven to acquire the conceptual instruments that would help her make sense of this pressing reality.
It must be emphasized that the concepts to which she resorted
with this in mind were not invented in an attempt to produce
her own system of ideas, but rather were borrowed from Abraham, in however modified a form, in order to meet the prob-
lematic reality she faced: varied sadistic attacks, overlapping
stages, an alteration of the notion of partial incorporation, etc.

In her description of the phase of sadism at its height—a concept which was entirely her own—only the epistemophilic instinct and the fantasy of the combined parents have the status of exclusively Kleinian notions. It should also be made clear that the latter is offered more as a fact to be observed in the imaginary scenarios it organizes—a fact to interpret, it is true, and in that sense constructive—than as a theoretical concept to be elaborated. It may be hypothesized that Melanie Klein, though capable of discovering the existence of a number of manifestations of extreme sadism during the early phases of development, was either perplexed or relatively uninterested when it came to the theoretical formulation of these facts. The remarkable thing is that she was hardly at all concerned with finding a deep-seated motive for sadism, as she did later for greed, projective identification, and envy. From 1927 on she used the first two concepts episodically, and had at her disposal all the clinical elements that enabled her to conceptualize the third in 1946. It was not because she lacked the means of making this conceptual study of sadism that she was uninterested in it. What is more, we notice that it was precisely when she was trying to identify a mechanism producing bad internal objects that Melanie Klein found herself, for quite a long time, in a theoretical impasse, clinging to the idea that an "introjected" object has been constituted in its most characteristic form—that is, "bad" to an unreal degree—by a mechanism of the introjective type.

As regards the description of the earliest and most extreme forms of sadism, the strength and scope of Melanie Klein's contribution must not be underestimated. However, it is precisely in the field of identification and analysis of the different procedures used by the ego to overcome sadism, or in any case to face up to it more or less completely, that Melanie Klein's genius shows itself in all its creativity. The discovery as early as 1929 of the reparation mechanisms brought in its wake the thematization of all the processes the recognition of which is characteristic of the Kleinian approach: splitting of the object; identification with (introjection of) the attacked object in sadistic fantasy; true guilt feelings as opposed to simple anxiety; repression proper; and sublimation. Around this pole of reparation are grouped the newest and most promising of all the ideas Melanie Klein brings into play in *The Psycho-Analysis of Children*. From the very beginning they are a system, so that anyone noticing the close ties existing from 1932 between splitting and genuine guilt feelings will never run the risk of confusing this "good" splitting with the schizoid mechanism described under the same term in the texts of 1946 and 1952, and will not be surprised to see the author of "Envy and Gratitude" (Klein, 1957) rediscover the adaptive strength of this defensive process.

But to make this observation is to say at the same time that in 1932 Melanie Klein was in possession of all the elements with which, by clarifying the bond between them, she could construct the theory of the depressive position. By a paradox which is only apparent, it was at the extreme point of a determinedly genetic attitude that *The Psycho-Analysis of Children* laid the foundations for the conception of 1934, which dismissed genetic preoccupations. It was by opposing more and more radically, in the very context of her genetic schema, the phase of sadism at its height and the reparation phase, that Melanie Klein was bound to see the concrete forms of their interaction, their overlapping, the regressions and progressions from one to the other—in short, the conflict-filled coexistence in which the distinction between the two phases takes, for the entire time of their overlapping, a sense that is more dynamic than genetic. To all intents and purposes they are no longer phases, but already positions, in the sense which a text of 1935 (Klein, 1935b) expressly assigns the term. That is to say, at the very moment the first Kleinian system finally took shape, it contained the germs of its own obsolescence.

References

Abraham, K. (1913), A constitutional basis of locomotor activity. In: *Selected Papers in Psycho-Analysis*. London: Hogarth Press, 1927, pp. 235–243.

—— (1920a), Manifestations of the female castration complex. In: *Selected Papers on Psycho-Analysis*. London: Hogarth Press, 1927, pp. 338–369.

—— (1920b), The narcissistic evaluation of excretory processes in dreams and neurosis. In: *Selected Papers on Psycho-Analysis*. London: Hogarth Press, 1927, pp. 318–322.

—— (1924a), The influence of oral erotism on character formation. In: *Selected Papers on Psycho-Analysis*. London: Hogarth Press, 1927, pp. 393–406.

—— (1924b), A short study of the development of the libido, viewed in the light of mental disorders. In: *Selected Papers on Psycho-Analysis*. London: Hogarth Press, 1927, pp. 418–501.

Alexander, F. (1923), The castration complex and the formation of character. *Internat. J. Psycho-Anal.*, 4:11–42.

Anzieu, D. (1957), *Le Psychodrame analytique chez l'enfant*. Paris: P.V.F.

—— (1973), *Les méthodes projectives*. 4th ed. Paris: P.V.F.

Baranger, W. (1971), *Posicion y Objeto en la Obro de Melanie Klein*. Buenos Aires: Editorial Paidos.

Bion, W. (1961), *Experiences in Groups*. London: Tavistock.

——, Rosenfeld, H., & Segal, H. (1961), Melanie Klein. *Internat. J. Psycho-Anal.*, 42:4–8.

Bolland, J., & Sandler, J. (1965), *The Hampstead Psychoanalytic*

Index: A Study of the Psychoanalytic Case Material of a Two-Year-Old Child. New York: International Universities Press.

Cassirer, E. (1923–1929), *The Philosophy of Symbolic Forms.* 3 vols. New Haven: Yale University Press, 1953–1957.

Chadwick, M. (1925), Uber die Würzel de Wissbegierde (The origin of the desire to know). *Internationale Zeitschrift für Psychoanalyse,* 11:54–68.

Devereux, G. (1970), Les pulsions cannabaliques de parents. In: *Essais d'ethnopsychiatrie générale.* Paris: Gallimard, pp. 143ff.

Ferenczi, S. (1908), Psycho-analysis and education. In: *Final Contributions to the Problems and Methods of Psycho-Analysis.* London: Hogarth Press, 1955.

——— (1909), Introjection and transference. In: *Contributions to Psycho-Analysis.* Boston: Badger, 1916, pp. 30–79.

——— (1913a), A little chanticleer. In: *Contributions to Psycho-Analysis.* Boston: Badger, 1916, pp. 204–213.

——— (1913b), The ontogenesis of symbols. In: *Contributions to Psycho-Analysis.* Boston: Badger, 1916, pp. 233–237.

——— (1913c), Stages in the development of the sense of reality. In: *Contributions to Psycho-Analysis.* Boston: Badger, 1916, pp. 181–203.

——— (1919a), Sunday neuroses. In: *Further Contributions to the Theory and Technique of Psycho-Analysis.* London: Hogarth Press, 1926, pp. 174–176.

——— (1919b), Technische Schwierigkeiten einer Hysterieanalyse. *Internationale Zeitschrift für Psychoanalyse,* 5:37.

——— (1924), *Thalassa: A Theory of Genitality.* New York: Norton, 1968.

Freud, A. (1926–1927), Introduction to the technique of child analysis. In: *The Psycho-Analytical Treatment of Children.* New York: International Universities Press, 1955, pp. 3–52.

——— (1965), *Normality and Pathology in Childhood: Assessment of Development.* New York: International Universities Press.

Freud, S. (1895a), On the grounds for detaching a particular syndrome from neurasthenia under the description "anxiety neurosis." *Standard Edition,* 3:90–115. London: Hogarth Press, 1962.

—— (1895b), Project for a scientific psychology. *Standard Edition,* 1:295–397. London: Hogarth Press, 1966.

—— (1900), The interpretation of dreams. *Standard Edition,* 4/5. London: Hogarth Press, 1953.

—— (1905a), Fragment of an analysis of a case of hysteria. *Standard Edition,* 7:7–122. London: Hogarth Press, 1953.

—— (1905b), Three essays on the theory of sexuality. *Standard Edition,* 7:130–243. London: Hogarth Press, 1953.

—— (1908), "Civilized" sexual ethics and modern nervous illness. *Standard Edition,* 9:181–204. London: Hogarth Press, 1959.

—— (1909a), Analysis of a phobia in a five-year-old boy. *Standard Edition,* 10:5–148. London: Hogarth Press, 1955.

—— (1909b), Family romances. *Standard Edition,* 9:237–241. London: Hogarth Press, 1959.

—— (1909c), Notes upon a case of obsessional neurosis. *Standard Edition,* 10:155–318. London: Hogarth Press, 1955.

—— (1910a), The antithetical meaning of primal words. *Standard Edition,* 11:155–161. London: Hogarth Press, 1957.

—— (1910b), Leonardo da Vinci and a memory of his childhood. *Standard Edition,* 11:63–137. London: Hogarth Press, 1957.

—— (1911), Formulations on the two principles of mental functioning. *Standard Edition,* 12:218–226. London: Hogarth Press, 1958.

—— (1913), The disposition to obsessional neurosis. *Standard Edition,* 12:317–326. London: Hogarth Press, 1958.

—— (1914), Remembering, repeating and working through. *Standard Edition,* 12:147–156. London: Hogarth Press, 1958.

—— (1915a), Instincts and their vicissitudes. *Standard Edition,* 14:117–140. London: Hogarth Press, 1957.

—— (1915b), The unconscious. *Standard Edition,* 14:166–215. London: Hogarth Press, 1957.

—— (1916–1917), Introductory lectures on psycho-analysis. *Standard Edition,* 15/16. London: Hogarth Press, 1963.

———— (1918), From the history of an infantile neurosis. *Standard Edition*, 17:7–122. London: Hogarth Press, 1955.

———— (1919), Lines of advance in psychoanalytic therapy. *Standard Edition*, 17:159–168. London: Hogarth Press, 1955.

———— (1920), Beyond the pleasure principle. *Standard Edition*, 18:7–64. London: Hogarth Press, 1955.

———— (1921), Group psychology and the analysis of the ego. *Standard Edition*, 18:69–143. London: Hogarth Press, 1955.

———— (1923), The ego and the id. *Standard Edition*, 19:12–66. London: Hogarth Press, 1961.

———— (1925), Negation. *Standard Edition*, 19:235–239. London: Hogarth Press, 1961.

———— (1926), Inhibitions, symptoms and anxiety. *Standard Edition*, 20:87–174. London: Hogarth Press, 1959.

———— (1933), New introductory lectures on psycho-analysis. *Standard Edition*, 22:5–182. London: Hogarth Press, 1964.

———— & Abraham, K. (1907–1926), *A Psycho-Analytic Dialogue*. London: Hogarth Press, 1965.

Giovacchini, P. (1972), *Tactics and Techniques in Psychoanalytic Therapy*, Vol. 1. New York: Aronson.

Glover, E. (1933), The psycho-analysis of children. *Internat. J. Psycho-Anal.*, 14:119–129.

Hoffer, W. (1961), Melanie Klein. *Internat. J. Psycho-Anal.*, 42:1–3.

Horney, K. (1924), On the genesis of the castration complex in women. *Internat. J. Psycho-Anal.*, 5:50–65.

Hug-Hellmuth, H. von (1921), On the technique of child analysis. *Internat. J. Psycho-Anal.*, 2:287–305.

✓ Isaacs, S. (1943), The nature and function of phantasy. In: *Developments in Psycho-Analysis*, ed. M. Klein, P. Heimann, S. Isaacs, & J. Riviere. London: Hogarth Press, 1952, pp. 67–221.

Jaques, E. (1974), Mort et crise du milieu de la vie. In: *Psychoanalyse du génie créateur*, ed. D. Anzieu. Paris: Dunod.

Jones, E. (1916), The theory of symbolism. In: *Papers on Psycho-Analysis*. 3rd ed. London: Baillière, Tindall, & Cox, 1938, pp. 87–144.

———— (1927), The early development of female sexuality. In:

Papers on Psycho-Analysis. London: Baillière, Tindall, & Cox, 1938, pp. 438–451.

———— (1929), Fear, guilt and hate. In: *Papers on Psycho-Analysis.* London: Baillière, Tindall, & Cox, 1938, pp. 304–319.

———— (1955), *The Life and Work of Sigmund Freud,* Vol. 2. New York: Basic Books.

———— (1957), *The Life and Work of Sigmund Freud,* Vol. 3. New York: Basic Books.

Klein, M. (1920), Der Familienroman in Statu Nascendi (The family romance in statu nascendi). *Internationale Zeitschrift für Psychoanalyse,* 6:151–155.

———— (1921), The development of a child. In: *Love, Guilt and Reparation and Other Works 1921–1945.* London: Hogarth Press, 1975, pp. 1–53.

———— (1923a), Early analysis. In: *Love, Guilt and Reparation and Other Works 1921–1945.* London: Hogarth Press, 1975, pp. 77–105.

———— (1923b), The role of the school in the libidinal development of the child. In: *Love, Guilt and Reparation and Other Works 1921–1945.* London: Hogarth Press, 1975, pp. 59–76.

———— (1925), A contribution to the psychogenesis of tics. In: *Love, Guilt and Reparation and Other Works 1921–1945.* London: Hogarth Press, 1975, pp. 106–127.

———— (1926), The psychological principles of early analysis. *Internat. J. Psycho-Anal.,* 8:25–37. Also in *Love, Guilt and Reparation and Other Works 1921–1945.* London: Hogarth Press, 1975, pp. 128–138.

———— (1927a), Criminal tendencies in normal children. In: *Love, Guilt and Reparation and Other Works 1921–1945.* London: Hogarth Press, 1975, pp. 170–185.

———— (1927b), Notes on "A dream of forensic interest" by Douglas Bryan. *Internat. J. Psycho-Anal.,* 9:255–258.

———— (1927c), Symposium on child-analysis. In: *Love, Guilt and Reparation and Other Works 1921–1945.* London: Hogarth Press, 1975, pp. 139–169.

———— (1928), Early stages of the Oedipus complex. In: *Love, Guilt and Reparation and Other Works 1921–1945.* London: Hogarth Press, 1975, pp. 186–198.

————— (1929a), Infantile anxiety situations reflected in a work of art and in the creative impulse. In: *Love, Guilt and Reparation and Other Works 1921–1945*. London: Hogarth Press, 1975, pp. 210–218.

————— (1929b), Personification in the play of children. In: *Love, Guilt and Reparation and Other Works 1921–1945*. London: Hogarth Press, 1975, pp. 199–209.

————— (1929c), Die Rollenbildung im Kinderspiel. *Internationale Zeitschrift für Psychoanalyse*, 15:171–182.

————— (1930a), The importance of symbol-formation in the development of the ego. In: *Love, Guilt and Reparation and Other Works 1921–1945*. London: Hogarth Press, 1975, pp. 219–232.

————— (1930b), The psychotherapy of the psychoses. In: *Love, Guilt and Reparation and Other Works 1921–1945*. London: Hogarth Press, 1975, pp. 233–235.

————— (1931a), A contribution to the theory of intellectual inhibition. In: *Love, Guilt and Reparation and Other Works 1921–1945*. London: Hogarth Press, 1975, pp. 236–247.

————— (1931b), Frühe Angstsituortionem im Spiegel Kunstlerisher Darstellungen. *Internationale Zeitschrift für Psychoanalyse*, 17:497–506.

————— (1932), *The Psycho-Analysis of Children*. Transl. A. Strachey. Rev. ed. London: Hogarth Press, 1975.

————— (1933), The early development of conscience in the child. In: *Love, Guilt and Reparation and Other Works 1921–1945*. London: Hogarth Press, 1975, pp. 248–257.

————— (1935a), *On the Bringing Up of Children*. London: Kegan Paul.

————— (1935b), A contribution to the psychogenesis of manic-depressive states. In: *Love, Guilt and Reparation and Other Works 1921–1945*. London: Hogarth Press, 1975, pp. 262–289.

————— (1936), Weaning. In: *Love, Guilt and Reparation and Other Works 1921–1945*. London: Hogarth Press, 1975, pp. 290–305.

————— (1945), The Oedipus complex in the light of early anxieties. In: *Love, Guilt and Reparation and Other Works 1921–1945*. London: Hogarth Press, 1975, pp. 370–419.

——— (1946), Notes on some schizoid mechanisms. In: *Envy and Gratitude and Other Works 1946–1963*. New York: Delacorte, 1975, pp. 1–24.

——— (1948), *Contributions to Psycho-Analysis* (trans. Essais de Psychanalyse). London: Hogarth Press.

——— (1952), *Developments in Psycho-Analysis*. London: Hogarth Press, 1966.

——— (1955), The psycho-analytic play technique: Its history and significance. In: *Envy and Gratitude and Other Works 1946–1963*. London: Hogarth Press, 1975, pp. 122–140.

——— (1957), Envy and gratitude. In: *Envy and Gratitude and Other Works 1946–1963*. New York: Delacorte, 1975, pp. 176–235.

——— (1961), *Narrative of a Child Analysis*, ed. E. Jaques. London: Hogarth Press.

——— (1968), *Essais de Psychanalyse*. Paris: Payot, 1968. See under 1948 for English trans.

——— Heimann, P., Isaacs, S., & Riviere, J., eds. (1952), *Developments in Psycho-Analysis*. London: Hogarth Press.

Lagache, D. (1964), Fantaisie, réalité, vérité. In: *La Psychoanalyse*, Vol. 5. Paris: P.U.F. [Fantasy, reality, and truth. *Internat. J. Psycho-Anal.*, Vol. 45]

Laplanche, J., & Pontalis, J.-B. (1967), *The Language of Psycho-Analysis*, transl. D. Nicholson-Smith. New York: Norton, 1973.

Levi-Strauss, C. (1958), Symbolic efficacy. In: *Structural Anthropology*. Vol. 1. New York: Basic Books, 1963.

Merleau-Ponty, M. (1953), Les relations avec autri chez l'enfant. Paris: Centre de documentation universitaire.

Nietzsche, F. (1887), *The Genealogy of Morals and Peoples and Countries*. Snowmass Village, CO: Gordon Press, 1974.

Pfeiffer, S. (1919), Manifestations of infantile erotic impulses in play: The position of psychoanalysis with regard to the principal theories of play. *Imago,* 5:243–282.

Piaget, J. (1923), La pensée symbolique et la pensée de l'enfant. *Archives de Psychologie,* Vol. 18.

——— (1945), La formation du symbole chez l'enfant. Paris: Delachaux et Niestlé. [*Play, Dreams, and Imagination in Childhood*. Routledge, 1962]

Pontalis, J.-B. (1954), Nos débuts dans la vie selon Melanie Klein. *Les Temps Modernes,* 105, August.

Rado, S. (1928), The problem of melancholia. *Internat. J. Psycho-Anal.,* 9:420–438.

Rodrigue, E. (1955), The analysis of a three-year-old mute schizophrenic. In: *New Directions in Psycho-Analysis,* ed. M. Klein, P. Heimann, & R. Money-Kyrle. London: Tavistock, pp. 140–179.

Roheim, G. (1923), Nach dem tode des Urvaters. *Imago,* 9:85–121.

Saussure, F. de (1915), *Course in General Linguistics.* New York: McGraw-Hill, 1966.

Segal, H. (1957), Notes on symbol formation. *Internat. J. Psycho-Anal.,* 38:391–397.

——— (1964), *Introduction to the Work of Melanie Klein.* Rev. ed. New York: Basic Books, 1974.

Sperber, H. (1915), Uber den Einfluss sexueller Momente auf Enstehung und Entwicklung der Sprache. *Imago,* 1:405.

Winnicott, D. (1965), A personal view of the Kleinian contribution. In: *The Maturational Processes and the Facilitating Environment.* New York: International Universities Press, 1965, pp. 171–178.

Name Index

Abraham, K., 3–4, 6, 8–13, 36, 46, 72–73, 86, 91, 98, 100, 108–110, 112, 118–119, 128, 146, 149, 152–156, 158–159, 161–162, 168, 175, 179–180, 184, 196, 201–203, 209–211, 217, 247, 252–253, 263–264, 283, 285, 288
Abraham, N., 14
Alexander, F., 49–50, 128
Anzieu, D., viii, 128–129

Baranger, W., viii, 196, 245–246
Bergeret, J., 232–233
Bion, W., 1, 58–59, 131–132, 185, 232
Boehm, 128
Bolland, J., xi
Breuer, 120
Brook, L., 9, 15

Cassirer, E., 219
Chadwick, M., 128, 189–195
Charcot, H., 81, 96–97
Colette, 266–268, 278

Deutsch, H., 166
Devereux, G., 260

Ferenczi, S., 3–9, 20–22, 36, 78, 81–85, 96, 100, 122, 128–129, 159, 161–162, 223, 235, 283

Freud, A., 59–60, 64–65, 134, 136–142, 144, 161–162, 238, 260
Freud, S., vii, ix, xii, 3–6, 9–10, 12–13, 16–17, 20–22, 34, 45, 48, 59–60, 67–73, 78–81 83, 85, 89–90n, 91, 95, 97–101, 108, 118, 120, 123, 128–129, 134, 140–141, 146–148, 151–152, 154, 158, 160–161, 170–171, 173, 183, 192–193, 195, 206, 210, 220–221, 224, 234–235, 241–243, 245–246, 252–253, 261, 272, 275, 277, 283, 287

Giovacchini, P., 211
Glover, E., 272
Grinstein, A., viii
Groddeck, 128

Heinmann, P., 245–246
Hoffer, W., 5, 6, 7n
Horney, K., 209
Hug–Hellmuth, H. von, 8, 64, 124–134, 136, 137, 162–163, 227

Isaacs, S., 60, 184, 245–246

Jacques, E., 110–111
Jones, E., viii, 3–4, 11, 13–14, 60, 78, 83–85, 97n, 100, 109, 128, 183–184, 209, 223, 245, 274–275

299

Subject Index